Online Cataloguing

Online Cataloguing

M. Ram

RANDOM

RANDOM PUBLICATIONS

NEW DELHI (INDIA)

Online Cataloguing

ISBN 978-93-5111-476-5

Published in 2015 in India by

RANDOM PUBLICATIONS

4376-A/4B, Gali Murari Lal, Ansari Road
New Delhi-110 002
Phone : +9111-43580356, 011-23289044, 011-43142548
e-mail: sales@randompublications.com,
info@randompublications.com, randomexports@gmail.com

Reprint 2021

Type Setting by : Friends Media, Delhi-110089
Digitally Printed at : Replika Press Pvt. Ltd.

Preface

A library catalogue is a register of all bibliographic items found in a library or group of libraries, such as a network of libraries at several locations. A bibliographic item can be any information entity that is considered library material, or a group of library materials, or linked from the catalogue as far as it is relevant to the catalogue and to the users of the library.

An online library catalogue is an electronic bibliographic database that describes the books, videotapes, periodicals, etc. carried by a particular library. It has evolved from a printed source, the library card catalogue. Before the advent of online catalogues, library catalogues were pieces of furniture that contained numerous small drawers. In these drawers were contained the records of particular items in the library.

Online cataloguing, such as Dynix, has greatly enhanced the usability of catalogues, thanks to the rise of MAchine Readable Cataloguing (MARC) standards in the 1960s. Rules governing the creation of catalogue MARC records include not only formal cataloguing rules like AACR2 but also special rules specific to MARC, available from the Library of Congress and also OCLC. MARC was originally used to automate the creation of physical catalogue cards; Now the MARC computer files are accessed directly in the search process.

In this book, an attempt has been made to reflect current practices in online cataloguing. With in-depth coverage and examples to illustrate even the most complex topics, it completely and comprehensively portrays the cutting edge scene in knowledge organization. The book maintains its supremacy in the field and is thus an essential reading for the students, teachers and practitioners in the arena of knowledge organization.

Author

Contents

1

Introduction to Online Cataloguing

Cataloguing is a form of order-making; it is a set of practices which quite literally put a library's collections in order and provide access through a set of systematically organized surrogates; and it is therefore a crucial part of the system by which books and other materials are maintained and made available to readers throughout the world. The work is ever ongoing, not just because new items are constantly being acquired, but because a collection will crumble—like the old barns one sees in the countryside—unless it is continually maintained: books disappear and need to be reordered, they are damaged and need to be repaired, they are misshelved, and so on; catalogues need to be similarly maintained. This might seem like an obvious enough point, but cataloguing shares with many other forms of order-making a certain invisibility.

For the ordinary library patron, the machinery by which the collection is maintained is out-of-sight, ill-understood, and the order it produces taken for granted. The typical library patron might be excused for not knowing how much work is being done behind the scenes to make an item available; indeed the invisibility of this system is largely a measure of its successful functioning. But it is more curious to observe that within the library community itself, in some quarters, at any rate, the work of cataloguing is denigrated; it is considered routine, at best semi-skilled, and unnecessarily detail-oriented work.

Cataloguing is not simply a matter of reading off self-evident properties of items, but is a highly skilled interpretative activity by which the properties of items are not simply described, but stabilized and even created. Over the last decade, discussion has ranged over many topics, including: how and whether to catalogue digital documents, the future of cataloguing, the politics of cataloguing, the relationship between cataloguing and reference services, teaching cataloguing in library schools, and cataloguing humor. But perhaps the central core of discussion is a steady, daily stream of questions, in which cataloguers ask one another for help with items they are cataloguing, for help in interpreting the cataloguing rules, and for advice with materials that the cataloguing rules don't address. What emerges is a much more complex—and interesting—picture than Manley's parody, or lay understanding, will admit. Bibliographic materials, it appears, do not always wear their bibliographic properties on their sleeve, and the rules for determining and "transcribing" these properties are quite complex and require interpretation to be applied. Anyone who has written a dissertation or a paper requiring a formal bibliography has encountered this problem in a small way: an item that is hard to categorize, that lacks an expected property, or one of whose properties is ambiguous.

Cataloguing is not just a matter of "reading off" the properties items have but of normalizing or regularizing the material to conform to standard categories of description and thereby making the properties in the act of describing them. That books have definitive titles and authors, that volumes are unambiguously of certain types, is a good first approximation to the truth, and the work of cataloguing is to maintain this first approximation as a useful and usable fiction. Cataloguing appears to be routine work so long as one believes that the materials just have a regular structure which can be trivially read off. But on inspection, it appears that this regular structure is the output of the work of cataloguers, not the input.

Cataloguing Rules

Cataloguing rules are the area where there is arguably the least international standardisation. This could be a barrier that remains when format issues etc are resolved. The Anglo-American Cataloguing Rules (AACR) is the most widely used code, but its influence is confined largely to the English-speaking world. However, the growing interest in AACR from other regions, including LIBER members, has prompted a review by the Committee of Principals for AACR, which is looking at internationalisation of the code's development and governance.

The virtual library environment means that not only must cataloguing rules cope with digital documents, but they must be also be capable of facilitating access to items from a collection that now expands well beyond the physical confines of one institution. The Committee of Principals held an international conference in 1997 to discuss how AACR might have to change for the new environment. The recommendations of the conference shaped the development process that has been going on ever since.

One of the major conference recommendations was that there needed to be a new logical data model underpinning the standard, to provide a solid foundation upon which to modify and extend the structure. The obvious choice for the data model was the IFLA Functional Requirements for Bibliographic Records (FRBR), and work is going on to fit the Rules to the model. This sounds quite radical, but it is more a question of rearranging the Rules rather than changing them. The aim is to avoid a step change like there was from AACR1 to AACR2, which required substantial conversion of existing catalogues.

The most significant changes are in the definition and cataloguing of serials. The situation has already been complicated enough in the print world with three codes in use: AACR, the IFLA International Standards Bibliographic description for Serials -ISB (S)- and UNESCO's International Serials Data System (ISDS). Fortunately, there has been a major breakthrough with the recent agreement to harmonise the codes. In parallel with this harmonisation the definition of what constitutes a serial has been substantially revised, and it is now much broader to reflect the changing patterns of publication, especially in the digital world.

Another area of change being considered is whether one continues to catalogue the work in hand (currently prescribed by AACR) or the intellectual work, where the physical manifestation acquired by the library is recorded at a secondary level. This has been characterised as the "content versus carrier " debate. The FRBR favours a tiered approach working from the intellectual work at the highest level, as does ONIX, since it has adopted the FRBR model. So work is well advanced to adapt at least one major cataloguing code to a hybrid print and digital environment.

What's more, provided AACR does increase its international appeal by being more welcoming to non-English speaking communities, it may offer a common code in which catalogue data can be more readily exchanged. However, the difficulty of overcoming cultural differences between national codes should not be underestimated. Cataloguing is often singled out for scrutiny in trying to pare costs. Cataloguing has adapted to these pressures by collaboration, and there are many success stories, e.g. OCLC, the Research Libraries Group and the Consortium of European Research Libraries. However, even more collaboration will be needed to contain costs in the digital environment.

Indeed, as libraries try to cope with constrained acquisitions and operating budgets, collaboration becomes a major driver in itself. For instance in the UK university and national library sectors much work is being devoted to developing collaborative acquisition, retention and preservation schemes, and cataloguing systems need to be able to cope with the demands this collaboration places upon them. Collaboration is also a major force in the trade sector. Book publishers, music publishers and video companies want to ensure their products are readily available from the on-line retailers. So they, too, are collaborating.

For collaboration to work interoperability is paramount. The trade does not want to have to re-key data between applications. Nor do libraries want to convert records between formats as they exchange records. Lastly, but of greatest importance for a service industry, are the users' and their needs. Users want a hybrid library; they don't want to search separate catalogues for print and digital documents. Neither are they interested in the distinction between what their library holds locally and what is on Web. So they are driving libraries towards providing seamless services, where again interoperability is the key.

Cataloguing in Digital Age

The development of film, video, microfilm, and photocopying technologies have all required changes and accommodations in the law, in library practices, in publishing and distribution, in patterns of consumption and use. None of these developments, however, has produced the uncertainty, confusion, and anxiety that has been occasioned by the increasing adoption of digital technologies, for none of these earlier developments challenged the order of the book, the order built around one central type of physical artifact and its modes of production, conservation, and consumption.

Perhaps the greatest uncertainty, from the perspective of cataloguing, is just what the new digital materials will be. Our current order carves up the bibliographic universe into discrete, stable, and long-lived units. But now, there is the potential at least for a great deal more variability and mutability of materials, and for a less rigid boundary between items. New genres, new categories of description, new institutions and practices have not yet arisen to stabilize this material. All of this together would constitute a new order, or substantial changes to the old order, as yet unrealized. Currently there is no lack of visionaries willing to sing the praises of this new order, and to proclaim their vision of the future as good, right, and inevitable. Having examined aspects of cataloguing and the larger order of which it is a part let us explore the question of cataloguing materials on the Net. From a cataloguing perspective, the Net is the wrong unit of analysis, for the Net does not constitute a library in any interesting sense.

It may be part of the technological infrastructure which could support a library, but it is not a library—not in the sense of an institution which oversees and provides access to a collection. Moreover, the materials on the Net do not constitute a library collection—not in the sense of a selection of items organized to serve a particular clientele. Instead, we should probably talk about cataloguing digital materials on the Net.

Digital collections will need to be organized and maintained if they are to remain stable and usable. To those within the library community this point may seem too obvious to make, since it is one of the central premises on which the modern library movement has been built. Yet it is not widely understood outside this community, to judge for example from the way the Web is often talked about. There seems to be a fairly wide-spread presumption, tacitly held, that materials can maintain their identity and their currency without continual intervention, without continual work. Moreover, it seems certain that the work of stabilizing and maintaining digital collections will require a great deal of systematic human activity. Certainly, powerful technologies will be involved as well as human labor, as is the case now. Again, this is obvious enough to librarians; technologists, by contrast, tend to see the technical infrastructure but not the "invisible" social infrastructure by which most things, not just library collections, are maintained. There can be no doubt that people will continue to make lists of digital resources which they will want to make available to others.

Some of these will have broad scope and utility (e.g. Yahoo and Alex), while others will be of limited scope. Whether we call these lists "bibliographies" or "catalogues,"there will be an ongoing need to maintain them, to keep them current and stable; and whether or not we call this ongoing maintenance work "cataloguing," it will no doubt be supported by a complex, and largely invisible, sociotechnical infrastructure. As with any new technology-based idea, there has been considerable controversy over the definition and possibilities of the term "digital library." To the computer science community, the new technical possibilities beckon enticingly. However, as traditionalists in the library community might point out, important issues are being ignored. According to Levy and Marshall, there is the "digital library" narrowly-construed and more broadly-construed. They argue for the broadly-construed digital library. The library community has been very successful in maintaining traditional libraries and has developed many practices and ideals to do so.

Among them are the ideas of unified collections and access methods. In fact, one could argue that many core library activities, such as circulation, technical services, and even shelving, were created by the library to maintain access to its collection over time. It is essential to note that this set of practices and ideals maintain the traditional library as institution and as community of practice together over time. This equilibrium is in the process of being disturbed or destroyed with the intrusion of new technical possibilities. Only some of the practices of the traditional library will carry into the digital world, perhaps only for a narrow conception of the digital library. Furthermore, the hypertext and computer science communities have no such traditions and practices for the broadly-construed library.

Libraries have always managed their collections, selecting and removing items from their shelves. This has been viewed as a critical function of library management. According to the collection management literature, the practices of collection management are dependent on the type of library collection. For example, Drew and Dewe distinguish ephemera in special collections from other items, and Kovacs distinguishes among types of libraries. We will argue here that new types of collections in the digital library will lend themselves to new types of maintenance issues.

In a traditional, or paper-based, library, there is considerable control over the collection. Versions of publications are stable. More importantly, because the collection is physically contained, there is considerable control over the collection. Library staff can decide what is and what is not in the collection. Maintenance of the collection is within the purview of the institutional members. At one opposite is the World Wide Web. The Web nodes often change, in content, location, and even existence. On the other hand, the content in a location does not shift rapidly; it tends to remain relatively stable. There is no control by any given individual over the entire Web. An individual has control only over his nodes and the selection of pointers to others' nodes (URLs) that provide the capability for extended collections.

At another opposite is Usenet or similar computer-mediated communication (CMC) systems. The locations do not change, but the contents of any given location change constantly. The control over the collection for this type is also very low for any given individual. In the middle of both dimensions is the organizational information repository.

Since the information resides within an organization and since the organization generally provides a sanctioned organizational member to manage the system, there is considerable control over its collection. Nonetheless, organizational memories tend to be more dynamic than traditional library collections; for example, they may include informal information, time-sensitive information, or bulletin board mechanisms. The variation in collection control determines the type of institutional and technical maintenance possible. Collections that are closer to those in traditional libraries can use more traditional control and maintenance mechanisms.

Digital libraries that incorporate more individualistic, dynamic, and informal information may need to find new maintenance mechanisms. Digital libraries, if self-contained in a manner similar to traditional libraries will be able to draw upon traditional methods and practices. Traditional libraries, as noted above, have developed methods for maintaining their core set of institutional ideals, their community of practice, and their collections of materials. Although many maintenance practices will need to be adapted—such as preservation and circulation control as extreme examples—the existing practices can serve as the bases for new norms and practices. We have argued above that such norms and practices are required for the long-term viability of the digital library as institution.

Therefore, if the adaptation of current practices is successful, then the narrowly-construed digital library will stand a much greater chance of success in the long run. These traditional practices, however, have had their limitations. They were based on a constrained collection; i.e., a selection from the bibliographic universe. A traditional library could never cope with much ephemera; it would require too many resources. To adequately index, catalogue, and otherwise conform to the institutional ideals for the broad range of ephemera would be overwhelming. In the past, there were strong institutional reasons to constrict the bibliographic universe.

Going digital, however, changes the cost structure, and collection and maintenance costs need to be revisited. It is not necessary, for example, in a digital universe to hand-index all materials; there are other methods of access. There is considerable evidence that this change in the cost structure is affecting organizational memories. However, the dynamism and volatility of organizational memories tend to be close to that of traditional libraries. That is, organizational members can reliably return to the same location in the organization's information repositories to find the same materials. However, the widespread interest in Lotus Notes, which combines electronic messaging and document storage, argues that combining formal organizational materials with informal is valuable.

Nonetheless, because institutional adaptation is much more manageable and amicable than extreme change, we expect that there will be pressure to have digital libraries as discrete and contained collections. The resource limitations of any social institution argue for defining a discrete collection as well. Of course, it will be possible to incorporate these narrowly-construed libraries in architectures that promote broad access. In addition, the broadly-construed digital library lacks practices that will maintain itself over the long run.

The same incentive that promotes use of the Web or of Usenet—namely that there is no intervening institution between the author and his potential audience—also brings its own disincentives to systematic use. As discussed, both the Web and Usenet have high levels of volatility. The location of Web nodes can change without notice. Usenet groupsdo not change locations, but the message traffic changes constantly. The individualistic orientation of both the Web and Usenet argues against easy control over the collection.

Without institutional control, each individual using the collection must deal with the maintenance issues himself. If the informal materials are dynamic or volatile, then there is a constant maintenance problem. Requiring every user to provide for collection maintenance raises the costs considerably. Users must determine whether materials will continue to be available, accessible, and even understandable. Collection maintenance, then, will be a critical limitation of the broadly-construed digital library. If the broadly-construed library, with its access to multiple sources, is to be viable, users cannot have a high maintenance cost over the long run. It will be necessary to reduce the cost of long-term use, and without mediating institutions, this reduction will need technical solutions.

Characteristics of Online Catalogues

Introduction of offline, computer-produced book and Computer Output Microform (COM) catalogues was a significant step in the evolution of the library catalogue, but almost exclusively in terms of production and maintenance. Computer-produced, offline catalogues addressed many of the problems inherent in card catalogue production and maintenance, and many labor-intensive tasks that were fundamental to card catalogues were eliminated with the use of computers and machine-readable records.

With offline computerized catalogues, only one unit entry record had to be created for each item; the computer expanded this record into as many individual catalogue entries as necessary and performed all alphabetization and filing tasks to maintain the catalogue. It was also much easier, at least in theory, to change a major catalogue heading; the change could be made once and applied to all effected entries by the computer-quite a difference from manually typing a new heading onto each which a change applied. As far ass the library user was concerned, the benefits of computer-generated offline catalogues were far less pronounced. The actual format of the catalogue certainly changed in some instances, but the basis content, and the basis avenues through which records in the catalogue could be found, rally did not. The principles used for access to entries in computer-generated book and COM catalogues mirrored those of the card catalogue, and the information was often identical and sometimes even less in amount.

From the users standpoint, computer-produced book catalogues were little more than card catalogues in bound volumes, and COM catalogues little more than card catalogues in a box. Given such frustrations as dealing with multiple parts of a catalogue issues in editions and supplements, and equipment breakdowns with COM catalogues, more advantages of computer-produced offline catalogues were not noticeable to the user and, at any rate, could often be overshadowed by the logistical difficulties in using them. In contrast, many OPACs, represent a radical departure both from card catalogues and from offline computerized catalogues in their implications for the user. Access to records can be enormously broadened in an online catalogue over what had typically been provided in other forms, but these benefits are accompanied by a new set of requirements and demands on the catalogue user. The relationship between user and online catalogue is fundamentally different from that in use of other catalogue forms.

The online catalogue is interactive, not passive, and requires the user to engage in a dialogue quite uncharacteristic of card, book and COM catalogues. Just to look into the catalogue requires new procedures on the part of the user. A search must be physically, not just mentally, initiated by typing onto a keyboard issuing a command through some other means. The system will respond according to the very specific action initiated by the user. In many instances, the user will then have to initiate further action based on the system's response, and so on back and forth until the user arrives at the desired end of the search or otherwise terminates the dialogue. This interaction and the nature of system responses represent a significant departure for the user from simply thumbing through catalogue cards or pressing a button, turning a knob, or sliding a handle on a microfilm or microfiche reader.

Online Public-Access Catalogues

The fact that a online public-access catalogues (OPACs) is intended for users of library materials in perhaps the fundamental distinction between this application of automation and those which serve strictly internal processing functions. Such matters as simplicity of operation or sophistication of retrieval capabilities should be important considerations in the design and selection of any automated system regardless of application, but self-evidence in operation may be less important in a technical processing system in which the library is able to exercise a certain degree of control over the selection, training, and monitoring of system users.

The design of an online catalogue must take into account a quite different set of circumstances. Considerable diversity exists among users in their level of knowledge about library catalogues and in the extent to which they are familiar with the use of computerized systems. The library will usually have little or opportunity to balance its diversity though a planned program of controlled instruction and monitoring. Most people will not use the OPAC as part of everyday routine, and hence their knowledge and skills will not be constantly reinforced.An example of the well-placed emphasis in discussions of OPACs on users and their interaction with the catalogue is the series of studies sponsored by the Council on Library Resources (CLR) during the early 1980s, aimed at gaining a better understanding of what users want and need in online catalogues, their likes and dislikes, and the dynamics of their interaction with catalogues.

Despite the vast array of differences among existing OPACs and lack of specific guidelines for development, at the base of these differences is a common goal: to design online catalogues that will allow the user maximum flexibility and yet will be easy to use. Investigations like those sponsored by CLR should help to establish a stronger foundation for realizing such a goal. Phrases such as "user friendly" have become almost meaningless because of their sometimes indiscriminate use to describe systems or features that commonsense observation show are 'anything but.' Yet the overuse, and ever misuse, of well-worn phrases does not negate the relevance of the concepts they represent. The degree to which OPACs are willingly accepted by library users will indeed depend in large part on just how user friendly these systems are. Technical processing systems can be evaluated largely in terms of functional capabilities, or what a system can do. But the circumstances in which OPACs are still used are too different for such a simple evaluation. Equally and perhaps more important is the question of how easily system functions can be learned, understood and applied to the fullest extent by a diverse group of users.

For any given characteristics in their operation, OPACs are still simply too new, and their use still too little understood, to be able to state categorically that one approach is somehow "better" than the other. Fundamental to all of the features described is the most basic improvement that OPACs have made on other forms of the library catalogue: the expansion of avenues of access to catalogue records. Although the purposes of the library catalogue are not case in stone and depend on one's perspective, one set of standards by which library catalogue functions have been measured throughout the twentieth century is the principles of Charles Ammi Cutter as noted in his Rules for a Dictionary Catalogue. Cutter enumerated three major "objects" of a library catalogue. A catalogue should allow someone to find book if its author, title, or topic is known. A catalogue should fulfill a gathering function, showing what a library owns by a given author, on a given subject or in a given type of literature.

A catalogue should provide assistance in the change of a book, either as to its edition or its literary or topical character. A fourth commonly recognized catalogue function, although not explicitly noted by Cutter, is collection, having to do with the arrangement and relationship of headings within the catalogue. Underlying most of these functions is the fundamental matter of access top bibliographic records in the catalogue: the points of entry through which a record for an item may be found. Cutter's first object—the finding function—is the essential basis for access, nut the gathering and collocation functions also have to do with accessibility to records.

The function least directly related to access is assistance in the choice of material, which has more to do with content of a bibliographic record than access to it. Whether Cutter's objects still provide the most viable criteria for defining the purposes of a library catalogue in an online era is debatable, and some have questioned the degree of completeness to which these objects have ever actually been realized in libraries. Cutter's principles stem from a time quite different from the 1980s.

New factors—including but not limited to those of a technological nature—should not be disregarded in defining the purposes of a library catalogue. Nevertheless, Cutter's principles serve as a point of departure in many decisions of online catalogues, and concerning access to bibliographic records they still provide a convenient framework for comparing online catalogues with one another and with other forms of the library catalogue.

Access to bibliographic records in library catalogues has traditionally been marked by a high degree of rigidity, requiring considerable knowledge and exactitude on the part of the user. Generally, access is gained through four types of bibliographic elements: author, title, series, and subject. Multiple author and subject headings are assigned to an item as rules or judgment dictates, but the number is usually kept to a minimum.

The terminology selected for headings is also tightly controlled, with the library usually trying to establish a one-to-one correspondence between headings and the persons, corporate bodies, or concepts they represent. These practices may be understandable from a practical point of view, but they do impose certain limits on accessibility to records. The user can indeed locate an item in the collection for which the author, title, or subject is known, but only under some rather inflexible conditions. To find a record under the title, the user must know the full and exact wording of the title—not some or most of the words, but all of the words, and in their correct order.

For access by author, because of the pre-AACR practice of establishing full and singularly valid forms of names, it has not always been enough to know the from of an author's name as it appears on publications or by which the person is popularly known. It has been necessary for the user somehow to know the exact from of a person's or corporation's name as it has been established by the library, often on the basis of considerable research. Where there are discrepancies in name form, it has been up to the user to figure out the form selected by the library. Access by subject is even more problematic.

Singularly valid forms of headings are selected from among all possible equivalents, but because of the greater conceptual complexity involved, there is even greater likelihood in subject searching that discrepancies will arise between the terminology selected by the library and the vocabulary chosen by the user.

The problem is further compounded by the general conservatism in libraries toward changing the vocabulary used in headings and by complicated subject heading formation and filling sequences. Such practices, which result in a lack of flexibility, are all but dictated by necessity in card catalogues; however, they were also carried over generally intact to offline versions of computerized catalogues as well. Given the capabilities of computers and the elimination of the need for manual filing, there is no strictly technological reason for some of these practices to have been retained so uniformly. Additional access points, such as by keywords appearing anywhere in titles or assigned subject headings, could have been provided with little or no appreciable increase in human labor.

Similarly, duplicate listings under variant forms of names could have been supplied in the catalogue. These expansions would have required greater sophistication in indexing and would have resulted in a far greater number of entries, and thus larger catalogues, but whether for economic reasons, ties to tradition, or something else, expansions of this type were never characteristic of offline computerized catalogues. Only with the introduction of online catalogues have such expansions taken firm hold, and they are changing the very concept of access to records in the library catalogue.

Some OPACs adhere quite closely to other forms of the catalogue in the ways in which access to records may be gained, requiring just as much exactitude and exhibiting just as little flexibility. These are essentially electronic card catalogues. Other OPACs significantly broaden, and even fundamentally change, the traditional concept of access.

Online Circulation Systems

One of the first online systems was at the Illinois State Library in Springfield, in late 1966, at a time when many other libraries were designing full offline systems. The backbone of the system was an IBM 1620 computer located in the state processing facility. The equipment in the library consisted of IBM 1033 prints and 1031 card readers, which were similar in operation to the 357 Data Collection System, requiring insertion of machine-readable book cards and borrower identification badges. Rather than producing transaction cards or recording transaction data on tape, however, the 1031 at the Illinois State Library transmitted data directly to the computer. By later standard, the online system at the library was primitive.

Although transaction information was conveyed directly to the computer as it occurred, it was stored on a separate daily transaction pack and was merged with the main circulation file only on a once-a-day batch processing basis. The system did not include item-specific online query, so that it was still necessary to use offline batch-produced circulation lists to trace circulation information pertaining to a given item. For these purposes, the system was much like wholly offline batch processing systems. What set it apart from those, however, was its ability to perform two important functions online: checking borrower registration numbers for validity and checking each returned item against an online holds file. Each time a borrower identification card was inserted into the designated slot of the 1031, the borrower number was automatically checked against a computer-stored file of valid borrower numbers.

If the borrower's number did not have a counterpart in the file, that fact was generated immediately on the 1033 printer. This was a major improvement over completely offline operations. Where such validation, if done at all, could be performed only by manual lookup in a printed directory of borrower numbers. The other important online function of the Illinois State Library system was checking holds, and that had equally important implications. When the book card of a returned item was placed in the 1031 for discharge, the call number was checked against an online list of call numbers of items placed on hold. If the cell number of the returned item matched a call number in the holds file, a message was automatically generated on the 1033 printer showing call number, identification number of the patron who had placed the item on hold, and the data when the hold had been placed. In this manner, greater control over holds was realized than was possible in offline batch processing computerized circulation systems.

Another early online circulation system was implemented in late 1967 at Midwestern University in Wichita Falls, Texas. The Midwestern system was unique in that it was, at least insofar as its designers know, the first and perhaps only online circulation system to operate on an IBM 1401 computer, a decidedly second-generation machine. Like the Illinois State Library system, Midwestern used IBM 1031 input stations and 1033 printers, validated borrower identification numbers, and checked items against an online holds file. But it went further than the Illinois system in several important respects. Not only did the Midwestern systems check borrower numbers during a charging operation for general validation, but it also determined if a borrower had any outstanding overdue items or unpaid fines.

If so, the computer generated an immediate list of the charges on the 1033 printer. The system had an online query capability, albeit restricted to searching on a borrower number. The keying in of a number prompted the computer to respond by printing a list on the 1033 containing all items charged to that borrower. But perhaps the fundamental difference in the Midwestern system was that the main circulation file was online in the strict sense of the term, with the file being updated immediately upon completion of each transaction, rather than in a batch mode. In September 1968, the Booth Library at Eastern Illinois University in Charleston began to operate its own version of a online circulation system using a third-generation IBM 360/Model 50 computer and the IBM 1031 input stations and 1033 printers. The Booth system had the basic functional characteristic of the Midwestern system, but with an important additional query feature.

The Midwestern system had query capability by patron number; the Booth system supplemented this with item query by call number. By entering a particular two-digit code followed by a call number, a terminal operator could retrieve bibliographic information and current circulation data about a specific item. Queries of this nature were made using an IBM Cathode Ray Tube (CRT) terminal located at the circulation desk. A further extension of this search capability was a scanning command that displayed bibliographic entries in call number sequence. Since the Booth Library online file was an inventory file containing an abbreviated bibliographic record for nearly even item in the library—not just items currently charged out—the scanning capability allowed shelflist searching of the entire library collection. The structure and search capabilities of this system suggested possible extension as a public-access tool, and in fact plans were announced to locate a public-access CRT terminal near the card catalogue in fall 1971. Still, the known item query capability of the Eastern Illinois system allowed more immediate information about the circulation status of an item than was possible in an offline system.

In the early 1970s, a number of academic libraries began to incorporate minicomputers in their circulation operations. A significant feature of these systems was that at least part of the processing hardware was located in the library itself, although a larger computer, outside the library, still played an integral role. Typically, the minicomputer in the library contained certain files for immediate online access and captured transaction data for later batch transmission to as larger computer located outside the library on which the main circulation file was stored. While some of the operations remained offline, this setup realized the benefits of online processing for certain critical purposes. One of the most common minicomputers in this type of configuration was the IBM System/7 in use in circulation control in at least six libraries by early 1974. In the system operational at the University of Pennsylvania in Philadelphia, five online files were stored in the minicomputer. Each of these contained critical information against which various types of transactions were checked. There were three item files against which renewal attempts and discharges were checked.

A call number file contained the call number of all items placed on hold, the access number file contained a list of all items recalled, and a reserve book file contained all items for which in request had been placed to transfer the item to a reserve book collection upon its return. Another file, against which all patron identification numbers were checked, was the restricted patron file, containing a lost of borrower identification numbers of all users whose further attempts to charge materials were to be blocked for some reason. The fifth online file was the daily transaction file, which recorded the day's activity. Once a day, this file was transmitted to the main computer, an IBM 370/Model 168, located at the university data processing center, for batch updating of the main circulation file. This transmission, usually involving information for about 3,000 transactions, required about 30 minutes. For the most part, improvements, gained in the Online circulation systems of the late 1960s and early 1070s over what was possible in an offline system were focused on immediate access to information about restricted items, such as holds, and better control of patron privilege. Although improvements regarding access to information about restricted items enhanced public service by allowing more rapid reshelving of returned items and a better system for regulating holds and ensuring identification upon return, these benefits were not always immediately evident to the average library user. The second common capability, immediate access to Online delinquent patron files, could as likely cause ill feelings as goodwill between the library and its users. The lack of reliable backup measures, inexperience in dealing with online systems, and continued reliance on batch-produced circulation lists combined to make early online circulation systems less than revolutionary in terms of public service. At least one facility, the Simon Fraser University Library, had so many problems and so much user discontent with its online system that it abandoned online and reverted to its earlier offline system."

Perhaps the outstanding example during the early 1970s of online circulation system that could, in fact, facilitate user services to a degree not possible in an offline system was demonstrated by Ohio State University's Library Control System. The entire philosophy behind the design and application of the system for the Ohio State University libraries was, as described by Hugh Atkinson, "that the system should be one which would speak to the problems of its users rather than simply the problems of the library." These problems included, among others, a decentralized library structure consisting of a main library and more than 20 branches. Only one catalogue—the main library's—contained complete information for all items in all 21 libraries. Similar to several earlier online circulation systems, Ohio State opted for an "inventory" file approach in which the main machine-readable database contained records for all items in the libraries rather than an "absence" file, which would have contained records only for those items in circulation. This principles as fundamental at Ohio State since the system was to be used as a locator file as well as for circulation operations.

A massive conversion effort—perhaps the largest of its kind carried out by any library to that date—was contracted to a vendor, which put into machine-readable form records containing call number, unique item number, author, title, date of publication. Library of Congress card number, language code, from of publication code, and holding for each of 1 million distinct titles and 2.5 million items. The key to the Ohio State system was its items query capability. Searching was possible by call number, title key, and a combination author/title key. When the desired item was retrieved, it was possible to see which library or libraries on campus owned a copy of the item, and whether each copy was charged out. Search terminals were available in the main library and in most of the branches. Thus, the entire union catalogue of the libraries' holdings could be assessed from any library in the system.

Although this in itself was a fundamental improvement over the single union catalogue in the main library. An item not already checked out in one library could be charged on terminals located in any a copy was found to be available in a different branch library, the circulation attendant could issue a command that would generate a charge slip in the branch library that had the copy. The item would be retrieved in that library and placed on a shelf to await later pickup by the patron. The online union catalogue, showing location and circulation status of each item throughout the system, combined with the capability of remote charging to remove much of the patron uncertainty that was inherent under prior circumstances. The Ohio State University library system, like all other online system, was not entirely free of problems, but many of them could eventually be alleviated by design changes and the system was such an improvement over earlier conditions that the problems were of comparatively minor consequence.

The impact of this system on library service was probably best exemplified by the fact that, during the first 18 months it was in operation, circulation at the Ohio State University libraries increased by more than 40 percent. The system was an important achievement owing to its scale of implementation, its query capabilities, and its emphasis on public service problem solving. The same system was later taken by Atkinson to the University of Illinois and implemented; today it is the basis of an important networking system in libraries throughout Illinois. Apart from circulation, the late 1960s and early 1970s saw the development of a number of online technical processing systems.

One of the earliest acquisitions systems was designed at the Washington State University Library in Pullman and was implemented in 1968; an online serials control system was up and running at University Level in Quebec the same year. Predating both of these was the beginning of a comprehensive online library system at the Redstone Scientific Information Center in

Alabama. Some parts of the system were operational as early as 1966. By the early 1970s, acquisitions, cataloguing, authority control, serials check-in, and circulation were online. Offline computerization had been an important development in acquisitions, providing for machine-assisted production of purchase orders, improved methods of fiscal control, and more timely updating and generation of status lists. Still, a significant amount of from handling and paper file maintenance remained in many of these systems.

The online acquisitions systems developed in the late 1960s and early 1970s represented major improvements by reducing the amount of manual handling and maintenance of paper products, as well as further enhanced those functions that had been performed well in offline computerized system. One of the more ambitious projects in the late 1960s was carried out at the Oregon State University Library at Corvallis. Christened LOLITA, this online acquisitions system required nearly seven "staff years" in programming, systems, and clerical labor to develop. It contained three Online files: order/in-process file contained three display screens of information input when an order was placed, and updated as an item passed through the acquisitions and cataloguing procedures. The first screen included basic bibliographic data, the second screen contained accounting data, and the third screen allowed for local cataloguing information such as call number and location.

The amount of time and file maintenance that this system saved the staff, particularly when compared with a manual system, was considerable. One of the greatest contributions made by online systems in general was the expansion of access points, and these early acquisition systems were no exception. It was possible with an offline system to produce lists or maintain paper copies of order forms by more than one point of access, such as by order number, author, and title if desired, but that merely increased the number of lists to be consulted or files to be maintained.

As a result, the number of listing parameters was usually minimized in offline systems. In online systems, all files and their indexes could be maintained in the computer, and multiple access points to a single record would not mean an increase in hard copy materials to be consulted or maintained. LOLITA, however, only provided to access points, order number and author, to each record in the system. The early online acquisitions systems retained some of the capabilities that had been included in their offline predecessors, but the newer systems were much improved in quality, speed, and ease of handling. LOLITA, along with several other early systems, provided for handling of partial shipments and authorization of partial invoice payments, capabilities that were handled, if at all, only with some difficult by offline systems. The fund accounting component of LOLITA was also successful.

A year-end encumbrance, could be generated in 20 minutes, and LOLITA was to only much faster, nut also judged more accurate and detailed in a controlled comparison with manual ledgers. Perhaps the most important characteristic of online acquisitions systems was that, in most cases, it was only one part of a broader integrated technical processing system that brought the acquisitions and cataloguing functions closer together. The online order record, upon receipt of an item, became an online cataloguing record. This greatly reduced duplication between acquisitions and cataloguing and also provided an end product consisting of a machine-readable bibliographic record for each item entering the collection.

In LOLITA, the final steps in the online processing after an item had been received were for a cataloguers to verify the bibliographic information originally entered by the acquisitions department and the complete the record by adding local cataloguing data. The completed record was removed from the online file, but not before it had been copied onto magnetic tape as a permanent machine-readable record. An important feature in the development of online technical processing systems was the incorporation of Library of Congress MARC records. Records on MARC tapes were transferred into the local online systems in various ways. A common feature across systems was that each new order was searched against a locally maintained MARC file, and when a match occurred, the appropriate MARC record entered the local system as the source for bibliographic information for ordering and eventual cataloguing.

One of the most comprehensive uses of MARC records evolved in the University of Chicago Library Data Management System. Orders could be searched against the MARC files, and there was a retrospective searching capability whereby incoming MARC records were searched against the local bibliographic file to identify previously created local records as potential candidates for bibliographic upgrading by the new matching MARC record. These features in one from or another could be found in other systems, but an interesting feature of the Chicago systems was its use of MARC tapes as a collection development tool. Subject profiles, defined by Library Congress classification numbers and ranges of numbers, could be maintained online, and each incoming MARC tape was matched against them. The result was an offline list of items falling into each subject profile for use in identifying potential orders for the library. The system also allowed access to these lists online if a bibliographer wished. The system also allowed access to these lists online if a bibliographer wished.

Supplementing the LC class number profiles were certain national bibliography online profiles used to identify potential orders from an area studies prospective. In addition to profiles designed to identify items of potential interest for the library, the University of Chicago system also included a capability designed to assist in better control over blanket orders from publishers. The first four digits of an International Standard Book Number (ISBN), MARC field 020, are unique to each publisher. Each record on the MARC tapes was automatically searched on these first four digits at Chicago. The system could then generate lists of items published by each publisher with whom Chicago had a blanket order arrangement, and these lists could be used to assist in monitoring receipt of blanket order items

Left with an alternative of in-house, single-library development projects, only the largest and most well endowed libraries could have used an online system for any technical support systems during the 1970s. As early as 1967, however, a second alternative was being formulated, and the outgrowth of this and similar efforts was the evolution of four system—OCLC, RLG, WLN, and UTLAS—whose use by the early 1980s, extended into several thousand libraries on the North American continent.

Ohio College Library Center (OCLC)

Although some libraries continued to develop their own in-house systems for certain library functions, it was apparent by the mid- 1970s that automated cataloguing in particular was evolving in a different direction. The basis of this transformation was the Ohio College Library Center (OCLC), a system based on the simple premise that, recognizing minor local variations, cataloguing data for a given item were essentially similar from library to library. The Library of Congress MARC project had been as major breakthrough in the concept of shared cataloguing information in an automated environment, but the general pattern of sharing had been unidirectional and on an institution-by-institution basis.

MARC tapes were sent from the Library of Congress to subscribing institutions, each of which then loaded the tapes and manipulated the data on its own computer. The idea that evolved for OCLC was a central file of cataloguing records that could be maintained on a single computer system and accessed through terminals sharing dedicated communications line connected to that computer. Not only would this enable libraries to share a MARC file, but it would centralize development costs of the system and virtually eliminated the need for each participating library to use the host institution's computer system.

Because the Library of Congress catalogued only portion of the universe of materials received by libraries, and since the MARC tapes included only the OCLC online system was the capability for allowing original input of records, using the MARC format, by the participating libraries themselves. The impact of this is seen by the fact that even by the end of the decade, less than one-fourth of the master bibliographic records in the OCLC database had been supplied by the Library of Congress.

OCLC was chartered in 1967 and Frederick G. Kilgour named as its executive director. System production first began with offline batch processing in 1970; 54 member academic libraries in Ohio submitted punched IBM cards with Library of Congress card numbers of items for which they wanted catalogue cards produced. The punched cards were searched against a file consisting of the Library of Congress MARC records, and when a match occurred, catalogue cards were generated and sent back to the requesting library within two weeks. In 1971, OCLC went online, installing terminals that allowed each library to search the growing OCLC On-Line Union Catalogue (OLUC), the bibliographic database of the system. The library could order catalogue cards merely depressing a couple of command keys on the keyboard attached to the CRT display terminal. During the first several years of OCLC online operation, a number of far-reaching decisions were made that would enhance-and sometimes plague—the cooperative effort.

The display format revolved around the concept of a bibliographic 'master record'; in theory there was to be only one record in the database for any given bibliographic entity. When this master record for an item was retrieved by a library, any of the MARC fields could be modified to reflect local practices with respect to subject headings, forms of name entry, local call number, and so on; virtually any element in the record could be modified. All local changes were reflected on the catalogue cards printed offline at OCLC and mailed to the library (and eventually on the library's magnetic tapes of its cataloguing activity when this service became available). These modifications, however, were not stored permanently online for the library. Therefore, when a library retrieved a record it had previously used for cataloguing, the bibliographic master record was displayed online, without the local modifications that the library had previously made. The lack of capability to permanently store local information was probably justifiable in OCLC's initial stages.

The amount of storage required to maintain this data for each cataloguing use of each record by each library would have been enormous, especially since most members of OCLC at that time had a low incidence of adding copies for titles they had already catalogued once. Nevertheless, it was not long after the system went online that some members began to express concern over the lack of a permanent online record containing local modifications for previously catalogued materials.

A characteristic of OCLC during the 1970s was a perpetual gap between announced plans and actual implementation, and the permanent storage and display of local cataloguing data—or at least of a scaled-down version of local holdings from selected fields—perhaps provides the most exemplary illustration. The strategy initially used in creating the online file of bibliographic master records in OCLC revolved around the creation of as large a database as possible in as little time as possible. This may be overgeneralization, but there is little doubt that it was prevalent enough so that a great many of the permanent master records entered into the database by member libraries in the early years suffered in quality and completeness of information.

Master records, particularly for retrospective cataloguing entered into the database, were frequently created from a description taken solely from the shelflist card of the first member library to convert the title. Thus quality and completeness depended in great part on any given library's past shelflisting practices, on the library's policy for input of new records into the database, and, beyond that, on the accuracy of the terminal operator.

The philosophy of rapid creation of a database at the expense of detail and completeness of record could bc seen in OCLC's approach in 1975 to providing records for serials titles, for which a specifically designed MARC format had only recently become available. To greatly increase the number of serials records in a short time, tapes of the Minnesota Union List of Serials (MULS) were loaded into the OCLC database. Although MULS contained accurate information as far as it went, it was primarily a locational tool and provided very abbreviated bibliographic data for cataloguing purposes. Perhaps the greatest quality control complication in the long run was the extreme difficulty of upgrading master records when a mistake was detected or information found to be incomplete.

Written forms had to be completed by a member library and mailed to OCLC; when received, the master record was examined by OCLC staff and modified according to the reported additions or changes. This process was time-consuming and cumbersome for member libraries, and not exactly a foremost staffing priority at OCLC. The result was that a library could easily retrieve a master record containing an obvious typographical error that presumably had been modified locally by any number of other libraries for their own card production, but that remained in the master record due to backlogs at OCLC in record upgrading. Owing to the prominent role of the OCLC database in the Conversion of Serials (CONSER) project, a limited number of libraries were given the capability of making permanent online modifications to OCLC serials master records from their own terminals, thus bypassing the manual error reporting procedure.

This proved a tremendous success. The possibility of enabling a small number of libraries a similar online capability for records in other formats was a topic of discussion for several years, and was finally initiated in mid-1984. The approach used in creating its database and the difficulty in correcting errors in master records earned OCLC a reputation in some quarters as a 'dirty database.' To be certain, many early records in the database did suffer from lack of quality control. An often overlooked factor by critics, however, was that OCLC was an experiment without direct precedent and included among its membership a segment of the library community that had virtually no previous experience with any type of library automation.

OCLC was not the first online system used for collective representation of cataloguing data fro a number of independent libraries, but immediate predecessors were based on centralized input and thus centralized control. This was quite different from the structure of OCLC, in which any member library could input an original bibliographic master record for an item. Given this degree of autonomy and decentralization, combined with the lack of previous experience with library automation on the part of most of its members, and a lack of precedence to gauge the implications of shared databases, the early 1970s were an individual and cooperative learning experience for OCLC members which served to demonstrate both the strong points and the problem areas of cooperative ventures in library automation.

During its first year of online operation OCLC remained a cooperative venture of Ohio academic libraries. During 1972, membership was extended to Ohio nonacademic libraries, and in 1973 to libraries outside the state. Although the major computer facilities were to remain centralized at OCLC headquarters, a decentralized approach to the provision of general support services emerged by the mid-1970s. OCLC and various independent state and regional agencies entered into contracts for the brokering of OCLC services and for provision of training and ongoing assistance. Some of these networks had predated OCLC; others were formed in direct response to the need for an agency to provide OCLC services in a particular area. Two exceptions to the general pattern of independent brokering were the formation of OCLC Western, consisting of several branch offices on the Pacific Coast, and OCLC Europe, both being service agencies under the direct administration of OCLC.

The independent affiliate networks, which have usually numbered about 20, have remained administratively separate from OCLC a relationship that has at times worked to the benefit of OCLC and at other times served as a source of conflict. Within four years after OCLC's decision in 1973 to expand its base of participation beyond Ohio, the number of libraries using the system had increased to more than 800. Increasing numbers of public and special libraries were joining, but the majority of new members continued to be academic libraries. These included many members of the Association of Rcsearch Libraries as well as medium-sized university libraries, but an influx of new participants continued from among the ranks of four-year colleges, a pattern that underscored OCLCs role in introducing automation into smaller institutions.

RESEARCH LIBRARIES GROUP (RLG)

The concept of resource sharing was the basis for the formation of a number of formal cooperative ventures during the 1970s. One such, begun in 1974, was the Research Libraries Group (RLG), comprised of Harvard, Yale, Columbia, and the New York Public Library. Its board goals focused on the sharing of resources, collection development, and preservation and conservation of library materials. RLG felt that a common automated bibliographic system would enhance cooperative efforts among member libraries. By early 1978, the four systems under final consideration for adoption included OCLC, Standford's BALLOTS, the University of Chicago Library Data Management System, and the New York Public Library bibliographic control system.

In spring 1978, RLG announced agreement with Stanford for the use of BALLOTS as the group's automated bibliographic component. Although RLG may merely have chosen what it considered to be the best available system, the choice drew strong reactions from within and outside the group. In June of the year, Harvard announced withdrawal from RLG, although Director of Libraries Douglas Bryant indicated that the choice of BALLOTS was not the motivating factor. A wide spectrum of emotions was expressed throughout the library community concerning RLG's decision not to go with OCLC, which many saw as the emerging national bibliographic network. In comparing the online features of BALLOTS and OCLC, there is no question that BALLOTS was the far more sophisticated and flexible technical processing system. Unlike OCLC, it also provided for online storage and display of an individual library's cataloguing data in a network environment, as well as other features such as searching by title keyword and subject, not available on OCLC.

Although on a smaller scale than OCLC, BALLETS had also proved capable of serving as a shared system as early as 1975 when seven public libraries in California entered into a networking arrangement with Stanford, and the number of libraries using it has increased since then. The greatest source of resentment among OCLC libraries about RLG's selection of BALLOTS was probably not so much the choice itself as it was the accompanying implicit, and sometimes explicit, attitude that OCLC and its 'dirty database' were unacceptable, and that the needs of RLG members were somehow quite apart from those of the rest of the library community—including those of many prestigious research libraries that remained ardent supporters of OCLC. Equally crucial in the reaction, OCLC had come to be recognized by then as much more than a shared cataloguing database. Because of library identifier symbols attached to each bibliographic record, OCLC had grown into a tremendous tool for facilitating interlibrary lending and, to many, was the most current and reliable source of occasional information available in the United States. The selection of another system by RLG virtually cut off those libraries and their collections from this source of information and ejected a major obstacle to their participation in resource sharing on a broader scale. To many OCLC libraries and even to those using neither system, this detachment seemed a conscious and motivated effort to minimize the role of RLG members in the broader context of American library cooperation. The reaction to RLG did little at that time or later to discourage the image of elitism.

A number of libraries did purchase their own equipment and designed applications software in-house in the 1970s, but another alternative began to emerge in that decade—the library-specific commercial vendor of automated library systems. In terms of the total computer market as viewed by larger corporations, libraries were too few to attract a great deal of attention, but the potential volume demonstrated a suitable market for smaller and specifically library-oriented commercial ventures.

References

American Library Association. Catalogue Code Revision Committee: *A.L.A. Catalogue Rules; Author and Title Entries.* Prelim. American 2d ed. Chicago, The Association, 1941.

Norris, Dorothy M.: *A History of Cataloguing and Cataloguing Methods, 1100-1850.* London, Grafton and Co., 1939.

Taylor, Arlene G., David P. Miller, and Arlene G. Taylor. *Introduction to Cataloguing and Classification.* 10th ed. Westport, Conn: Libraries Unlimited, 2006.

Wynar, Bohdan S. *Introduction to cataloguing and classification.* 6th ed. Littleton, Colorado : Libraries Unlimited. 1980.

2

Functions of Library Cataloguing

Cataloguc is very important in a library whenever its collection is growing too large. Its function is to remember the items available in a library. In contrast with a large library, a small or private library will have less need for a formal catalogue. Its collection can be accessed through author, or title. However, when the collection becomes a bit growing, an informal arrangement for a grouping the books by subject categories may provide access to them.

When a library collection becomes too large for simple approach, formal records are necessary. Any information represents in a record is called an entry. In a library, each entry in the catalogue is the representation of a bibliographic record at a particular point in the catalogue. A bibliographic records transcription of the complete cataloguing information for any item. The purpose of a bibliographic record is:

— to provide all the information to describe an item both physically and intellectually in order to distinguish it form other item

— to provide its location in the collection

A library catalogue provides information about the books, periodicals, videos, databases, and other materials owned by a library. In the past, library catalogues were kept on cards in wooden drawers. Today, it is common for the records to be kept online, allowing you to search them by computer. Regardless of the form of access, the function is the same: to describe the materials owned by the library so that you can locate them by author, title, or subject.

The card catalogue was a familiar sight to library users for generations, but it has been effectively replaced by the online public access catalogue (OPAC). Some still refer to the online catalogue as a "card catalog". Some libraries with OPAC access still have card catalogues on site, but these are now strictly a secondary resource and are seldom updated. Many of the libraries that have retained their physical card catalogue post a sign advising the last year that the card catalogue was updated. Some libraries have eliminated their card catalogue in favour of the OPAC for the purpose of saving space for other use, such as additional shelving.

Functions of a Library Catalogue

The objectives of a library catalogue are to enable a user to find a book when one of the author, or title, or subject is known; to show what the library has by a given author, on a given subject, in a given kind of literature; and to assist in the choice of a material as to the edition or as to its characteristic

The main functions of a library catalogue are to enable the library users to determine :

- — whether the library has a certain item
- — which works by a particular author are in the collection
- — which editions of a particular work the library has, and
- — what materials the library has on a particular subject

Charles Ammi Cutter made the first explicit statement regarding the objectives of a bibliographic system in his *Rules for a Printed Dictionary Catalog*ue in 1876. According to Cutter, those objectives were

1. To enable a person to find a book of which either (Identifying objective):
   a. the author
   b. the title
   c. the subject
   d. the category
2. To show what the library has (Collocating objective)
   a. by a given author
   b. on a given subject
   c. in a given kind of literature

3. to assist in the choice of a book (Evaluating objective)

a. as to its edition (bibliographically)

b. as to its character (literary or topical)

These objectives can still be recognised in more modern definitions formulated throughout the 20th century. 1960/61 Cutter's objectives were revised by Lubetzky and Lubetzky and the Conference on Cataloguing Principles (CCP) in Paris. The latest attempt to describe a library catalogue's goals and functions was made in 1998 with Functional Requirements for Bibliographic Records (FRBR) which defines four user tasks: find, identify, select, and obtain.

Types of Catalogues

Traditionally, there are the following types of catalogue:

— *Author card:* a formal catalogue, sorted alphabetically according to the authors' or editors' names of the entries.

— *Title catalogue*: a formal catalogue, sorted alphabetically according to the title of the entries.

— *Dictionary catalogue*: a catalogue in which all entries (author, title, subject, series) are interfiled in a single alphabetical order. This was the primary form of card catalogue in North American libraries just prior to the introduction of the computer-based catalogue.

— *Keyword catalogue*: a subject catalogue, sorted alphabetically according to some system of keywords.

— *Mixed alphabetic catalogue forms*: sometimes, one finds a mixed author/title, or an author/title/keyword catalogue.

— *Systematic catalogue:* a subject catalogue, sorted according to some systematic subdivision of subjects. Also called a *Classified* catalogue.

— *Shelf list catalogue:* a formal catalogue with entries sorted in the same order as bibliographic items are shelved. This catalogue may also serve as the primary inventory for the library

History of Library Catalogues

Library catalogues originated as manuscript lists, arranged by format (folio, quarto, etc.) or in a rough alphabetical arrangement by author. Printed catalogues, sometimes called *dictionary catalogues* enabled scholars outside a library to gain an idea of its contents. These would sometimes be interleaved with blank leaves on which additions could be recorded, or bound as *guardbooks* in which slips of paper were bound in for new entries. Slips could also be kept loose in cardboard or tin boxes, stored on shelves. The first card catalogues appeared in the nineteenth century, enabling much more flexibility, and towards the end of the twentieth century the OPAC was developed.

One the earliest catalogues was that of a collection of books given by Gregory the Great to the Church of St Clement in Rome in the eighth century AD, was written in the form of prayer. Alcuin's metrical catalogue produced for the monastic library at York is the only catalogue known to have been written in verse. The demand to give locations of books was not respected until the fourteenth century and the alphabetical arrangement did not become generally used until the sixteenth century. Even though there were some efforts to standardise of cataloguing methods as those by Concrad Gesner and John Durie catalogues mostly fuctioned to list stock rather than to gain books or bibliographical functions.

The first national cataloguing code was the French code of 1791, and was a result of the French revolution. This was characterised by a compulsory author entry, defining the form of the card catalogue and also covering rules for accessing and guiding. Panizzi with his publication '91 Rules' in 1839 improved the cataloguing code which may be supposed the first modern catalogue. Panizzi's 91 Rules lead to the Anglo-American code of 1908, or, ALA code of 1941 and 1949, or, AACR of 1967, 1978, and 1988. MARC format, what we known today for online cataloguing, would not have been possible without the international acceptance of a standard code of cataloguing rules, e.g. AACR.

Cataloguing Rules

Cataloguing (or cataloguing) rules have been defined to allow for consistent cataloguing of various library materials across several persons of a cataloguing team and across time. Users can use them to clarify how to find an entry and how to interpret the data in an entry. Cataloguing rules prescribe:

— which information from a bibliographic item is included in the entry;
— show this information is presented on a catalogue card or in a cataloguing record;

— show the entries should be sorted in the catalogue.

The larger a collection, the more elaborate cataloguing rules are needed. Users cannot and do not want to examine hundreds of catalogue entries or even dozens of library items to find the one item they need.

Currently, most cataloguing rules are similar to, or even based on, the International Standard Bibliographic Description (ISBD), a set of rules produced by the International Federation of Library Associations and Institutions (IFLA) to describe a wide range of library materials. These rules organize the bibliographic description of an item in the following areas: title and statement of responsibility (author or editor), edition, material specific details(for example, the scale of a map), publication and distribution, physical description (for example, number of pages), series, notes, and standard number (ISBN). The most commonly used set of cataloguing rules in the English speaking world are the Anglo-American Cataloguing Rules, 2nd Edition, or AACR2 for short. In the German-speaking world there exists the *Regeln für die alphabetische Katalogisierung*, abbreviated RAK. AACR2 has been translated into many languages, however, for use around the world. AACR2 provides rules for *descriptive cataloguing* only and does not touch upon *subject cataloguing*.

Library items that are written in a foreign script are, in some cases, transliterated to the script of the catalogue. Library catalogues originated as manuscript lists, arranged by format (folio, quarto, etc.) or in a rough alphabetical arrangement by author. Printed catalogues, sometimes called dictionary catalogues enabled scholars outside a library to gain an idea of its contents. These would sometimes be interleaved with blank leaves on which additions could be recorded, or bound as guardbooks in which slips of paper were bound in for new entries. Slips could also be kept loose in cardboard or tin boxes, stored on shelves. The first card catalogues appeared in the nineteenth century, enabling much more flexibility, and towards the end of the twentieth century the OPAC was developed.

Sorting

In a title catalogue, one can distinguish two sort orders:

— In the *grammatical* sort order (used mainly in older catalogues), the most important word of the title is the first sort term. The importance of a word is measured by grammatical rules; for example, the first noun may be defined to be the most important word.

— In the *mechanical* sort order, the first word of the title is the first sort term. Most new catalogues use this scheme, but still include a trace of the grammatical sort order: they neglect an article (The, A, etc.) at the beginning of the title.

The grammatical sort order has the advantage that often, the most important word of the title is also a good keyword (question 3), and it is the word most users remember first when their memory is incomplete. However, it has the disadvantage that many elaborate grammatical rules are needed, so that only expert users may be able to search the catalogue without help from a librarian.

In some catalogues, person's names are standardised, i. e., the name of the person is always (catalogued and) sorted in a standard form, even if it appears differently in the library material. This standardisation is achieved by a process called authority control. An advantage of the authority control is that it is easier to answer question 2 (which works of some author does the library have?). On the other hand, it may be more difficult to answer question 1 (does the library have some specific material?) if the material spells the author in a peculiar variant. For the cataloguer, it may incur (too) much work to check whether *Smith, J.* is *Smith, John* or *Smith, Jack.* For some works, even the title can be standardised. The technical term for this is *uniform title.* For example, translations and reeditions are sometimes sorted under their original title. In many catalogues, parts of the Bible are sorted under the standard name of the book(s) they contain. The plays of William Shakespeare are another frequently cited example of the role played by a *uniform title* in the library catalogue.

In a subject catalogue, one has to decide on which classification system to use. The cataloguer will select appropriate subject headings for the bibliographic item and a unique classification number (sometimes known as a "call number") which is used not only for identification but also for the purposes of shelving, placing items with similar subjects near one another, which aids in browsing by library users, who are thus often able to take advantage of serendipity in their search process.

Standardisation for Automation

Automation offers individual library the opportunity to develop its function throughout the world, which has been termed 'international cooperation'. This cooperation has such functions as the following : creation and maintenance of the national union catalogue, coordination of national services, international exchange of publication, coordination the acquisition policy, realisation of the automation of documentation and creation of new technology. To achieve these functions an individual library needs the international cataloguing standard or formats, powerful computer networks with bibliographic utility and highly trained cataloguing specialists, programmers, and so on.

The reason for standardisation is that—along with the benefits of accessing catalogue records from the bibliographic utility—any member of a network has the responsibility to maintain the integrity of the database. Any record contributed to database does not exclusively belong to individual library and, therefore, must be kept in agreeing standard for accuracy, completeness, and ease of retrieval and access.

When the automation of processing library materials began over two decades ago there were in libraries only a few standards concerning the application of electronic data processing which were implemented self-made systems and had their own programming. The first efforts were to create standards in technical domain, e.q. coding and exchange of electronic signals, or, data formats. The further attempts, however, were joint products of : the individual library, the great institution such as the Library of Congress, university libraries, and commercial vendors companies which were interested in developing libraries. The move toward international standardisation of cataloguing code and practices - as exemplified in manuals, the ISBD (International Standard Bibliographic Description) change - means that cataloguers have to be aware of the development of this standard. The trend towards a common approach to standardised ways is to use the already overwhelming and growing commercial databases in the market.

There are seven layers of standardisation for a union catalogue, e.q. :

— *Data carrier and data transfer*. When a national library starts cataloguing automation, this library receives bibliographic and data holding from regional libraries on various data carriers : worksheets, punched paper tapes, magnetic tapes of various sizes. It is thus necessary to convert them to mainframe machine.

— *Character coding*. The need keyboard with international reference.

— *Character sets.* Standardisation of character sets is very important, because database includes files in all language, and edits in a amount of different scripts.

— *Cataloguing rules.* Libraries should adapt international cataloguing rules.

— *Data format* Data format depends on the cataloguing rules, most libraries use MARC formats.

— *Common agreement about rules and formats* In a union catalogue, any library must have a very detailed agreement on, and instructions for, all data fields. Even though libraries have rules and a sufficient format, there will remain doubts about how to handle certain fields for the serials cataloguing practice, such as how subsequent publishers and places of publication of one serial should be recorded, how irregular publication should be indicated, etc.

— *Authority control.* This means standardisation of names of authors, corporate bodies and uniform titles. In a union cataloguing of serials, for example, mainly the heading of corporate bodies are concerned. Serials Database is very strict in authority control, because the file for corporate bodies is entirely under the responsibility of a group of specialists. That is why all entries for names of corporate bodies have to be sent on worksheets to the database and are keyboarded after bibliographic control by that group.

The MARC Formats for Bibliographic Data are a series of rules for coding bibliographic data into a form that can be understood and used in a computer. The MARC formats are also called communication formats by which it is meant that data in this form can be transfered by one computer to another. This format was primarily designed by the Library of Congress and reflects the need to catalogue products and processes. By bibliographic data is meant all of the elements of a bibliographic records : bibliographic descriptions, access points, subject headings, and classification numbers.

Trends in Bibliographic Networks

One of the future trendy of cataloguing library materials in the 1990's is the more powerful features of Bibliographic Networks. A bibliographic network is a network consisting of a central computer system with a large database of catalogue records linked by telecommunications facilities to libraries. As many other networks, it has the same common attraction to its users. Distant users can require access to the data and processing functions of the host computer. The most interesting aspects of the bibliographic network to librarians is the huge amount of the database required for library applications and the various ways of processing this data.

A general service in bibliographic networks is the sharing functions of cataloguing, or, online cataloguing. Evidence of this success was the introdution of online cataloguing by a bibliographic utility, such as RLIN (the Research Libraries Information Network), OCLC (Online Computer Library Center), UTLAS (the University of Toronto Library Automation System), and WLN (the Western Library Network). A cataloguer can make catalogues for specific items by accessing from the host computer which contains millions of records contributed such as by the Library of Congress or the British Library or other members of Networks. If the cataloguer finds records for such items, he can choose to accept them and command the system to produce particular products, such as card catalogue sets, microfiche, magnetic tape records and indexes. At the same time, the holdings data of the cataloguer's library is generated on the database which is then to be a union catalogue to function for all clients of networks. If the records are not presented in the database or he may not accept the standard of cataloguing recorded, new records and holdings information for the items can be added to the system. The common term for these practices is 'copy cataloguing'.

Copy cataloguing is a method of cataloguing library materials by which a source record is copied as found or edited instead of creating a new record. Simply stated, the purpose of copy cataloguing is to provide bibliographic access to books and other library materials and to get those materials to the shelves to be available for use promptly. New technology and system in cataloguing capability influence thinking on the organisational structure of the library. The online catalogue has made it possible from any branch library to access the complete holdings of the other libraries' catalogue via a remote terminal. Thus, suggestion for the centralising of library operations may now be reconsidered.

It seems as if traditional cataloguing for an item is being replaced by more efficient ways of retrieving and verifying existing millions of bibliographic records. However, the individual cataloguer is still required to perform thoughtful accurate work. All cataloguers concerned with an online bibliographic networks should also have to verify their own copy of any bibliographic record which may contain errors or may not be suitable for their institution. Or in other words, an individual cataloguer of a local library which contributes to the central bibliographic system should input data for items carefully. Any mistake means that other members of networks suffer. The technology and systems used in cataloguing library materials have been gradually growing. It is clear that successful Bibliographic Networks for cataloguing cannot be separated form the history of cataloguing itself. Bibliographic Networks enable the cataloguer to access and retrieve libraries' databases the worldwide, which makes it possible for a library to perform more functions.

Physical Forms of Catalogues

The types of physical form of a library catalogue are : book catalogues, card catalogues, microform catalogue and online catalogue. Any kind of these types has advantages and disadvantages. Thus, in deciding whether a library uses any type of a catalogue, certain considerations should be made. The library catalogue should, for example, be flexible and up-to-date to the changing of library collection; easy to use; and easy to produce in multiple copies. Since the catalogue is a record of what is available in the library, entries should be added or removed as a certain material is added, removed or discarded from the library.

The printed book or book catalogue is the oldest type of catalogue which was commonly used in American libraries. The characteristic of this type was expensive to produce and quickly became out of date or inflexible in changing of the collection. The libraries using this type should provide more copies, this is due to provide access for more users. Thus this type was gradually replaced by card catalogues. However, with the more modern, cheaper methods of printing and with the advent of automation for quicker cumulation that the book catalogue again became popular in certain type of libraries. It is produced in more modern production techniques, such as by National Library of Medicine, the Library of Congress, and the New York Public Library. This catalogue is easy to be sent to other libraries or information agencies.

The card catalogue is the library most often found in the worldwide. Each entry is prepared on a standard 7.5 x 12.5 cm. card. These cards are then filed in alphabetically order by author, subject, title, or call number in the drawers to provide access to the collection. The card catalogue is very flexible, it can be easily added or removed whenever necessary. Changing can be made on cards and they can be refiled. It can be provided by references. In large library, however, filing a large of new entries takes a long time and, of course, it needs more spaces. Other disadvantages are any changing is made manually and the users tend to manipulate the trays or drawers, so that other users may have to wait them.

Microform catalogues have become much more popular with the development of computer-output microform (COM). COM catalogues are produced in microfilm or microfiche. It provides a complete data of library holding which is periodically updated. Both book and COM are inflexible in changing, they cannot be added or deleted until the new editions are produced. But, by which they are computer-produced, they are flexible in making changes of entries. With a certain command can be made to change many entries. To meet the users demand, COM should be made in many copies. They are also easy to be sent to other libraries or information agencies

The online catalogue is the newest. The bibliographic records stored in the computer memory are printed on the video screen in response to a request from a user. Entries may comprise the full bibliographic record, or medium, or only a brief, it is depending on the system and/or the desires of the users. Online catalogue is the most flexible and current. Additions, deletions, and changes of entries can be made at any time, and the results are immediately available to the users. However, it is quite expensive to build up compared with other three types.

The primary advantage of the online catalogue is that database can be searched in almost any item of information of interest to the users or the users can retrieve information in a variety of ways, and it provides very rapid search. Other advantages are, such as : it can be used from far a way location, so that the users can access a local, national and international cataloguing database; filing of indexes is no longer a consideration; database in online catalogue can be updated online or at frequent intervals, as needed; provided instructional help; provided links to card form catalogues, reference help and circulation; online database, with a certain instruction in the system, can be produced in any other physical form of catalogues; and global changing can be made.

However, some of the disadvantages are, for example: it is much more sensitive in spelling, any error means unexpected or different information is printed on the computer screen; its users may be frustrated by getting a quite few citations or sometimes too many citations; it requires a new way of getting information, or training for its users; and it will be unavailable if there is no power or if the computer breaks downs.

Online vs. Card Catalogues

The card catalogue is an alphabetical file of authors, subjects, and titles for material acquired by the University Library before 1978. It is located throughout the corridors on the second and third floors of the main library. The thesis file is located in the Information Desk/Circulation area of the second floor.

The card catalogue provides the only subject access to the Library's collection for many items acquired before 1978. The locations given in the card catalogue may not be accurate. Once a call number is obtained through the card catalogue, do a call number search on the online catalogue to find the item's current location. In addition to providing complete bibliographic information, the card multiple cross-references that make it particularly useful if you have incomplete or questionable information. For example, the card catalogue has cross-references linking:

— pseudonyms to real names

— titular names (such as Earl or Duke) to given names

— current to previous names of journals

— separate titles of a series to the series title

— second or other authors to the main author

The card catalogue is useful, as well, for locating translations and works by editors or important illustrators. Browsing through a few cards may reveal that the title sought is actually a sub-title or a separate volume of a larger work. The Library's collection is extremely diverse: if you don't find something through the online catalogue and the item may have been acquired prior to 1978, try the card catalog!

The card catalogue has a card for the author as well as cards for each of the tracings (the Arabic and Roman numerals at the bottom of the card). The online catalogue, however, only provides access to the title and first author for many items found in the card catalogue.

General Information for Using the Card Catalogue

First-word articles (a, an, the) in any language are ignored in filing the cards. Certain other common words are also ignored for filing purposes. A list of the ignored words is posted at the end of each group of card catalogue cases. Words are alphabetised exactly as spelled without regard to diacritical marks. Thus, ü= u, but æ=ae and so, for example there will be entries under both Encyclopaedia and Encyclopedia. Initialisms and acronyms (e.g., AFL-CIO) are filed at the beginning of each letter of the alphabet. Identical words are file in Author-Subject-Title order:

— Music Antonio Zoran, 1909- (Author)

— Music (Subject)

— Music at Midnight by Muriel Draper (Title)

Subject Searching

The first step in subject searching is translate your topic into the terminology of the catalogue. This is usually a straightforward process, but language and perspective change over time, and the heading used by a library may sometimes be surprising. The University Library used the ninth edition of the Library of Congress Subject Headings for cataloguing books by subject in the card catalog; a copy of this edition of Subject Headings is located in the main catalogue area.

Begin searching under the narrowest term that encompasses your topic; cross-references will help lead you to the correct heading. The Library uses various approaches of subdividing larger topics and this may be confusing. Geographical regions may be subjects subdivided into smaller topics or subjects may be subdivided by geographical region. When a term used in the Subject Headings is followed by (Indirect) it means that the subject may have geographical subdivisions. For example, if you were interested in obtaining information on rodeo traditions in Montana, you would first look in the Subject Headings under "rodeo." The entry reads:

Rodeos (Indirect)

sa Rodeo clowns Trick riding Western riding Women in rodeos

xx Cowboys Horse-shows Horse sports Horsemanship Sports Western riding

The "Indirect" indicates that this heading may have subdivisions by geographic region, e.g., Rodeos—Montana. Note also the specificity of the "see also" (sa) suggestions. The "xx" entries are slightly broader headings at the next level of specificity. All of these headings are also "Indirect" and may have Montana as a subdivision. It may be, however, that even these headings are too specific for the Library's collection. In this case, you might try searching directly under a subdivision of Montana. Some possibilities are listed under "Montana" in the Subject Headings.

Alternatives to Card Catalogue

The record-keeping world has learned from librarians the real advantages of a card catalogue, based as they are on recording one unit of information on one card, duplicating the card in quantity, and filing copies of it in as many places as are necessary. The advantages and disadvantages deserve recapitulation below, to serve as background for what is to follow:

— Advantages
  - — *Flexibility*: A new card can be inserted at any point in the catalogue at any time, or a card can be removed.
  - — *Currency and completeness*: Because of flexibility, a card catalogue always can be maintained and revised to any degree of currency and completeness of which the cataloguers are capable.

— Disadvantages
  - — *Difficulty of consultation*: Only one card can be seen at a time. Guide cards in a catalogue tray, even when freely used, are a poor substitute for an arrangement seen on a page.
  - — *Limited availability*: Card catalogues are so difficult to prepare, distribute, and maintain that it is impractical to provide duplicates outside the library systems to which they apply.

The principal attempt at such duplication, the deposit of Library of Congress printed catalogue cards in author order only, grew to 105 sets in forty-five years, yet eighty-seven libraries have given up the maintenance of their depository catalogues since 1947, when the same information was made available in book form.

Printed library catalogues afford the converse of the advantages and disadvantages of the card catalogue. They are easy to consult because many titles and the plan of arrangement can be seen on the opened pages, and they are widely accessible since they may be published in many copies. They are never current and complete, because additions are impossible once the pages have been printed. Yet the advantages of printed catalogues are those desired by scholars, while those of the card catalogue are those which are of greatest convenience to librarians in administering their libraries. A good many surveys confirm this observation by showing that scholars do not make as much use of the dictionary catalogue as they do of printed bibliographical sources of information.

Unfortunately for librarians and scholars, library technology has not advanced to the state where a combination of orderly arrangement, flexibility, currency and completeness, ease of consultation, and widespread availability can be provided for any library's catalogue, or for that matter for any union catalogue showing the contents of many libraries, or for any indexing and abstracting service, or for any bibliography. In actuality, library technology has succeeded only in refining and combining the techniques which were known a century ago. Thus, the sheaf or loose-leaf manuscript catalogue provides a compromise between the ease of consultation of the printed catalogue and the flexibility and currency and completeness of the card catalog; and when the leaves are printed, the loose-leaf catalogue has the further advantage of widespread distribution. The cumulative plan of publishing catalogues in book form furnishes a further compromise which overcomes the difficulty of maintaining a loose-leaf catalogue but introduces the necessity of consulting a succession of alphabets if a complete search is desired. Strangely enough, the most modern and advanced substitutes for the card catalogue employ the earliest form of record used in libraries, a chronological list of receipts, better known to librarians as the accessions record, because they entail sequential scanning of the complete compilation to locate information. Since an accessions list offered no orderly author-title-subject approach, Liberians gave it up long ago as a means of access to their collections and adopted various orderly arrangements—first, classifications and then alphabetic subject headings and alphabetic arrangements of author and title entries—because it was not practical to read the entire record for every search. Whereas an accessions record grew only at one end of the sequence, the orderly arrangements expanded anywhere within themselves. This situation was a real obstacle in catalogue production until the card catalogue provided a practical solution to the problem of unrestricted growth.

The new machines which accomplish sequential scanning of the complete record rapidly enough to be practical employ electronic devices to achieve their speed. They include two International Business Machines sorters, which search 650 cards per minute; the Rapid Selector, which scans 500 feet of microfilm or 120,000 choices a minute; and the various electronic analog and digital computers, whose records consist of charges on wire, tape, and disks. There is already sufficient experience with the sorters and the Rapid Selector to assure the recovering of information by using them. While experts have asserted that computers can be used for storing and recovering bibliographic information, there has been no experimental confirmation of their claims.

The new machines are commonly thought of as solving the problem of subject control; and while they could be employed in searching for author and title entries, they are not being used experimentally in that way now. Yet our research librarians know that author and title entries are fully as valuable and as frequently used as are the subject entries in their catalogues, especially in the present state of cataloguing and bibliography. It cannot be said, moreover, that a complete record by subjects will make author and title records unnecessary, for they are legitimate objects of search and identification in themselves. A universal catalogue or bibliography will need all three kinds of entries. If the machines are viewed as opening up the possible achievement of a universal catalogue, a little arithmetic soon reveals that one scanning of a universal catalogue with any of the machines will still require many hours and probably many days to accomplish. A realisation of this situation has already led to searching several questions on the sorters for each use of the complete record, thus dividing the operating time by the number of questions which can be asked simultaneously.

The alternatives to a conventional card catalogue really are few. They are:

1. Sheets (Books)
    a. Bound printed catalogues
        — Successive editions
        — Basic catalogue plus supplements
        — Cumulative editions
    b. Loose-leaf manuscript and printed catalogues
2. Punched Cards (fully mechanised)
3. Continuous Strips

a. Microfilm

b. Magnetic Tape and Wire

c. Magnetic Disks

In the late 1930's a committee of the Association of Besearch Libraries, with William Warner Bishop as chairman, proposed the photo-offset reproduction of Library of Congress printed catalogue cards in one alphabet arranged by author entry. The activities of this committee resulted in the publication of *A Catalogue of Books Represented by Library of Congress Printed Cards Issued to July 31, 1942,* and later its *Supplement, Cards Issued August 1, 1942 to December 31, 1947,* altogether 209 volumes of about 600 pages each. Familiarly known from the publisher's name as the Edwards Catalogue, this set, recording about 2,500,000 titles at once, took its place among the great book catalogues of the world.

The success of the Edwards Catalogue, and the realisation that its depository card catalogues represented a burden most depository libraries could not long afford to bear, lead the Library of Congress to seek means of continuing the publication of its cards in book form as well as their sale for use in card catalogues. The depository catalogues had been valued as a contribution to bibliography from the first, and issue of the cards in books was advocated as an extension of this. During the investigation Theodore Besterman visited the Library of Congress, and responded to its invitation to suggest a method by advocating a printed loose-leaf author catalogue. In his article, "The Library of Congress and the Future of its Catalogue," he wrote:

> Any acceptable solution of this problem must satisfy the following conditions: (1) the resulting catalogue must be complete; (2) it must always be up to date in one alphabet; (3) it must be universally available; (4) it must be convenient to use; (5) it must economize space; and (6) it must not be unduly costly.

The Library of Congress studied the matter seriously, and encountered the following disadvantages, in addition to the reservations expressed by Besterman in his article:

1. Whereas the Edwards Catalogue had been reproduced by photo-offset lithography from cards prepared during forty-five years of printing, there was no type standing for 2,500,000 entries from which the basic sheets could be printed. In 1946 it was estimated that composition,

proofreading, type metal, and storage facilities to put 2,500,000 entries into standing type would cost over $3,000,000.

2. The Government Printing Office was unwilling to hold so much standing type, and in addition, was unwilling to adopt a cumulative plan of publication which would have involved holding type for periods of even five years.
3. The expense of printing new leaves and of inserting them into costly loose-leaf binders for several hundred sets was considered to be greater than subscribers would care to pay.

The Library of Congress also was aware of the potentialities of fully mechanised punched card installations, of the Rapid Selector for high speed subject searching and reproduction of selected information, and of the rapid development of electronic computers, but these were recognised as inadequate for making the catalogue widely available. The cumulative catalogue method, adopted late in 1946, was a carefully chosen compromise which took advantage of conditions peculiar to the Library of Congress to obtain the best results possible in printing a book catalogue from catalogue cards. Photo-offset lithography was considered the most effective printing method, and it was readily available at the main buildings of the Government Printing Office. Philip L. Cole, then Director of Planning there, suggested that a great deal of space could be saved, in comparison with the Edwards Catalogue, which reproduced only eighteen cards to the page, if the slugs of type could be rearranged to eliminate the white spaces before the cards were photographed in page form. Secure in the knowledge that the rearrangement could be done in the Branch Printing Office, located in the Library's Annex Building, Cole and R. C. Smith invented the Card Aligning Device on which the cards could be laid out and taped to cardboard to form pages for the camera, at about thirty-eight or thirty-nine entries per page.

The Library then adopted the following schedule of cumulative publication for what is now called the *Library of Congress Author Catalogue:*

> Monthly Issues: January, February, April, May, July, August, October,
>
> November, and December. Quarterly issues: January-March, April-June, July-September. (The January-March number replaces that of January and February, for example.)

Annual volumes. These replace the three quarterly and three monthly numbers which make up one year's issues.

—ennial volumes. The largest cumulation to date is quinquennial, now in preparation to replace the annual volumes of 1948 through 1952.

The adoption of the cumulative style of publication solved the problems of flexibility and currency and completeness by requiring the user to consult more than one alphabet, but provided alphabets which are large enough to compensate for the need to consult several. The adoption of the printed book format meant that any arrangement could be used for the entries, that searching could be done faster than in any card catalogue, and that users outside the Library of Congress would have the catalogue available in what has since proven to be eight times as many locations as formerly. Sixty-three sets, of both the *Author Catalogue* and *Subject Catalogue,* are used within the Library.

The value of adopting a method which permits any arrangement was demonstrated in 1950, when the *Library of Congress Subject Catalogue* was first published. Its entries are alphabetically arranged by the subject headings regularly assigned and traced on the cards. Variations of the cumulative catalogue techinque are used in the Library of Congress for its copyright catalogues; and further variations, employing a numerical record plus author and subject indexes, are utilised in the Department of Agriculture Library and the Armed Forces Medical Library to publish the *Bibliography of Agriculture* and the *Current List of Medical Literature,* respectively.

Since no library catalogue is a complete record of the holdings of its library, and since few catalogues provide more than limited subject access to the catalogued material, librarians and scholars rely heavily on bibliographies, indexing services, and abstracting services, and on the published catalogues of large libraries, for access to information in their own libraries and for notice of information contained in other libraries. Collectively these published catalogues, bibliographies, indexes, and abstract journals are more than a substitute for the card catalogue, as just noted, yet there is no evidence that any one or any combination of the current publications in this field can be used to replace the card catalogue of any research library or of any large public library. All libraries have possessed publications for many years which are not listed in these services, and notably acquire them currently before they are listed. No published register is likely to supersede, for flexibility currency, and completeness, a library's individual card catalogue as an author record of its materials. It is too difficult, for one thing, to transfer the list of a library's holdings from one edition of a catalogue to a later edition, or from a number of small cumulations to a larger cumulation. It can be considered impossible to display a library's holdings in any of the services which are arranged by subject, when they do not show the headings or class marks under which individual entries are made; and impractical even if such entries are traced, as they are to a very large extent in the *Library of Congress Author Catalogue.*

A test was made at the University of California Library at Berkeley to ascertain whether the *Library of Congress Subject Catalogue,* which has been since 1950 the world's most comprehensive listing of general publications in a subject arrangement, could be substituted for its subject card catalogue without recording California's holdings in the printed volumes. The report on it includes the following:

> The results of this investigation give partial support to the idea of substituting the LC *Subject Catalogue* for our own subject cataloguing. A sample comparison of the cards and LC *Subject Catalogue* for the letters A and B, excluding UC theses, shows that 65 percent of the locally manufactured subject entries produced in 1950 were found in the LC *Subject Catalogue* for 1950. On the other hand, of the 2,789 1950 imprints in letters A and B of the LC *Subject Catalogue* for 1950, only 16 percent were found in the CU file. Other parts of the investigation showed that as time goes on more and more UC acquisitions appear in the LC *Subject Catalogue* and theoretically it can be assumed that in the course of time substantially everything acquired by the University of California will appear in the LC *Subject Catalogue.* Nevertheless, this information is imbedded in the record of vastly larger LC acquisitions and the probability of increasing numbers of abortive searches by users of the LC *Subject Catalogue* as a local substitute is certain.

Consequently, it has been concluded that the substitution of the LC *Subject Catalogue* for local subject cataloguing is not feasible.

The daily experience of the Union Catalogue Division staff in using the National Union Catalogue at the Library of Congress provides another view of the great complexity of what has been termed bibliographical control. That catalogue, with some 12,300,000 cards representing approximately 8,500,000 titles held in hundreds of U.S. and Canadian libraries, is the most comprehensive author catalogue in existence. There is no accurate information of how complete a record it provides of North American holdings, but year after year the staff is unable to locate 25 per cent of the requests which reach it by mail, telephone, and personal inquiries. This record is not an undue reflection on the catalogue and its staff, but rather emphasizes the remarkable improvement over the record of thirty years ago, when 75 per cent of similar requests could not be located. The present effectiveness is achieved with the additional aid of any catalogue, bibliography, or indexing and abstracting service which the individual searcher chooses to use; but balanced against these remarkable resources are exceedingly difficult searches, for most of the titles have been sought by competent librarians in their own libraries before being sent to Washington on behalf of the persons needing the material, most of whom are well qualified in their own subject fields.

Since the National Union Catalogue was microfilmed in 1952, and can be purchased in its entirety on 2,706 rolls at a cost of $10,824, for use in any microfilm reader accommodating 16 mm. film, it is physically available to any library as a substitute for its author catalogue. There have been no purchases to date, however. In spite of its comprehensiveness and usefulness for locating books, there are the following disadvantages to the microfilm copy:

1. It is expensive, although not prohibitively so for very large research libraries.
2. It is filmed in several alphabets.
3. Although current receipts are filmed, they cannot be photographed in convenient arrangements.
4. It must be used in a microfilm reader.
5. Although a majority of the cards bear classification symbols, subject headings, or both, these are not coded, and consequently the film copy cannot be searched by subject with the Rapid Selector.

Are these disadvantages sufficient to prevent purchase, or has its undetermined incompleteness prevented purchase?

Published library catalogues, bibliographies, and indexing and abstracting services have been recognised almost since their first appearance as supplements to the catalogue of any one library, and as the possible foundation of a universal catalogue or bibliography. In recent years Liberians have been seriously concerned about the deficiencies of these tools, which may be summarised as inadequate coverage and inadequate analysis (both author and subject); uneconomical duplication of entries by various individual publications; lack of currency; uneven distribution of the published volumes; and the high expense of production, purchase, and use. With the weaknesses so numerous it would seem that none of the services could be of much value, yet most of them are self-sustaining and actually are invaluable to their purchasers and users.

Online cataloguing has greatly enhanced the usability of catalogues, thanks to the rise of MAchine Readable Cataloguing = MARC standards in the 1960s. Rules governing the creation of catalogue MARC records include not only formal cataloguing rules like AACR2 but also special rules specific to MARC, available from the Library of Congress and also OCLC. MARC was originally used to automate the creation of physical catalogue cards; Now the MARC computer files are accessed directly in the search process. OPACs have enhanced usability over traditional card formats because:

The online catalogue does not need to be sorted statically; the user can choose author, title, keyword, or systematic order dynamically.

Most online catalogues offer a search facility for any word of the title; the goal of the grammatic word order (provide an entry on the word that most users would look for) is reached even better.

Many online catalogues allow links between several variants of an author name. So, authors can be found both under the original and the standardised name (if entered properly by the cataloguer).

The elimination of paper cards has made the information more accessible to many people with disabilities, such as the visually impaired, wheelchair users, and those who suffer from mold allergies.

Cataloguing Process

A catalogue is a list of library materials contained in a collection, a library, or group of libraries, organised according to some definite plan. Obviously, cataloguing, or bibliographic control, is the process of preparing such a list. The catalogue consists of a description of each item, which is retrievable by several of its important characteristics used as headings, or access points: the author, title or subject matter. In a manual system, there are several copies of each description which are filed under the appropriate access points for the respective item. But in an automated system there is only one copy of the description which can be displayed using any access point for searching. The description is now called bibliographic record or just record.

Preparing and maintaining a catalogue require:

1. Intellectual activity for the cataloguing process based on selected standards and rules, or for locating and using bibliographic records created externally;
2. Choice of an overall organisation of records within the catalogue and their specific filing sequence;
3. Choice of the physical form(s) for the catalogue and the production of records in that form;
4. Developing procedures for adding new records and modifying existing ones.

Every record may normally have two distinct parts for describing an item:

Descriptive Cataloguing

This embraces the description of the bibliographic or physical significance of the item except its subject content. The cataloguer also decides here which bibliographic elements should be used as access points for the item in the catalogue and determines the appropriate form of access points used. The description normally has many different elements arranged in standard formats.The rules that should be followed for descriptive cataloguing in a medical library are the Anglo-American Cataloguing Rules, second edition (AACR2) and its revisions. As these rules are more or less the most used rules internationally in both manual and automated systems, using them will enable the user to see the same descriptive record format in any library he may use, and enable the library to use records produced in other libraries.

Defining the Subject Content

This is normally done using two types of tools which produce a subject description in a coded form or in thc language(s) used in the catalogue, which is the only difference between using them, otherwise the processes are identical. The two processes are:

1. *Classification*: Classification, through the notation of the classification scheme used, decides the general area in the collection where the item will be shelved. Most classification schemes lead to an arrangement

of items based on their subject content. This allows the user to browse the shelves. Normally, a more specific shelving number or symbol must be added after the class number to give the item a unique place among other items in the same class. The resulting number is called " call number".

Standardisation in classification, contrary to descriptive cataloguing, has not yet been achieved internationally. The library may choose a generalised scheme or a specialised one. The general schemes most widely used in medical libraries are :

a. Dewey Decimal Classification (DDC), which is now in its 21st edition and the second on CD-ROM;

b. Library of Congress Classification (LCC), which is continuously subjected to revision;

c. Universal Decimal Classification (UDC), which is widely used in Europe.

Among the specialised schemes the most widely used one in medical libraries is NLM Classification.

2. *Subject Cataloguing or Indexing*: The problem of this process is that it is language dependent and thus no standardisation can possibly be achieved. The process depends on two types of tools:

a. *Lists of subject headings*: These may be general or specialised. Among the general ones, the most widely used list is Library of Congress List of Subject Headings (LCSH), while Medical Subject Headings (MeSH) is the most widely used list by medical libraries ; it is now available in many languages.

b. *Thesauri*: These are more recent than lists of subject headings and are more associated with automation in libraries. Most thesauri are specialised in their nature.

The choice between lists and subject headings and thesauri is mostly dictated by the indexing method, whether it is precoordinated or postcoordinated, as the former favours the lists while the latter adopts thesauri. Automation has introduced yet another way of indexing using free text search or selecting keywords as access points.

Cataloguing as previously stated may involve original cataloguing, that is the creation of cataloguing records in the library from scratch, or using existing records elsewhere which is known as copy cataloguing. This may be carried out manually or automated.

3. *Cataloguing-In-Publication (CIP)*: The data in CIP is created on the basis of prepublication galley proofs or preproduction information for the item. This data is usually given on the verso of the title page. CIP data has to be handled with care and should be compared carefully with the item itself when it is used as the basis for a cataloguing record, as it may have erroneous elements or is not in conformance with standards and rules adopted by the library.
4. *Published Bibliographies*: Whether these bibliographies are catalogues of library holdings or published bibliographies, such as national bibliographies, they may be used for creating cataloguing records.
5. *Machine-readable Records on Tape*: Some major libraries, such as NLM, may distribute their records on tapes in MARC format. The subscribing library may get such tapes, then use local computer system to select the records needed for the local catalogue. This approach requires significant local hardware and software. Recent development for this is the use of CD-ROM instead of tapes which is cost-effective.
6. *Online Services*: Some files simply offer copies of cataloguing records, other online services allow user libraries to modify or create cataloguing records in a variety of formats for incorporation into their local catalogues. Among these are OCLC, RLIN, WLN, UTLAS, and BCMP. NLM has three online files with cataloguing data : CATLINE (Catalogue-on-line) for printed materials, AVLINE (Audiovisuals-on-line) for audiovisuals since 1975, and NAF (Name Authority File) for name and series authority records.
7. *Service Bureaus*: Several agencies and companies in some countries produce catalogue cards or other catalogue formats on demand. The cataloguing copy is provided in a form that is immediately usable in a local catalogue.
8. *Book Suppliers*: Some book suppliers provide catalogue records (cards or otherwise) with the books they ship to their library customers.

Regardless of the source of the cataloguing copy, individual libraries may modify or augment cataloguing records they find in order to make them more useful in local catalogues. Among such amendments the following are necessary:

9. If the copy has subject headings and/or classification which the library does not use;
10. If the edition of cataloguing rules used for the copy is different from the one applied by the library;
11. If the library may wish to add further access points and explanatory notes to records to emphasize some local interest.

    But if the cataloguer comes across an error in an access point or in another part of a cataloguing record, he should write to the appropriate institution and ask for clarification.

    Other kinds of modifications are probably unnecessary, such as:
12. Eliminating data to simplify records;
13. Deleting data that the library feels does not assist users very much, such as ISBN or ISSN.

Organisation of the Catalogue

In a manual system, most library catalogues are divided into at least two sections:

1. The shelflist.
2. The main catalogue. This provides access to records by authors, titles and subjects.

Shelflist

The shelflist contains one record for each item in the collection. It is usually arranged by call number in exactly the same order of items on the shelf. It is useful for assigning individual shelving numbers, in making an inventory of the collection, provided it is annotated when the library has multiple copies in the same order. This shelflist may not be available for serials when they are not classified. A list of serials may replace it.

Main Catalogue

The main catalogue contains several copies of the record for each item in the collection. A copy of each record is entered : under the author's name, the names of any of the other persons or corporate bodies associated with the work described, its title, its series title, and various subject headings. It also includes cross-references, guiding users from unused forms of names and subject headings to those that have been used. Many catalogues may also include guide or special heading to enable a user to determine quickly where in the overall sequence of records a particular catalogue file drawer, page of book catalogue, or part of a microform catalogue is located.

Dictionary versus Divided Catalogue

There are three major arrangements for manual main catalogues:

1. Dictionary catalogue, in which author, title and subject access points are interfiled.
2. Divided catalogue, in which subject access points are arranged in a separate sequence from author and title sequence. Some libraries divide even author and title access points as well.
3. Classified catalogue, in which the call numbers serve as subject access points and are in a separate sequence from author and title access points. This arrangement usually requires a language subject index to class numbers used in the catalogue, although some libraries may be satisfied with the published index of the classification scheme used.

In an online catalogue there will be no need for such arrangements although the automated systems produce any arrangement as a by-product.

Authority Files

The authority file is the file that contains the forms of names (of persons, corporate bodies or places), title, series, or subject headings and descriptors used in the bibliographic record, as well the required cross-references to and from these forms, and their relationship with other used forms.

Authority records may be interfiled in the main catalogue, or may be kept in separate authority files, in a manual system. They must be accessible to cataloguing staff. In automated system, they are usually separate from the bibliographic records database but transparently interlinked with the number or symbol of the authority record. The following is a brief description of the types of authority files:

1. *Name authorities*: A name authority record consists of:
   a. The authoritative name form chosen for use in the catalogue;
   b. Alternate forms of the name, and an indication as to whether cross-references from these forms are maintained in the catalogue;
   c. Any related names such as previous names of an institution;

d. Source of the authoritative name;

e. Any historical or biographical information about the name necessary to distinguish it from another name;

f. An indication as to which set of cataloguing rules was used to establish the authoritative form.

Name authorities may be imported from cooperative ventures or from major libraries that have such files, such as NLM.

They may be initiated also on cooperative basis particularly among libraries with a common language such as Arabic, because the forms of names may differ among the speakers of that language, and the library in the respective country is the best to verify them. With automated systems, it may be easier to use as a search tool as well if the file is constructed in a thesaurus form. These systems and the thesaurus structure will enable making the file multilingual.

2. *Title authorities*: These files will be particularly useful if the library uses uniform titles in its catalogue, or when variant titles exist among various editions of the same work.

3. *Series authorities*: A series authority record is required only for a monographic series, where individual works bear individual title and authorship information, in addition to an overall series title. This file should record the decision on how to handle series.

4. *Subject authorities*: The library may consider the list of subject headings or the thesaurus it applies as a subject authority, or restrict the file to the subject headings or descriptors it actually uses. This latter type has been eliminated when an automated system is used as it is going to do both purposes.

Catalogues of Special Collections

Some libraries maintain separate catalogue for special types of materials, such as audiovisuals, in addition to their inclusion in the main catalogue. In automated systems, such catalogues may be produced as by-product from the bibliographic database.

Filing Rules

Records in main catalogue in a manual system must be filed alphabetically according to standard filing rules, while those in the shelflist according to the filing order of the classification scheme in use. In an automated system, the system itself contains filing values for the elements of description that are considered in filing. These values are in fact interpretation of the filing rules adopted. As filing is always language dependent, the rules must cope with all languages represented in the catalogue, whether the characters are in roman or non-roman alphabets. The major existing filing rules are:

1. *ALA filing rules*/Filing committee, Resources and Technical Services Division, American Library Association. Chicago : ALA, 1980.
2. *Blaise filing rules*/British Library Filing Rules Committee. London:British Library, 1980.
3. *BS 1749:* British standard recommendations for alphabetical arrangement and filing order of numbers and symbols. London: BSI, 1985.
4. ISO 7154—ISO bibliographic filing rules. Geneva : ISO, 1985. and ISO/TR 8393-1985, Exemplification of bibliographic filing principles in a model set of rules. Geneva : ISO, 1985.
5. *Library of Congress filing rules*/prepared by John C. Rather and Susan C. Biebel. Washington, DC : Library of Congress, 1980.

The set of filing rules for Arab libraries discusses the agreement and disagreement of these filing rules and those used in some major libraries in the Arab region as well as standard rules for the region:

1. ARIS-Net filing rules for catalogues, bibliographies and directories. Tunis: ALDOC, 1989.

The basic principles behind all these rules are;

1. Filing is word by word rather than letter by letter.
2. Filing must be strictly as is rather than as if which means that the word is filed as written not as it sounds or means, whether written in full or abbreviated form.
3. A numeral files before the alphabet.
4. Order of characters must be strictly adhered to. This order is as follows:
   a. Space, dash, hyphen and diagonal slash are given equal filing character and come first
   b. Ampersand
   c. Arabic numerals

   d. Alphabet letters

5. Different forms of the same letter have equal value and must be interfiled.
6. All records in the same catalogue must be filed according to the same principles -the same rules.

Descriptive Cataloguing

The major contribution in cataloguing at the international level is that of IFLA. This is in the form of international standard bibliographic descriptions (ISBDs) which have influenced almost all existing cataloguing rules. IFLA has so far issued the following ISBDs and is continuously subjecting them to revision:

1. ISBD (G) : general
2. ISBD (M) : monographs
3. ISBD(NBM) : non-book materials
4. ISBD (CM) : cartographic materials
5. ISBD (A) : antiquarian books
6. ISBD (PM) : printed music
7. ISBD (S) : serials
8. ISBD (CF) : computer file, Machine-Readable files (MRF)
9 ISBD (CP) : component parts
10. ISBD (ER) : electronic resources (replaced ISBD (CF)

Other international efforts include those of Unesco particularly the creation of the International Serials Data System (ISDS). ISDS seeks to develop a registry of world serials publications. Containing sufficient bibliographic information for their identification and bibliographic control. The cornerstones of ISDS are the ISSN and a corresponding " key title ", to which geographic qualifiers may be included in parentheses at the end of the title when necessary to make the key title unique.

Another international organisation is the International Standardisation Organisation (ISO) which is responsible for many relevant international standards, in addition to those previously cited on filing rules :

11. ISO 690 : Bibliographic references : contents, form and structure.
12. ISO 9115 : Bibliographic identification (biblid) of contributions in serials and books.
13. ISO 2108 : International standard book numbering (ISBN).
14. ISO 3297 : International standard serial numbering (ISSN).
15. ISO 3901 : International standard recording code (ISRC).
16. ISO 2709 : Format for bibliographic information interchange on magnetic tape.
17. ISO 10444 : International standard technical report number (ISRN).

AACR2

AACR2 incorporates the ISBD system aiming at eliminating inconsistency in the descriptive treatment of various types of materials. It allows local cataloguers to choose among three levels or degrees of detail in constructing descriptive cataloguing data and also includes some optional rules. This flexibility improves the utility of the rules by a wide range of sizes and types of libraries.

1. *Levels of Description*: Rule 1.OD of AACR2 specifies these levels as follows:
   a. *First level*: Title proper / first statement of responsibility if different from main entry in form or number or if there is no main heading.
      — Edition statement
      — Material (or type of publication) specific details.
      — First publisher, etc., date of publication, etc.
      — Extent of item.
      — Note(s).
      — Standard number.

b. *Second Level*: Title proper [general material designation] = Parallel title: other title information / first statement of responsibility.

— Edition statement/first statement of responsibility relating to the edition.

— Material (or type of publication) specific details.

— First place of publication, etc : first publisher, etc, date of publication, etc.

— Extent of item:other physical details ; dimensions.

— (Title proper of series / statement of responsibility relating to series, ISSN of series; numbering within the series. Title of subseries ; ISSN of subseries ; numbering within subseries).

— Note(s).

— Standard number.

c. *Third Level*: All the elements set out in the rules that are applicable to the item being described.

The information stated here is considered the minimum to be given by the cataloguer, as he may add additional elements in the first two levels. Moreover, the cataloguer may use different levels for different materials ; if he does he must be consistent. From what has be given above, it is noted that a punctuation pattern is used, which is very important element in bibliographic standardisation. This pattern is defined for every element of description.

2. *Areas of Description*: The description is divided in both AACR2 and ISBDs into eight areas or fields. They are as follows:

a. *Area 1*: Title and Statement of Responsibility Area

— Title proper

— General material designation

— Parallel title(s)

— Other title information

— Statement(s) of responsibility

b. *Area 2*: Edition Area

— Edition statement

— Parallel edition statement(s)

— Statement(s) of responsibility relating to the edition

— Statement relating to a named revision of an edition

— Statement(s) of responsibility relating to a named revision of an edition

c. *Area 3*: Material (or Type of publication) Specific Details area (Used only for cartographic materials, printed music, computer files, and serials).

d. *Area 4*: Publication, production, Distribution, etc, Area

— Place(s) of publication, distribution, etc.

— Name(s) of publisher, distributor, etc.

— Date of publication, distribution, etc.

— Place of manufacture

— Name of manufacturer

— Date of manufacture

e. *Area 5*: Physical Description Area

— Specific material designation and extent of item

— Other physical details 5.3 Dimensions

— Identification of accompanying material

f. *Area 6*: Series Area

— Title proper of the series

— Parallel title(s) of the series

— Other title information of the series

— Statement(s) of responsibility relating to the series

— International Standard Serial Number (ISSN) of the series

— Numbering within the series

— Enumeration and/or title of subseries

— The same as for 6.2 through 6.6 for subseries

g. *Area 7*: Note(s) Area (repeatable, each note being a separate area)

h. *Area 8*: Standard Number, etc Area (a repeatable area)

— Standard number : ISBN, ISSN, ISRC etc.

— Key-title (associated only with an ISSN) 8.3 Terms of availability and/or price

— Qualification(s) following 8.1 and/or 8.3

3. *Access Points (Headings) and References*: AACR2 is of two parts : the first covers descriptions as stated before and consists of (13) chapters where the first covers all types of materials, and chapters 2-12 cover a certain type each, while chapter 13 concerns analytical cataloguing. The second part starts with chapter 20 which is an explanation of the rules of this part, while no chapters 14-19 exist. Chapter 21 covers the choice of access points, chapter 22 deals with headings for persons, chapter 23 deals with headings for geographic names, chapter 24 deals with headings for corporate bodies, chapter 25 deals with uniform titles, while chapter 26 collects together the various rules for references. The rules are completed by four appendices:
   a. A: capitalisation
   b. B: abbreviations
   c. C: numerals
   d. D: glossary

Numerous handbooks and illustrations have been published in different languages, as well as in the local formats adopted such as CEHANET procedures manual.

Subject Analysis

Classification

Classification is basically grouping similar objects or ideas together. This grouping is done through the notations assigned as class numbers from the classification scheme adopted. As mentioned earlier there are three major general classification schemes that may be encountered in some medical libraries :

Library of Congress Classification

This is a general enumerative scheme consisting of 21 classes in individual schemes, although they are now available on CD-ROM as well. The main classes and subclasses are designated by capital letters. Further subdivision is by integral numbers ranging from 1 to 9999, which may be extended decimally. The classes of this classification that concern medical libraries are:

1. GN : Anthropology
2. HN : Social History and Reform
3. QR : Bacteriology
4. TC : Hydrology
5. TD : Sanitary and Municipal Engineering
6. TH : Building construction
7. TX : Domestic Sciences

Note here that medicine is assigned class R which is not recommended for medical libraries. This class is subdivided as follows:

1. R : Medicine in General
2. RA : Government Medicine and Public Health
3. RB : Pathology
4. RC : Practice of Medicine
5. RD : Surgery
6. RE : Ophthalmology
7. RF : Otorhinolaryngology
8. RG : Gynecology and Obstetrics
9. RJ : Paediatrics
10 RK : Dentistry
11. RL : Dermatology
12. RM : Therapeutics
13. RS : Pharmacy
14. RT : Nursing
15. RV : Herbalism
16. RX : Homeotherapy
17. RZ : Various Schools and Arts

LCC uses auxiliary tables for individual classes, but not for the scheme as a whole. There are five types of these tables: form, geographic, historical, topical and mixed.

Dewey Decimal Classification

Knowledge in this scheme is divided into ten major classes using arabic numerals 0-9 provided that the number is of three digits. After this base number numbers may be expanded decimally. Medical sciences are placed in the main class 600 - Technology as follows :

1. 610 : Medical Sciences Medicine
2. 611 : Human Anatomy, Cytology, Histology
3. 612 : Human Physiology
4. 613 : Hygiene
5. 614 : Forensic Medicine, Disease Incidence, General Preventive Medicine
6. 615 : Pharmacology
7. 616 : Diseases
8. 617 : Various Medicine Branches. Surgery
9. 618 : Other Medicine Branches. Gynecology and Obstetrics
10. 619 : Experimental Medicine

In addition, there is a large number of class numbers relevant to health sciences, among which are:

1. 334 : Social Law, Social welfare, Labour, Health, Safety, Education and Culture Law
2. 363 : Social Issues and Services
3. 574 : Biology
4. 628 : Sanitary and Municipal Engineering, Environmental Protection Engineering
5. 632 : Plant Injuries, Diseases, Pests
6. 636 : Veterinary Medicine

The scheme has seven auxiliary tables for using with the various class numbers as instructed in the schedules. The scheme is now in its twenty-first edition in four volumes, of which the fourth volume is an alphabetical relative index and a manual. It is also on CD-ROM (2nd version).

Universal Decimal Classification

This scheme is originally based on DDC but deviated from it in many aspects particularly the obligation of using the three digits base numbers. But the major classes are nearly the same except for cancelling class 4 to be combined with class 8. Medical sciences have 61 and its subdivisions are as follows:

1. 61 : Medical Sciences (Medicine)
2. 611 : Anatomy. Human and Comparative Anatomy
3. 612 : Physiology. Human and Comparative Physiology
4. 613 : Hygiene in General. Personal Health and Hygiene
5. 614 : Public Health and Hygiene. Accident Prevention
6. 615 : Pharmacology. Therapeutics. Toxicology
7. 616 : Pathology. Clinical Medicine
8. 617 : Surgery. Orthopaedics. Ophthalmology
9. 618 : Gynecology. Obstetrics
10. 619 : Domesticated Animal Diseases. Veterinary Medicine

Class numbers related to health sciences are also scattered in nearly the same way as DDC. The scheme also uses ten auxiliary tables. The latest medium English edition was published in 1993, and its amendments in 1996. It is also on CD-ROM.

NLM Classification

This scheme covers medicine and other related sciences using the classes QS-QZ and W-WZ permanently excluded in LCC. So, LCC may be considered supplementary to this scheme for classifying other disciplines, except QM (human anatomy), QR (microbiology) and R (medicine) in LCC which cannot be used in this scheme. The classes are subdivided as follows:

1. QS-QZ : Preclinical Sciences
2. QS : Human Anatomy
3. QT : Physiology
4. QU : Biochemistry
5. QV : Pharmacology
6. QW : Microbiology and Immunology
7. QX : Parasitology
8. QY : Clinical Pathology
9. QZ : Pathology

10. W-WZ : Medicine and Related Subjects
11. W : Health Professions
12. WA : Public Health
13. WB : Practice of Medicine
14. WC : Communicable Diseases
15. WD100 : Nutrition Disorders
16. WD200 : Metabolic Diseases
17. WD300 : Immunologic and Collagen Diseases. Hypersensitivity
18. WD400 : Animal Poisons
19. WD500 : Plant Poisons
20. WD600 : Diseases and Injuries caused by Physical Agents
21. WD700 : Aviation and Space Medicine
22. WE : Musculoskeletal System
23. WF : Rispiratory System
24. WG : Cardiovascular System
25. WH : Hemic and Lymphatic System
26. WI : Digestive System
27. WJ : Urogenital System
28. WK : Endocrine System
29. WL : Nervous System
30. WM : Psychiatry
31. WN : Radiology. Diagnostic Imaging
32. WO : Surgery
33. WP : Gynecology
34. WQ : Obstetrics
35. WR : Dermatology
36. WS : Paediatrics
37. WT : Geriatrics. Chronic Disease
38. WU : Dentistry. Oral Surgery

39. WV : Otorhinolaryngology
40. WW : Ophthalmology
41. WX : Hospitals and Other Health Facilities
42. WY : Nursing
43. WZ : History of Medicine

In addition the scheme has two types of auxiliary tables, the first covers form subdivisions which are listed under main class numbers, and the other is list (G) which is common to all schedules and covers the geographic subdivision. This list divides the world into nine geographic regions, and one notation for international organisations that publish materials related to medicine. It has an alphabetical relative index, which uses terms derived from Medical Subject Headings (MeSH), and includes subjects outside the scope of the scheme and have LCC numbers.

Controlled Vocabulary

There are two types of tools for controlling vocabulary to be used in subject cataloguing and indexing :

Lists of Subject Headings

Library of Congress Subject Headings (LCSH)

This is the largest list of subject headings in English. It is a general list originally constructed for the use of the Library of Congress. Now it is published annually, as well as quarterly on CD-ROM under the title: CDMARC subjects. Recent development include:

1. The use of accepted abbreviations such as BT and NT, generally used in thesauri.
2. Eliminating inverted forms of subject headings gradually.

   Gradual elimination of subject headings that have the conjunction " and " or qualifiers.

The list has four types of subdivision:

1. Topical subdivision
2. Form subdivision
3. Geographic subdivision
4. Chronological subdivision

The list is not recommended for medical libraries as it is too general and lacks the subject headings required in health sciences.

Medical Subject Headings (MeSH)

This is the largest list of medical subject headings in English and in other languages to which it has been translated. It is published annually by the NLM, and is used in Medline and in most large medical libraries in the world. It is unique in having the following features that are absent in traditional lists of subject headings:

1. Subject headings have classification numbers based on the tree structure of the list. Some headings bear more than ten different numbers each. The major categories of the tree structure are:

   A : Anatomy

   B : Organisms

   C : Diseases

   D : Chemicals and Drugs

   E : Analytical, Diagnostic and Therapeutic Techniques and Equipment

   F : Psychiatry and Psychology

   G : Biological Sciences

   H : Physical Sciences

   I : Anthropology, Education, Sociology and Social Phenomena

   J : Technology, Industry, Agriculture

   K : Humanities

   L : Information Science

   M : Named Groups

   N : Health Care

   Z : Geographic Locations

   Each main category is further subdivided once or more as required using arabic numerals and decimal points.

2. The list has an index to the tree structure which is published as a separate volume.

3. The list has a KWOC index for the terms used. This feature is used in thersauri.
4. The topical, geographical, chronological and form subdivisions are not repeated in the list under the related headings but the notes give instruction on their use.
5. The print edition has the following lists as appendices:
    a. *Types of publications*: The types are also listed in the main list.
    b. Topical subdivisions which are only used with main headings. They are also given in the main list.
    c. *Form subdivisions for cataloguers with annotations*: They are also given in the main list.
    d. *Geographical locations for cataloguers*: They are not given in the main list.
    e. *Language subdivisions*: These are not given in the main list.

Entries of MeSH are of three types:

1. Entry of the main heading which typically includes the following information as required:
    a. The Heading
    b. Consider also cross-reference to other terms
    c. Tree number(s)
    d. Indexing annotation
    e. Cataloguing annotation
    f. History note
    g. Online note
    h. See related
    i. X See cross-referencc, for entry vocabulary
    j. XR See related from other headings
2. *Subheading*: This is printed in lower case and preceded by a slash. The entry includes the following information:
    a. Subheading
    b. Indexing annotation
    c. History note

d. Online note

Note that tree numbers are not assigned for subheadings.

3. *Vocabulary terms*: These include synonyms, near-synonyms, abbreviations, alternative spelling and alternate forms that may be more familiar or easier to type. The entry includes the following information:

   a. The vocabulary term

   b. The word " see "

   c. The main heading preferred

   d. The tree number(s) of the main heading

Thesauri

A thesaurus is the vocabulary of a controlled indexing language, formally organised so that the relationships between concepts are made explicit.

Fortunately the establishment and development of thesauri have been handled by ISO:

1. *ISO 2708, Documentation*: Guidelines for the establishment and development of monolingual thesauri.
2. *ISO 5964, Documentation*: Guidelines for the establishment and development of multilingual thesauri.
3. *ISO 5963, Documentation*: Methods for examining documents, determining their subject and selecting indexing terms.

According to these standards, the relationship or function of term or note which follows is expressed by the following abbreviations and symbols.

1. SN : Scope note; a note attached to a term to indicate its meaning within an indexing language.
2. USE : The term that follows the symbol is the preferred term, when a choice between synonyms or quasi-synonyms exists.
3. UF : Use for; the term that follows the symbol is a non-preferred synonym or quasi-synonym.
4. TT : Top term; the term that follows the symbol is the name of the broadest class to which the specific concept belongs. It is sometimes used in the alphabetical section of a thesaurus.

4. BT : Broader term; the term that follows the symbol represents a concept having a wider meaning.
5. NT : Narrower term; the term that follows the symbol refers to a concept with a more specific meaning.
6. RT : Related term; the term that follows the symbol is associated, but is not a synonym, a quasi-synonym, a broader term or a narrower term.

Although these abbreviations have acquired status as generally recognised conventions, some agencies have developed different symbols such as using -> instead of USE, = instead of UF, < for BT, > for NT and- for RT.

The concepts that are represented by indexing terms may be:

1. Concrete entities
   a. Things and their physical parts
      — Limbs
      — Microforms
   b. Materials
      — Adhesives
      — Drugs
2. Abstract entities
   a. Actions and events
      — Treatment
      — Marketing
   b. Abstract entities, and properties of thing, materials or actions
      — Elasticity
      — Speed
   c. Disciplines or sciences
      — Chemistry
      — Microbiology
   d. Units of measurement
      — Hertz
      — Kilometres
3. Individual intities, or classes-of-one, expressed as proper nouns

a. World Health Organisation

The indexing term should preferably consist of a noun or a noun phrase. The latter occurs in two forms:

1. Adjective phrase
    a. Handicapped children
2. Prepositional phrase
    a. Hospitals for children

The adjective, the adverb or the verb used alone should be avoided as far as possible. Abbreviations and acronyms such as UNICEF may be used.

To choose a singular versus plural form, the standards recommends that count nouns are expressed as plurals

Documents

Injuries

But when there is only one of the entity, the noun should be expressed as singulars

Hands	but	Head
Lungs	but	Nose

The non-count nouns are expressed as singulars

Steam

Brass

But if they are regarded as a class with more than one member, they are expressed as plurals

Poisons

Plastics

The other aspects that are considered in thesauri relate to the following: spelling, loan words versus translations, transliteration, slang terms versus jargon, common names and trade names, popular names versus scientific names.

There are three basic relationships between terms:

1. *The equivalence relationship*: The relationship between the preferred (descriptor) and non preferred (non-descriptor) terms. The symbols used are USE and UF.
2. *The hierarchical relationship*: This shows the degree or level of super-ordination and subordination. The symbols used are BT and NT. It has

to be noted here that there are whole-part relationships (which are usually considered as associative relationships) that are considered hierarchical relations, which are:

a. systems and organs of the body
   — Cardiovascular System
   — NT Arteries
b. geographical locations
   — Arab Countries
   — NT Jordan
c. disciplines and fields of discourse
   — Science
   — NT Biology
d. hierarchical social structures
   — Parents
   — NT Mothers

3. *The associative relationship*: This relationship is not equivalence or hierarchical relationships. The symbol used is RT.

   Most thesauri have designation of categories of terms, called facets. This is some sort of classification.

Finally, it has to be stated that there is presently no thesaurus that comprehensively covers health sciences the way MeSH does. The major sources of useful thesauri for this purpose are those produced by indexing and abstracting services. One example of a thesaurus in environmental health is " Inter-water Thesaurus ". This thesaurus complies with ISO standard. One case, not common among most traditional thesauri is the multi-hierarchical structure as exemplified here:

1. Surface Water
   a. BT1 Water Resources
      — BT2 Natural Resources
   b. NT1 Canals
      — NT2 Irrigation Canals
   c. NT1 Estuaries
   d. NT1 Lakes

e. NT1 Ponds

— NT2 Fishponds

— NT2 Village Ponds

f. NT1 Rivers

g. RT Impounding Reservoirs

h. RT Runoffs

Uncontrolled Vocabulary

Uncontrolled, or natural language, words and terms can be of considerable value as subject access points when they come from such sources as the title of a document, cataloguer's note on its bibliographic record, abstract or full text. Such words are often called keywords. Use of these keywords was made for creating KWIC (Keyword-in-context) and KWOC (keyword-out-of-context) indexes particularly by using the computer. In addition they are used for searching databases particularly those without controlled vocabulary. This requires compiling stop-list to identify those words of natural-language text which the computer program is not to make accessible in an index, thus marking accessible only those words which are highly significant for retrieval purposes.

But natural language indexing compared to that of controlled vocabulary has some stronger and weaker characteristics.

1. *Synonym Control*: suppose that we consider " renal stone " as the keywords to be searched. We must look into several places if our search is to be fairly comprehensive. We have look under renal calculi, kidney calculi, and kidney stones, as well as their singulars. If the system develops some sort of synonym control then searching will be efficient.
2. *Singular and Plural*: The same problem occurs here as in synonym control. This has to be solved through truncation and other devices that enable the retrieval of singulars and plurals.
3. *Different Spelling*: An important example is the different spelling in British and American English.
4. *Hierarchical Relationships*: Prevalent in controlled vocabulary.
5. *Specificality*: This is represented better in natural language indexing than in controlled vocabulary.

6. *Up-to-date Vocabulary*: Natural language indexing is always up-to-date.
7. *Ease*: Natural language is easier to use than controlled vocabulary, if the need is for few articles, but is very hard if the need is for comprehensiveness.
8. *Lower Cost*: Natural language is quicker and cheaper for the index producer to develop. There is no need for well-trained indexers.
9. *Compound Terms*: The controlled vocabulary takes care of this problem fairly easy. Natural language should have the required capability in the system.
10. *Inconsistency of the Indexer*: This is not existing in natural language indexing.

Whatever we do in technical processing our target must always be the satisfaction of user needs.

References

Chan, Lois Mai. *Cataloguing and Classification: An Introduction.* New York: McGraw-Hill, 1994.

Fayen, Emily Gallup. *The online catalogue : improving public access to library materials.* White Plains, NY : Knowledge Industry Publications, 1983.

Hanson, James C. M. *Catalogue rules; author and title entries.* Chicago: American Library Association. 1908.

Hunter Eric J. and KGB Bakewell. *Cataloguing.* 2nd ed. London : Clive Bingley, 1983.

Hunter, Eric Joseph and KGB Bakewell. *Cataloguing.* London : Clive Bingley, 1979.

Intner, Sheila S. and Jean Weihs. *Standard cataloguing for school and public libraries.* Englewood, Colorado : Libraries Unlimited, 1990.

3

Practices of Digital Cataloguing

Today, with computer systems librarians started to challenge some of the basic concepts of catalogues of the past, like main entry–realizing that both access by works and access to individual manifestations are important to some users. Now there is no need to prefer bibliographic unit or literary unit over the other, because the bibliographic and authority information can be rearranged by computer systems to display the elements that have included in description and access points – showing the works (literary units) when that is useful and showing the individual manifestation(bibliographic unit) when that is needed. However to do this intelligently, the cataloger needs to clearly identify the elements: that is, specify the primary author, identify the work, and be clear about the elements that identify the work, expression, manifestation, and item he or she is cataloguing. In fact, we have been doing this since the late 1960's with the MARC format, but we could do even better.

Libraries gave up trying to catalogue everything a long time ago. At the end of the 1800's after a brief attempt to collaborate with publishers in creating catalogue records for every article in selected journals, it was found to be uneconomical, and H.W. Wilson took up the challenge and started his own indexing company. Libraries catalogue the materials in traditional collections (books, serials, maps, sound recordings, films, prints and photographs, manuscripts, archives), but also provide their users with access to resources through abstracting and indexing services and other reference tools that can be combined in searches through metasearch engines, portals, and gateways. Catalogues were once used side by side with other reference tools, but with the online access of all of these tools, they can now be searched together. Catalogues are going through a metamorphosis, merging with other tools to improve bibliographic control over a wider range of resources, and the resulting future tools will need to do a lot more. We not only want to retrieve the surrogate bibliographic records or citations that describe resources, we want the resources themselves, and increasingly we can get them in digital form or at least be told of a nearby library where we can obtain a copy or be told of an online vendor that will sell us a copy of what we want.

Even though libraries don't catalogue everything in their collections, today they are going beyond their own collections to inform their users of relevant resources anywhere in the world. Web resources are being selected and added to catalogues and other Internet resources are being linked for our users to access on the tool that is also their online catalogue. Not only do they get the search tool, they may also get to see the digital object itself.

A catalogue consists of a set of entries, each of which stands for an item in the collection and which describes certain characteristics of the item, such as its author, title, publisher, subjects, and so on. The catalogue is itself a collection -- a collection of surrogates for items in the primary collection; these surrogates must be arranged as well. There is a highly articulated set of strategies for organising catalogues, e.g. alphabetically by author and/or by subject. Current cataloguing practices involve both strategies.

Surrogates are created for the items and arranged in a catalogue. The items themselves are also arranged —e.g. books are placed "linearly" on the shelves of a library's stacks. This is typically accomplished via a classification scheme, such as the Library of Congress Classification (LCC) or the Dewey Decimal Classification (DDC), in which a hierarchy of possible subjects is given a linear ordering and each subject is given its place on the shelves. This means that an item's call number not only specifies an item's location in the stacks but collocates it with other items that address the same putative topic. A distinction is made between two types of cataloguing activity, both of which are practiced to catalogue a particular item: descriptive cataloguing and subject cataloguing. Descriptive cataloguing is concerned with creating catalogue records for items, describing their characteristics as just noted — author, title, and so on. Subject cataloguing is concerned with classifying the subject matter, the intellectual content, of an item. It is the subject cataloguers who assigns an item to a class within a classification scheme which in turn determines a place on the shelf.

A distinction is also made between bibliographies and catalogues. Both of these in practice describe items. The difference is that a bibliography describes works and editions of works, but not actual physical items. A catalogue, by contrast, primarily describes particular, physical items in a particular collection. It does this partly by describing aspects of a work, as does a bibliography, and partly by indicating physical properties, including its location. The development of highly sophisticated, systematically organised catalogues and cataloguing procedures is a product of the modern library era, which dates from the second half of the last century. Book catalogues were the first kind used in the U.S.; these began to be displaced by the familiar card catalogues around the turn of the century. Digital catalogues began to appear in the 1970's and are now widespread; they are rapidly displacing card catalogues Entries in OPACs are commonly encoded in MARC (Machine Readable Cataloguing) format, a standard which permits them to be shared among institutions. To a great extent, the MARC standard encodes those features previously recorded on cards; it enables a fairly straightforward translation of card contents into digital form.

In libraries today, cataloguing is considered part of "technical services" — those services generally concerned with the maintenance of the collection, such as acquisition and binding. Technical services are distinguished from "public services," such as reference services, which involve direct contact with library users. Nearly all libraries have cataloguers, although in very small libraries one person may handle other tasks, e.g. reference work and acquisition of new materials, in addition to cataloguing. The cataloguers's job is to produce catalogue records for newly acquired materials.

"Original cataloguing" is the process of creating catalogue records from scratch — creating a record primarily using the item itself, e.g. by inspection of the book, including, but not limited to, its title page. This is distinguished from "copy cataloguing," in which the cataloguers makes use of a previously existing catalogue record for the item to create a new record tailored to the needs of their own library. Catalogue records that can be used as sources for copy cataloguing are maintained by several institutions, including the Library of Congress, OCLC, and RLG. While it may take only a few minutes to copy catalogue an item, it is not unusual for the original cataloguing of an item to take on the order of an hour. The whole scenario of information management can be divided into two worlds. These two worlds-the seemingly unorganised Web and the organised world of libraries- have much to offer one another. The Web can offer automated tools for searching raw information and the library world can offer experience organising and understanding information of all types.

By combining their talents and techniques, these two communities can bring powerful resources to bear on the problems of accessing, maintaining, and supplying electronic information. But this is not an easy task. Even though using latest technologies, searching the raw content of every document still seems to be almost impossible since it's not uncommon to retrieve hundreds of documents for a given search.

Modern Approaches to Cataloguing

For over a century we have tried to reduce costs through cooperative or centralised approaches to cataloguing. The business model for cooperative cataloguing is based on the notion that resources are created in multiple copies and that a bibliographic record can be reused to describe a copy held anywhere, that is, cost savings by sharing the work of cataloguing. The records created by one library can be reused by many libraries worldwide. Those costs can be lessened through cooperative cataloguing initiatives to catalogue more with fewer people, by using shared standards that in turn enable the reuse of the resulting bibliographic and authority records on a global scale. "Catalogue it once for all!" to save the cumulative cost of redundantly cataloguing the same manifestations in each library that acquired a copy. One cataloguer would catalogue the manifestation once for all cataloguers and for all time.

This is also the idea behind IFLA's "Universal Bibliographic Control" or UBC – where each national bibliographic agency is responsible for creating bibliographic records for its nation's published products and for creating authority records for all of its authors. (IFLA is the International Federation of Library Associations and Institutions.) The idea is that those records would then be used worldwide by anyone else acquiring those materials or needing the authority record for the person or corporate body represented by the authority record. The problem with that concept is that not all libraries use the same language or script or cataloguing rules, so records created in France, for example, might be of minimal use in Russia or China where they might prefer to transliterate to a script their users can read. IFLA is taking a new view of Universal Bibliographic Control to link records for the same entity and take more advantage of today's technology to enable greater sharing of bibliographic and authority information. We can retain the diversity of cultural differences and citation practices with cataloguing rules to meet the local user needs, while agreeing on basic elements and clear identification of the elements of description and access for increased interoperability worldwide.

The economies of scale make sense for published materials that are typically printed or produced in multiple copies. That does not hold up so well for unique materials, like objects in museums or archives and many special collections of rare materials or other resources that we may want to make available to a targeted group of users, like in-house technical reports and unpublished reports of research or courseware or instructional materials. So we don't get the economies from cooperative cataloguing for these special materials but we could reduce costs for those through better tools that support the cataloguer systems that help suggest controlled subject terms and classification numbers and help with authority work for names. Such systems can help all types of cataloguing.

Just as we have many times in the past, we can take advantage of the technology available to us at the time. For example, librarians made the most of printed card technology to mass-produce cataloguing records that could be purchased and added to local catalogues. With the development of the MARC format in the late 1960's we saw online systems that helped cataloguers enter bibliographic information and enable wider sharing of that information eventually worldwide. Bibliographic utilities since the 1970's have provided a rich resource of centralised sharing of bibliographic and authority data through networked systems.

With integrated library systems, we could not only bring in those shared records from the bibliographic utilities, but we could reuse bibliographic information at various stages of acquiring and cataloguing materials, and on through the life cycle of resources to their binding, storage, circulation, interlibrary loan, and preservation. Now with Web OPACS and catalogues merging with other tools in gateways and portals, our users can be anyone in the world and our collections can be global as well. Library systems are still in their infancy, just as the card catalogue was a century ago, and our systems have yet to realize the full potential of enabling access to the world's information resources. Information in libraries will be one of the prime resources for future search and retrieval systems. Google has already recognised that and is courting libraries to digitize their collections. Our bibliographic and authority records are a treasure that can be shared for the benefit of users worldwide in many communities even beyond libraries.

Today we are working towards greater global standardisation in order to more easily share bibliographic and authority information and thereby help to reduce the costs and also increase the ability to meet changing user needs. IFLA has led the way for generations and recently offered a conceptual model of the bibliographic universe to provide a framework for rethinking cataloguing and catalogues.

This conceptual model is part of the "Functional Requirements for Bibliographic Records" also known as FRBR (sometimes pronounced "ferber"). Very importantly, FRBR describes the entities in this universe and their attributes and relationships. It reminds us of the importance of bibliographic relationships to collocate the works and expressions associated with a person or corporate body – something lost in many online catalogues of today. It also reminds us the user comes first, that we catalogue in order to meet specific user tasks to: 'find,' 'identify,' 'select,' 'obtain,' and I add 'relate.'

FRBR describes fundamental concepts that have been stated in many ways in the past and now puts those concepts in new terms. It reinforces those concepts just at this point in time when librarians are working closely with other knowledge managers and information providers (from publishers to museums, archives, rights management organisations, and the Internet and computer system developers) to organize and provide access to both the traditional materials and the growing corpus of digital objects. These new digital forms of material and new packages for information introduce an opportunity for tremendous change in how we provide bibliographic control. Understanding the same concepts and sharing a vocabulary among all information providers are essential steps in enabling change.

In 1961 IFLA sponsored a meeting of cataloguing experts to promote international cooperation and standardisation of cataloguing practices to facilitate the sharing of bibliographic information. The product of that meeting was the "Paris Principles" that are the foundation of nearly every cataloguing code used throughout the world today. This was a giant step towards global bibliographic control.

In 2003 IFLA began a multi-year series of meetings of the world's cataloguing rule makers and national cataloguing experts to re-examine the Paris Principles, to update them for today's environment, and to expand them to cover both descriptive and subject cataloguing now reflected in online catalogues and planned for future systems. The 2003 meeting, held in Frankfurt, Germany, brought together 54 experts from 32 European countries to compare their current cataloguing codes. We just held the 2004 meeting in Buenos Aires, Argentina for the Latin American and Caribbean countries. One goal of these meetings is to see if the existing cataloguing codes could be harmonised and perhaps to recommend rules for an international cataloguing code that would still allow for cultural and national variations where that was important to users. The resulting draft "Statement of International Cataloguing Principles" (Frankfurt Draft Principles) is being refined over the course of further annual regional meetings worldwide through 2007 and a subsequent "worldwide" review beyond the cataloguing experts and rule-makers themselves.

The Frankfurt Draft statement declares that it is "built on the great cataloguing traditions of the world, and also on the conceptual models of the IFLA documents *Functional Requirements for Bibliographic Records* (FRBR) and *Functional Requirements and Numbering of Authority Records* (FRANAR)." The introductory text goes on to say, "It is hoped these principles will increase the international sharing of bibliographic and authority data and guide cataloguing rule makers in their efforts to develop an international cataloguing code." An international code would be rules and principles to guide rule makers with rules that have worldwide acceptance while also allowing for options when needed to meet cultural differences. There will continue to be the need for codes that reflect the needs of different cultures, sometimes due to different scripts, different citation traditions, different conventions of naming, and so on.

Anglo-American Cataloguing Rules (AACR)

This also implies there will be a continuing need for *Anglo-American Cataloguing Rules*. AACR is the cataloguing code now used in all the Anglo-American countries as well as in many other places throughout the world. Following the 1997 International Conference on the Future of AACR held by the Joint Steering Committee for Revision of the Anglo-American Cataloguing Rules (JSC), the JSC recommended the analysis of AACR and reviewed the logical structure of AACR2 with the desire to restructure the rules so they would be easier to apply and to articulate the underlying principles to build cataloguer's judgment. Plans have been underway for several years now to create a new edition of the rules. One of the goals for restructuring the rules is to increase the consistency in application of the underlying principles across all types of materials. The Introduction for AACR3 will explain the FRBR terminology and basic cataloguing concepts, including the FRBR user tasks and objectives for library catalogues, and eventually will include the future IFLA Statement of International Cataloguing Principles. The timing with the IFLA initiative is quite good, as IFLA will probably have a nearly final version of the Statement of International Cataloguing Principles by late 2006, which is when AACR3 will be sent to the publishers.

One of the beauties of including the FRBR concepts in the new edition of the rules is to remind us of the basic objectives to enable finding and collocating bibliographic records. This has been the objective of library catalogues, but should also apply equally to search engines of the future. FRBR describes the model to facilitate the collocation of related entities in the vast bibliographic universe. FRBR specifies the basic attributes or data elements that need to be present in national bibliographic records. The FRBR model also identifies important relationships in the entity-relationship model and those are already in the rules but can be made clearer. Records built on the FRBR concepts will clearly identify the bibliographic entities, so displays in online catalogues or retrieval systems can show the families of works and related works, as well as their expressions and various manifestations in multiple physical formats, even down to specific distinctive items and where they are located or accessible. Hopefully this will result in clearer displays for users to get a better picture of what is available related to what they are looking for.

In the past few years there have been several test systems and prototypes based on the FRBR concepts. One test of the FRBR relationship information is OCLC's research into "XISBN" whereby a searcher of an online search engine or of an online bookseller's Web site can invoke an application that would capture the ISBN (International Standard Book Number) of the retrieved item and find the FRBR related expressions and manifestations. It grabs their ISBNs and displays the resulting set of bibliographic records to suggest to the user that there are other manifestations beyond the single one searched for. This ISBN information can also be used to provide information on where specific items for each manifestation are located in the user's geographic area (based on the user's zip code linked to libraries in that location). This capability builds on the objective to collocate the various manifestations of a work.

The ISBN in FRBR terms is an identifier for the manifestation, one of its attributes. The provision of the ISBN in bibliographic records comes through cataloguing rules, and in turn a system can use that attribute to suggest other manifestations to the user that may equally meet his or her needs and equally to a requestor for inter library loan or to a patron at a reference or information desk. The user may not care which edition, as long as it is one in a language he or she can read and contains the content he or she wants. The format of being a paperback or a CD or a cassette also may not matter, as long as the user has the means for using that format to get to the content. So using the connections to the literary unit, to the work/ expression, a system can help a user fulfil the task of obtaining desired information.

MARCit

MARCit is an aid to easy cataloguing of web sites, working with a web browser. Cataloguing a site involves viewing the site with the browser, clicking on the MARCit icon, adding other information to the cataloguing screen, saving the cataloguing to a file, and importing the file into a library automation system.

A user's manual, which can be downloaded, is very helpful and written so that it can be understood by a non-technical person. The web browser opens when MARCit is opened. Then, while viewing a web site, one can click on the MARCit icon. The URL and title information appear in the MARCit screen directly from the web site. Several fields are catalogued automatically; other fields can be filled in manually. The software allows the cataloguers to rate the site. Different records can be saved to different files. A saved file can be emptied, renamed, and deleted without leaving MARCit. The method used for importing the file into the library's online catalogue depends on the automation system used. After cataloguing Internet resources, if the user searches for items on "Monalisa" for example, s/he might find a web site dedicated to Monalisa's art. The user can then access the site and get the information needed.

The user doesn't have to wade through the millions of hits a search on Monalisa might yield with a search engine. MARCit makes cataloguing such sites simple. The librarian who catalogues it can also rate each MARC record. Users seeking the best information available can use the ratings as a valuable guide to quality sites. MARCit has been designed taking into consideration that accessing the information would be easier and more efficient if a librarian has designed it.

MARC Format Adherence

MARCit adheres to the July 1997 Library of Congress MARC Standards. The comprehensive MARC records it generates comply fully with these standards and include all mandatory fields. Indicators are set automatically. MARCit even sets whether the site is a web site (http) or an FTP site automatically in the 856 fields, in accordance with the MARC Standards.

MARCit also automatically handles one main author entry, which can be either personal or corporate, but not both, and several other author entries - both personal and corporate. MARCit also sets the correct MARC fields, subfields and indicators for different types of subjects and subject divisions. It automatically checks ISBNs entered. It makes sure whether title is entered. MARCit does all of this automatically, ensuring that the records are of the highest quality. Computer running Windows XX or NT, 5 MB hard drive space, 16 MB RAM, Netscape Navigator v.3.0 or later OR Microsoft Internet Explorer v.3.0 or later and Internet connection.

Features

- MARCit will work with any library automation system that can import USMARC records from a PC-based hard or floppy disk.
- One can specify Dewey, LC, or local as primary call number. One can also choose to catalogue using all three call numbers. These and other default parameters can be changed at any time.

The explosive growth of the Internet and the World-Wide Web in recent times has caused great excitement in many quarters. Suddenly an extraordinary wealth of materials on a huge range of subjects is instantaneously available from desktops all over the world. This excitement is tempered somewhat by the awareness that this material is poorly organised, and of variable quality and stability; it is difficult to conceptualise, browse, search, filter, or reference. Increasingly, people are wondering how this situation can be improved. At one extreme are those who believe it is up to current institutions to take on the task of cataloguing, and generally organising, these materials; at the other are those who imagine new sorts of tools and techniques — sophisticated search tools and "agents" — will obviate the need for these traditional methods.

Cataloguing Codes

Cataloguing is an expensive business, and the economic pressures will be made worse by the increase in publishing in both digital and print formats. This will force the even wider re-use of records than is already occurring, but efficient re-use is only possible if records are prepared to common standards. The web and digital publishing communities have realised the importance of standards, and there is a flurry of activity to develop them. Unfortunately there is a multiplicity of standards in development, and it can be difficult to find one's way through the maze. Cataloguing standards - leaving aside communications and catalogue search protocols such as Z39.50 -can be categorised as:

— data dictionaries (lists of data elements)

— formats (how the data are carried)

— identifiers (to uniquely identify documents, authors etc)

— cataloguing rules (by which data are presented consistently to facilitate retrieval).

The data dictionaries with greatest significance for libraries are Dublin Core, which originated at a conference hosted by OCLC in Dublin Ohio, and ONIX (Online Information eXchange) which has emerged from the book trade as a subset of the wider EPICS (EDItEUR Product Information Communication Standards) data dictionary. EItEUR is the international organisation concerned with developing standards to support trade applications, but who are also keen to ensure collaboration with the library sector. In the formats category we have MARC (MAchine Readable Cataloguing), which has been building up its capability to accommodate records for digital documents.

Meanwhile the new kid on the block is XML (eXtensible Mark-up Language) with its specially designed metadata format, the Resource e-scription Framework (RDF) for embedding records in XML documents. Identifiers are important to uniquely identify an item to facilitate the reuse of common components and to minimise data traffic. The library world has through the International Federation of Library Associations (IFLA) been working towards a standard identifier to allow the unique identification of persons and the re-use of accurate name authority data packages. However, this requires name authority registries in each country, and there has not been the resource to achieve that. Meanwhile in the trade sector rights management is a hot topic.

The final component of the information architecture is the cataloguing codes used to provide the intellectual structure for the data. Without that structure the data loses much of its meaning was originally developed for resource discovery of digital documents on the Web. It comprises 15 data elements and is meant to be simple and cheap to apply, especially by the originators of the documents. The ONIX subset emerged from the Association of American Publishers discussions on how to get e-commerce applications under way in the trade sector. It is driven in particular by the needs of on-line booksellers where rich metadata, e.g. reviews, blurbs, extracts and images, is necessary to make up for the inability of customers to browse the books in the flesh. ONIX is implemented in XML.

Version 2.0 has been published, which can accommodate multimedia publications and e-books. ONIX is being adopted by an increasing number of trade bodies, for example in the US, UK, Germany and Latin America, and by international bodies like the ISBN network and the International OI Foundation as their preferred metadata standard for descriptive data associated with the International Standard Book. A study was commissioned recently to examine the potential for ONIX to be used in the library sector.

The fact that ONIX is based on the IFLA Functional Requirements for Bibliographic Records model means that there is basic compatibility with library applications. Indeed the trade sector can be commended for not trying to reinvent the wheel and for drawing on the best of what the library world can offer. Librarians who were consulted as part of the study were enthused by the potential for trade-library collaboration, and saw ONIX as having tremendous potential for acquisitions functions and for enriching cataloguc records.

Indeed some foresaw ONIX as having the potential eventually to replace MARC as the format for carrying cataloguing data. Obviously extension to wider library applications will require more data elements, e.g. preservation data, but the format is expansible. This raises the question for libraries -which data dictionary does one choose? Are Dublin Core and

ONIX competing or complementary? For a time there was concern that they were competing. However, the messages one hears more recently are of convergence, e.g. with the adoption of qualifiers by DC, and of dialogue between the communities. Which one predominates in the library sector will depend on the capabilities of library systems, on the availability of records in the different formats and on the investment that is put in to developing the systems and schemes. In this situation it is obvious that interoperability will be paramount, and that realisation is gaining ground.

The preexisting format in widespread use in libraries is MARC. It is well established in the library sector, but not so well in the trade sector. This makes cross sector collaboration more difficult. The main drawback of MARC is the number of national variants and the apparent competition between UNIMARC and MARC21.The difficulties of exchanging records are pushing countries like the UK and organisations like LIBER to pursue harmonisation of formats. The predominance of the US in research -and to a degree in publishing -means that the target format of choice is becoming MARC21.

The UK is almost certainly going to harmonise its UKMARC format with MARC21, provided the role for non-US organisations in the governance of MARC21 satisfies the UK community. XML, the major new format that carries out the same function as MARC in a digital environment, grew out of the Standard Generalised Mark-up Language (SGML) originally developed to support computer typesetting, and the Hyper-text Mark-up Language (HTML) developed for writing Web pages. Combined with Java script XML is an even more powerful web authoring language. R F, the Resource description Format, was developed by the World Wide Web Consortium (W3C) as a metadata format designed to be held within XML documents.

XML/R F covers technical and rights data as well as the description of the digital document. Both Dublin Core and ONIX records can be represented in XML/R F; indeed ONIX was explicitly designed for use in an XML environment. Two interesting features of RDF are that it tracks the sources of individual data elements -very useful when records are built up by a variety of organisations enhancing data along the line -and that it can provide an envelope for data in other formats. So it would be possible, say, for a library supplier to embed a MARC record for library use in a publisher's metadata record. If libraries were to invest in changing their systems to MARC21 only to find that within a few years MARC is replaced, say, by ONIX or Dublin Core records encoded in the XML format.

One leading light, closely involved with developing the MARC format, saw MARC lasting at least 15 years in to the future and probably longer, because of the huge investment by libraries in systems and data. Crosswalks between formats were seen as the way of achieving interoperability, and continuing development of the format would accommodate new applications and data types.

Future Cataloguing Systems

The FRBR entities of work, expression, manifestation, and item are often confused with the current MARC record structures by some cataloguers. They want to know how FRBR maps to what we are doing now. In fact, the bibliographic records we create in MARC format contain attributes of all of the FRBR entities. You do not have to have separate records for each entity, but it is helpful to separately identify or code the specific attributes – as we do now with MARC tagging or XML DTDs (data type definitions). In that way we can more easily manipulate that data for various displays, and many of the attributes can be used for collocating or clustering together the manifestations of the same expression and the expressions of the same work and even the family of related works. If we clearly identify or label the attributes, they can be manipulated by machines for searches and displays.

Our systems for creating bibliographic descriptions should keep MARC or other communication formats invisible to the cataloguer and the user. For example, cataloguers could be assisted in the creation of bibliographic descriptions through the use of style sheets that capture as much as possible in terms of transcribed information from the object to be catalogued. We could provide automatic transliteration when needed. The systems of the future could suggest possible related resources. They could suggest possible subject headings and classification numbers based on information already in the database of bibliographic and authority records for similar material.

We can also envision putting subject headings and classification numbers at the work and expression levels that would then link to data for the various manifestations that embody that work and expression. For now, we could enter that subject information in an expanded authority record for the citations (or we now call them uniform title authority records) for the works and expressions. If we assign the classification numbers and subject headings to the work and expression, that information could be linked to or reused for the bibliographic records describing the various manifestations without needing to redundantly assign subject headings and class numbers to each manifestations separately. We'd just need to add to the call number to provide a unique location for each item or copy. When we have systems that can use data from authority and bibliographic and holdings records (with today's MARC record constructs), there are many exciting opportunities for data entry and displays. It liberates the data within MARC records themselves to be applied to displays that fulfil the objectives of the catalogue and fulfil user tasks.

Future systems could also suggest controlled vocabulary terms and names that would be verified by the cataloguer and would offer the possibility to connect to a virtual international authority file to check for controlled names created by other authoritative sources worldwide. That virtual international authority system would also be a means for future switching of display forms for names and terms, again to keep the user first. The user would specify their preferred language and script, and the system for controlled vocabularies would enable switching to their preferred choice.

Applying cataloguing concepts and fulfilling objectives for catalogues would help future systems to gain the benefits for end-users of improved precision of searches and better clustering of related entities. Those future systems will help the user search all potential sources of information through intelligent systems, like the Semantic Web or similar global networked environments.

We have other prototypes of what systems could do in applications like Red Light Green from RLG. It incorporates some of the FRBR concepts in a Web-based search engine. It uses a Google-like search to retrieve the works and expressions in its database and alerts the user to available translations and editions (which are a type of expression in FRBR terms). The user focus of Red Light Green is on undergraduate students, so the system lets the student know the local libraries where he or she can get the desired item, and it enables that student to reuse the retrieved bibliographic information (the FRBR attributes) repackaged in their choice of standard citation format to use in bibliographies and footnotes in papers they are writing.

There are also systems that enable end-users to go to online sellers, like Amazon, Barnes and Nobel, Borders, etc. to purchase items they have found. This bridges libraries with bookstores and vendor systems to give users the option to borrow or purchase. Our library concepts and research can benefit the development of those commercial products as well.

There are also new front-end systems, like Endeca, for guided searching of databases. Endeca has built on library concepts of giving users suggested terminology to refine their search and to point out related resources not only through the traditional reference structures and links from authority records, but through suggesting related search terms and concepts found anywhere in associated bibliographic and authority records. It re-purposes the traditional elements of bibliographic and authority records to assist the user in seeing the range of possibilities for searching. The user enters any term or name or piece of information they want to search and the system responds with a screen of clustered terms used in the database that are associated with the information the user keyed in. From the research of Marcia Bates and Karen Markey Drabenstott , we know users very likely don't know the vocabulary or controlled forms used by the library system; and with systems like Endeca, they don't need to know, because the system knows and can offer up an array of suggested terms, names, places, times found anywhere in the bibliographic and authority records that are connected to the term used for the search. The system makes full use of the attributes and terms we have provided through cataloguing and presents the information in a creative new way to give the user a better picture of the universe they are exploring.

Combining Bibliographic Description with Items

Our bibliographic records more and more include links to the digital objects themselves or to related electronic finding aids and other resources. Some systems now embed our bibliographic descriptions with the digital information objects themselves either copying the MARC record or mapping it to a METS record with MARC XML or just by cutting and pasting the contents of the MARC records to use as the descriptive metadata for the digital objects.

Combining the description of an object with the object itself isn't new. We could say we've been doing that for many years with Cataloguing-in-Publication (CIP) information, that is, bibliographic description in the items themselves. That CIP data or bibliographic description is printed on the verso of the title page, so it's not directly searchable by a computer system. The analog content of the item also is not searchable, but once we provide the

MARC record for the CIP data to computer systems, particularly those searchable through the Web, we increase the access to that information. And once we digitize the content of the item, both the description and the full content of the digital object can be searchable by computer systems right on the user's own PC, fulfilling the user task to obtain the item they want.

The cost of cataloguing digital or electronic materials might also be reduced through the availability of more tagged or labelled descriptive metadata built in to the objects themselves as they are created. Microsoft and other companies could design systems to automatically provide basic metadata as electronic resources are being created, going beyond what they do now in suggesting a title and providing the name of the creator, and providing the date of creation. Those systems could help the creator to access easy to use keywords from controlled vocabularies and authority files to include with their creations for future indexing and retrieval. OCLC has already experimented with such a tool using the latest XML-enabled version of Word. Cataloguers, who get copies of the resulting works, could enhance the basic descriptive metadata, adding other controlled subject terms and classification numbers as needed and providing relationships to names of persons, corporate bodies, works, etc. to enhance the Web discovery of both the descriptions and the items themselves.

For images, we have cameras now creating their own metadata when you take a picture with them certainly the date the picture was taken, and some add the photographers' name (or rather the name of the owner of the camera who entered the information at the start), and it captures information about the settings used. It could even include the satellite geospatial positioning information to indicate where the picture was taken – and all of that could be used later for retrieval. For documents, when we use software like Microsoft Word, the software automatically indicates the date the document was created or modified, the author (based on the registered owner of the software), the document's file size, the software used to create it (type of file), and it suggests a title for the document when you save it using the first words of the first line of text ironically that is how the Babylon clay tables, scrolls, and early manuscripts were identified the first lines of text; and music- by the first few notes of the work. All of that is metadata that can be used to retrieve that document later.

Some bibliographic and authority records already include hotlinks to digital items for online access, to "obtain" in FRBR terms. This brings with it the need to alert the user to access restrictions for obtaining some materials that require licenses or other payment for use or those that are restricted, confidential, or top secret materials. There are several experimental systems for digital rights management, and some integrated library systems include such alerts as well.

We have some adjustments to make in bibliographic descriptions to be more precise about what we are describing – a work, an expression, a manifestation, an item – we already do that to some degree in our MARC records, but the MARC format itself has benefits and drawbacks for enabling future manipulation of the data elements for different displays. Some systems have experimented with "FRBR-ising" legacy data, like VTLS and Innovative Interfaces. The Library of Congress and OCLC each have different kinds of FRBR algorithms that are available for experimentation and map MARC data into FRBR concepts.

As we re-examine cataloguing practices in light of FRBR, we see the usefulness of explicitly identifying the roles of persons and corporate bodies with respect to the bibliographic entities, more than the MARC format does through the tags of main or added entry, to use what the MARC format already includes as relator terms and codes. Through another cost-cutting decision many libraries in the United States agreed to stop providing such role information for nearly all types of roles (exceptions being for some illustrators and some roles in music like composers and arrangers). These are things that could be built into the creation of descriptive metadata in future cataloguing systems in ways that are easy for the cataloguer to use. This "role" information is not part of the heading for the person or corporate body, but instead is an identification of the relationship between that person or corporate body and the bibliographic entity being described. It is useful information for filtering large search results.

We also see the value of standardised citations for works and expressions (what we now call uniform titles for works and expressions) to collocate the small but important percent of materials that exist in multiple manifestations. Some of OCLC's research has shown less than 20% of their WorldCat database of over 56 million records have more than a single manifestation per work. We can see the potential for decreasing cataloguing work and costs by linking subject headings and classification numbers to those citations that in turn can be linked to records for the manifestations that embody those works and expressions – or they could be linked to or embedded with the digital object they describe, increasing the precision of retrieval for that object.

Benefits of Digitisation

Today, we could access information by words or sounds or images found in the digital objects themselves, but retrieval would be more precise if we included controlled vocabularies (names, titles of works, and subjects). Brewster Kahle of the Internet Archive was cited recently in the *BBC News* World Edition as follows: "Using a robotic scanner, Mr. Kahle said the job of scanning the 26 million volumes in the US Library of Congress, the world's biggest library, would cost only \$260m...He estimated that the scanned images would take up about a terabyte of space and cost about \$60,000...to store. Instead of needing a huge building to hold them, the entire library could fit on a single shelf."

Besides the point that the Library of Congress has over 116 million items and not just the 26 million book volumes in its collections and that we continue to add thousands of new items in analog form to the collections each day, the point Mr. Kahle was making is that digitising it all is probably doable with today's technology, and someday those scanned digitised texts, images, and sounds will also become searchable with advances in optical character recognition and sound and image recognition. It's not good enough just to digitize it all we must be able to retrieve individual items and groups of items that meet user needs to find, identify, select, and obtain information.

In the future, for the born digital and the digitised items, all the "chief source" information will be there, and we will find ways to give more weight to information found on a chief source (that's the title page for books, remember), just as Google can now give more weight to metadata in titles and from highly ranked sources in addition to frequency of occurrence of searched terms or frequently accessed sources. But we know from history that searching is improved when we used controlled vocabularies. Libraries have been in the business of selecting the most relevant resources for its users, and we could continue to augment the machine-generated metadata for those selected resources with added access information using our controlled vocabularies.

We need application software to enable retrievals and displays such as topic maps and other cluster display capabilities and guided search engines, utilising information we provide in bibliographic and authority records that augments information we could use from digitised objects themselves. Tomorrow's cataloguers will continue to develop and maintain the most useful controlled vocabularies and authority databases worldwide.

We need the virtual international authority file as a functioning building block along with other name and topic lists and mappings of vocabularies to enable users to search and see names and terms displayed in the language and script they can read while enhancing the precision of Web searching. The virtual international authority file would help cataloguers reduce the costs and labour of authority work through more international sharing of the work and automatic incorporation of found authority information into local systems. It will speed up their work and avoid redundant effort. In the future, a virtual international authority file system would enable creators and realisers of intellectual and artistic content to automatically include (or link to) controlled forms of names and topics at the point of recording the content they create.

We need international cataloguing rules (or compatible national rules) to make it easier to reuse the products of cataloguing and to help reduce global costs for bibliographic control. Future rules would provide guidance for those serious about description and access, while providing general principles anyone could use. The description and access points provided by creators and publishers will be enhanced by cataloguers, just as we do now, but we can expect to get more usable information from publishers, who have trained cataloguers on their staff. Sharing bibliographic and authority information worldwide will help reduce costs.

We will see new information retrieval systems, that is, corporate integrated systems, which enable the creation, maintenance, and use of XML-based data packages. Those data packages would build on the FRBR entities, attributes, and relationships for elements we now place in bibliographic and authority records but in future with links to the objects themselves.

Cataloguing requires skilled people to save users time and effort in locating information they need. We want to continue to let users know about related material and some of those relationships will be provided by machine-generated links, but others will need human intelligence to identify. Cataloguing follows some basic principles and concepts and objectives that put the user first, providing collocation and differentiation of entities that are meaningful to users. Those principles should be enhanced by future search engines and global networks. The skills and knowledge of cataloguers will help future generations develop even better systems and methods for organising the ever-increasing universe of information.

Trained Cataloguers

Reducing costs can happen through better use of people and technology and through a cataloguing process that returns (once again) to the basics for providing bibliographic control over a large volume of diverse material. It requires skilled people and smart systems to make it easier for the user. It is a fallacy to think an untrained person can produce a "good enough" product. Training is necessary so the product is more easily indexed and usable. Sir Thomas Hyde wrote in his preface to the Bodleian Library catalogue of 1674 that inexperienced people who make indexes for their collection of private books think all it takes is writing down the titles from the title pages. He goes on to say that to create an alphabetical catalogue for a large collection of a multitude of books from all over the world brings up "intricate and difficult problems that torture the mind."

We see this today in trying to use metasearch engines to retrieve materials across a wide variety of source databases that are built by people of varying degrees of training, based on different metadata standards. One example is the National Science Digital Library. The NSDL uses software to massage the metadata they get from the various contributors and typically have to "dumb-down" the transformed data. Some of it is simply not usable, because it is not structured in a clear way that lets a machine recognize the components. For example, Dublin Core metadata elements are used, but the element "creator" may contain a single name in any order or multiple names with no indication for the machine to know what's going on. Some contributors to the NSDL include full information, others provide very minimal information, so trying to make sense of the resulting searches is challenging.

It's interesting to note that non-librarian designers of digital libraries discovered they needed authority control once they got beyond their prototype systems of a few hundred records. Names and titles can be presented in a wide variety of ways and in many scripts, so librarians follow standards to enable gathering like things together. Controlled vocabularies for names and subjects are proven components of good retrieval systems.

So here's another cataloguing tradition that has value into the future controlled vocabularies. And we know authority control is expensive. To build and maintain controlled vocabularies and authority files requires trained experts, but the value becomes clear for the precision of searching and enabling the collocation objective of catalogues especially when you want to obtain resources in a very large, multilingual, diverse collection. Yes, it may be expensive, but we'll look in a moment how to help reduce that cost.

Creating a subject heading string requires knowledge of the syntax rules, so there have been proposals to get rid of the need for that by using faceted terms that can be post-coordinated. Yet we know that post-coordinated searching reduces the precision of searches and increases the recall, making it harder for users to find what they need in very large databases.

Doing authority work takes skill and time, so there have been decisions to eliminate access points by using minimal level or core records, such as the "core records" in the Program for Cooperative Cataloguing. This results in the abandonment of some of the basic objectives of catalogues to enable a user to find all the works of an author and to collocate the various manifestations of a work and to find all the works under a given subject. Cost-cutting decisions to eliminate subject access run against studies that tell us subject access is so vital, especially for digital materials and Web resources. Cutting costs by reducing or eliminating name and subject access and the corresponding authority control result in serious disservice to users and remember that users include library staff who need some of that information to do their jobs of selection, acquisitions, cataloguing, and reference.

Beyond access points, descriptive elements have also been reviewed and reduced or eliminated. Panizzi argued for a base set of elements, justifying them by the usefulness of each element to the user, and cataloguing rules since his time have refined his choices. We now have the ISBDs (International Standards for Bibliographic Description) that give us prescribed elements and their order in a bibliographic record. However, we have also seen how short-sighted decisions to eliminate some of the basic elements have resulted in inconsistent records that are lost in retrievals and collocations again the user is the loser.

Another effort to reduce costs has been the development of special processing for special types of materials. The result has been a proliferation of processing streams to meet special needs and the resulting special case law approaches have led to complex documentation to record the myriad conditions and pathways. We have justified this by explaining that with a large workforce you need to document all these special conditions in order to assure consistent products. This wasn't just the warning of Andrew Osborn in 1941 about the "crisis in cataloguing," and the proliferation of case law rules, but it's again a major concern today. We need to step back again to see where consistency is important and to assure there are general rules to cover those situations and also to recognize other areas of description where consistency doesn't matter, provided that the resulting information in the cataloguing record accurately reflects the item being catalogued and is clearly understood by the user. Back to basic principles.

In 1932 Keyes Metcalf in expressing concern about the cost of cataloguing suggested giving up cataloguing as we do it now; finding some way of increasing production; or through centralised or cooperative cataloguing reducing the amount of cataloguing that must be done. Today we are trying all three approaches and still need to do more.

We know we cannot continue to catalogue as we always have certainly not as we did in the days of handwriting cataloguing information on slips and cards or even typing card sets or buying them from the Library of Congress or a vendor. We know we can't even catalogue as we have for the past nearly 40 years of online cataloguing through our still very primitive library systems and online catalogues (OPACs). The online catalogues actually lost some of the benefits of earlier catalogues. We lost the use of the full array of original scripts the Japanese, Chinese, Hebrew, Arabic and many other beautiful scripts of languages that we used to transcribe when creating descriptive information we've been limited to those languages that the MARC format would accept, and even those could not be displayed in most integrated library systems this remains a limitation of most integrated library systems today. We lost the collocation of many works and expressions in OPACs that, to this day, typically do not properly index uniform titles. Just talk to your music librarian colleagues to hear their dismay about current online catalogues displaying musical works. Our tools are not as good as they should be or as they can be.

Yet, those OPACs brought us the ability to filter and limit searches and to bring together records in ways we could not do in book or card catalogues. They gave us the mixed blessing of keyword searching for great recall at the expense of precision. And now we see the Internet capabilities of Google and Yahoo and Amazon for even faster keyword access to information. We have the promise of even newer search engines than Google that are built on graph theory to retrieve the richness of the data we've been providing in bibliographic and authority records; systems to help guide users by enabling them to see the wealth of terms and names associated with the topic they are looking for. Still the cataloguing remains expensive.

References

Anglo-American Cataloguing Rules. North American Text. Chicago, ALA, 1967.

Bliss, H. E.: *The Organisation of Knowledge in Libraries,* 2d ed., rev. New York, H, W. Wilson, 1939.

Fayen, Emily Gallup. *The online catalogue : improving public access to library materials.* White Plains, NY : Knowledge Industry Publications, 1983.

Fellows, Dorcas. *Cataloguing Rules with Explanations and Illustrations.* 2d ed. New York, H. W. Wilson, 1922.

4

Online Library Classification

According to the Online Computer Library Center, Inc., the DDC system is used in more than 200,000 libraries throughout 135 countries, making it the most widely used library classification system in the world. This system is used in most public and school libraries. Adults may remember using the Dewey Decimal card catalog system. But as library users turned high tech -—using library search engines to find books online—the DDC system responded with WebDewey. This online version of the complete DDC system is available to librarians via a standard Web browser. With online updates, WebDewey makes it easy for librarians to keep their collections organized, even as advances in science and technology are creating a demand for new classifications every day.

The Library of Congress Classification system was originally designed to organize the books of the world's biggest library: the Library of Congress. Today, this system is also used in many large academic libraries. This system organizes all subjects using 21 basic classes, each identified with a different letter of the alphabet. Librarians can access the LCC system through 41 printed volumes, or via Classification Web, the LCC system's online version.

The Superintendent of Documents, or SuDocs, is a specialized classification system that organizes U.S. government documents according to government author. The U.S. Government Printing Office provides these documents free to depository libraries throughout the United States. Free electronic access to a digital library of government publications is available to depository librarians through GPO Access.

Classification Schemes

Classification is a process of grouping. It involves putting together like entities and separating unlike entities. In ordinary classification, we deal with the arrangement of ideas and objects. But in library classification we are concerned with documents, and the aim is to arrange these in the most helpful and permanent order.

Classification is the arranging of things according to likeness and unlikeness. It is the sorting and grouping of things, but in addition, classification of books is a knowledge classification with adjustments made necessary by the physical form of books. Classification is thus a process, which brings together like documents and separates unlike ones.

The four major classification schemes are:

Library of Congress Classification (LCC)

The scheme of classification drawn up by Herbert Putnam in 1897. Although based in some respects on the Dewey Decimal Classification and Cutter's expansive schemes, it does not conform to theoretical rules for classification. It was quite explicitly compiled to meet the needs of the library's huge collection of books and is too detailed and complex for use in small libraries. It has, however, been adopted by research and university libraries throughout the world.

Dewey Decimal Classification (DDC)

Devised by Melvil Dewey and first published anonymously in 876, since when it has been revised nineteen times. Knowledge is divided into the ten main classes, each designated by a numeral from zero to nine, which can then be subdivided by the addition of two numerals before a decimal point and further numerals after it. It has a relative index which shows the relation of each subject that is indexed to a larger subject (or class or division). The published schedules have been extended and modified in successive editions.

Universal Decimal Classification (UDC)

Essentially an elaborate expansion of the Decimal Classification of Melvil Dewey, using various symbols in addition to Arabic numerals to create long and expressive notations for particular documents. This makes it particularly appropriate for use in specialist libraries and collections, and its adoption by the International Organization for Standardization (ISO) has ensured its worldwide use. It was developed by the Institut Internationale de Bibliographie, now FID, under the direction of Paul Otlet and Henri la Fontaine.

Colon Classification (CC)

Designed by Dr. S.R. Ranganathan, it is based on the classification of any subject by its uses and relations, which are indicated by numbers divided by a colon ':'. It was the first example of an analytico-synthetic classification, in which the subject field is first analysed into facets, and class numbers are then constructed by synthesis. Ready-made class numbers are not provided for most topics but are constructed by combining the classes of the various unit schedules of which the scheme consists. It has proved particularly popular in India and has inspired classification researchers in many parts of the world

Uses of Classification Systems

Classification as a library tool sprung up with the development of the public library movement; but what was an adequate tool for the small public libraries of the early twentieth century has proved quite unable to cope with the demands of research and industrial libraries of later years.

The Universal Decimal Classification, which set out to meet their requirements, falls deeper and deeper into the morass of involved construction, extravagant use of notation, and ambiguity. As for the Decimal Classification itself, the fifteenth edition seems to indicate that it has quite given up the struggle to control knowledge. It seems to be settling comfortably back into the routine of meeting the comparatively simple demands of the small-town American library, leaving the real task of organising knowledge to the dictionary catalogue, and contenting itself with providing a means of assembling books on the shelves. This leads to an enunciation of the three levels at which a librarian may use classification in his daily work:

1. As a convenient method of assembling books on shelves, and for arranging pamphlets and clippings in vertical files.
2. As a basis for systematic organisation of knowledge in catalogues and bibliographies, classification being employed to show the more permanent relations between subjects, alphabetical arrangements to indicate others, including authorship.

3. As a discipline in reference service, to enable the librarian to sort the wheat from the chaff in a subject inquiry, and to handle a question with maximum efficiency.

In the United States the concept of classification seems, in the main, to halt at the first stage, due doubtless to the numerical preponderance of small-town libraries there, and also to the failure of Decimal Classification to measure up to the demands of large libraries in universities and colleges. In Great Britain the greater interest of the profession in classified catalogues has led to a fairly general acceptance of the second stage. This is reflected in the demand of the national scheme of certification, conducted by the Library Association, for an understanding of the construction of the classified catalogue by "competent practising librarians." It is significant that when the Library Association, in collaboration with the British Museum and other institutions, promoted the *British National Bibliography,* it went without saying that the bibliography should take the form of a classified catalogue. The third stage of classification is only glimpsed here and there, although all good librarians use it intuitively. S. R. Ranganathan refers to it in his *Classification and Communication,* while D. J. Foskett of the Metal Box Company, England, has touched upon it as an important bibliographical discipline.

As long as discussion of classification continues to be based only upon an appreciation of its use at the first stage, it will remain largely abortive. There are no more problems to discuss in respect of "books-on-the-shelves," and not sufficient demonstrably solid advantages to make it worth all the trouble of overcoming inbred prejudices. There even seems to be a school of thought arising in the United States which favours a return to *numerous current,* plus bigger and better dictionary catalogues! This, of course, only passes on the problem of organisation of knowledge to the catalog; for readers must have the benefit of systematic order, and this is achieved or sought through the "pyramid of references," which itself derives from a hidden classification of knowledge. In the case of Sears' list of subject headings, the hidden classification is an early edition of Decimal Classification, as comparative examination will show.

If the use of classification is to advance from the primary to the secondary or tertiary stage, a far more advanced type of classification scheme is required. All indexing must refer to something, if only the pages of a book. The smaller the unit to which reference can be made, obviously the more detailed the indexing will be. When indexing the subjects in a catalogue, it is necessary to have every major aspect of a subject represented in the notation, in order that the alphabetical index, by picking up each digit of the notation, may overlook nothing of importance. Any attempt, therefore, to set arbitrary limits to the number of symbols to be used in a classified catalogue necessarily restricts the penetration of the alphabetical index. This is a warning against trying to organize knowledge through any simplified arrangement, whether of classification or of subject headings.

In this brief review of criticism of the major schemes, no attempt has been made to rehearse the familiar arguments. As can be seen from *Library Literature* too many papers have already been devoted to the failings of Decimal Classification, which is the most widely used plan. Indeed, it has been said that to many librarians classification and Decimal Classification are synonymous. The more fundamental work of Ranganathan, to which an attempt has been made to provide a simple introduction recently, supplies a sharper set of criteria upon which to base criticism of any scheme of classification.

Having taken cognizance of the great volume of criticism which has been expended upon the Decimal Classification over the last half century, one is naturally led to wonder what the effect has been on the widespread use of the plan. The answer is, as far as public libraries are concerned, very little. There is small evidence that criticism has resulted in action, except in American university and college libraries, which have swung over to the Library of Congress Classifications in the last quarter century. Out of 6,000 libraries in the United States, only 213 were classified in 1940 on the Library of Congress plan, and it is fairly safe to assume that no other scheme has been favoured in this way, so that Decimal Classification still holds the field.

Yet one must not be too hard. Admittedly it is possible for the captious critic to refer to the "vested interest of sloth"; but few librarians are in the happy state of having more staff than immediate needs demand, and, though the task of reclassifying is not itself insuperable, the burden of consequential revision of the catolog is sufficient to daunt the bravest innovator. The only workable method is to fix a deadline when the new scheme will come into effect, classifying and cataloguing all new books in accordance with it, and reclassifying and recataloguing the *live* older books on their way back from reader to shelf. To what an unendurable age of manipulating two sequences this would condemn a library staff! In the writer's own experience, with quite a small bookstock the task spread out over years, despite hours of voluntary overtime worked by a library staff on stand-by for air raid precautions from 1939 to 1941.

Criticism of the Decimal Classification, and particularly discussion of its drawbacks, has proceeded for nearly half a century. The arguments have gone round and round—mainly superficial in content, and all stemming ultimately from a few tentative suggestions from W.C.B. Sayers and a full-dress discussion by H. E. BlissfMuch of the debate was valuable in early years, but as time has passed, and the scheme has been shown to work in spite of its drawbacks, we ought to be able to draw one of two conclusions. Either the volume of criticism has been wrongly focused, or classification is such a powerful tool that even so bad a scheme as the critics would have us believe D.C. to be is of considerable value in organising knowledge.

The Library of Congress Classification, on the other hand, has been approached with a certain measure of restraint. In the first place, it did not demand any action by the rank and file of librarians; it was of concern only to its operators in Washington, and to young students who, the foreign pupil of Shakespeare, "anaphrased, paralysed and pulverised" it. Sayers' criticism amounted to little more than a questioning of the "inconstant repetition" of common subdivisions and geographical divisions, leading to great bulk, and to the charge that there appears to be no natural or philosophical order in the main classes. Bliss gave extensive criticism to this scheme also.

All of these schemes set out to list specific subjects as they existed, or seemed likely to exist in some cases, at the time of their construction. But it is demonstrably impossible to list all existing subjects even to the moment the author lays down his pen; and the anticipation of future subjects is beyond the power of men. In certain respects this was recognised at various stages in the progress of the Decimal Classification; and provision was made to divide geographically by the subdivisions of class 900, or subjectively by appropriate schedules from other parts of the classification, or even by the main scheme itself, and thus to avoid infinite enumeration. Such devices were introduced in successive editions, with the grafting of new ideas onto the old stock, and without rethinking the whole according to the new patterns of knowledge.

Bliss, coming later in the field, was able to take advantage of many new devices, and with his second book introduced the conception of synthetic classification, at least in respect of certain recurrent features of knowledge. Nevertheless, he still adhered fundamentally to the enumerative form, and the praise that was accorded his work echoes the pronouncement "scholarly."

In all these schemes, any considerable advance in knowledge demands revision of the basic schedules by the author. None of them grows by itself, save insofar as the tables of constants, i.e., geographical tables, linguistic tables, and common subdivisions, provide for this. Yet the recognition of the need for such tables ranging over wider fields than place, time, language, and form is growing—except, in a limited way, in the Library of Congress scheme. This is evidenced by the provision for interrelation between subjects provided for in the Universal Decimal Classification, and by the new Metallurgy schedules, which are built on the principles of allotting numbers to certain processes wherever they appear. This greater preoccupation with the thoroughgoing control of knowledge springs from the demands of scientific and technological libraries which are concerned with that part of knowledge which is growing most rapidly.

Bibliographic Classification

The picture remains much as it was in 1938, when over 90 per cent of American and British libraries used Decimal Classification. There is one new feature to be observed, namely, the growing use of the Bibliographic Classification of H, E. Bliss. In the newer countries, where no entrenchment of the Decimal Classification existed to bedevil the new librarians, the more modem approach of the Bibliographic Classification has attracted a number of adherents. In New Zealand, Otago University has adopted the scheme, and in Africa it is in use at Ibadan University College, and at the Gordon College in Khartoum; Kumasi College of Technology also employs it, as does the Public Library Service of the Northern Region of Nigeria. Note that these are mostly university and allied libraries. Here the scholarly approach of Bliss, whose work is claimed to be based upon educational and scientific consensus, as reflected in the university syllabus, proves very attractive, and not unnaturally. It is significant too that in Great Britain, where the Institutes of Education (often attached to the universities) are latecomers in the field of provision for libraries, this scheme has been chosen in a number of instances. Certain British polytechnics and other training colleges have succumbed to its lure, and at least one British government library Ministry of Health has adopted it.

Why the Bibliographic Classification? Probably because the cumulated criticism of many years has led librarians to look elsewhere than to Decimal Classification when forming new libraries, or classifying old ones for the first time. Because, too, the basic plan of the Bibliographic Classification is more in line with modem thought than that of Decimal Classification. And because basically it is similar in design to Decimal Classification.

The Library of Congress Classification also has had its conquests in Britain, notably among governmental libraries (e.g., Board of Trade, Ministry of Transport). Here the reason is not far to seek. The extremely detailed schedules, and their sectional revision and publication, make this scheme relatively easy to apply, once the decision to do so has been taken. Such a decision may be influenced, too, by the availability of the Library of Congress catalogue cards.

The main schedules of both of the foregoing plans are enumerative in form, and do not demand the fundamentally different approach required by the Colon Classification, which is the only other contemporary general scheme. One should add, however, that awareness of the Bibliographic and Congress schemes has been a long time growing, while knowledge of Ranganathan's work is a postwar, and still rare, phenomenon in the West. It is too much to expect it to have met with wide adoption yet.

Nevertheless, the underlying concept of Colon is more in line with the needs of a changing society than is the case with any other library classification. It steadfastly refuses to "fix" at any stage the specific subjects that together make up knowledge. Beyond listing the fundamental constituent parts of each major subject, and providing geographical tables and common subdivisions, it enumerates nothing except Indian literature, which is "worked out" as an example. It implicitly recognizes that in enumeration lie the seeds of decay of any classification, and that as far as there can be a truly permanent scheme, it must be one which is potential, and never reaches finality. Colon Classification does not accept the permanence of any piece of knowledge, but gives hospitality to all theories, hypotheses, or guesses at the answers to problems, without elevating any of them to a more lasting place than is justified by the output of literature concerning it. If there is no literature there is no number.

The particular contribution of Ranganathan has been his idea of fundamental categories. He contends that if one goes beneath the surface of specific subjects he finds them made up of parts which correspond to the five fundamental divisions of Personality, Matter, Energy, Space, and Time. Certainly, choosing a simple example of human activity such as "Furniture Making," one can say that in order to fashion a certain item or part of an item of furniture, one must take raw materials and work upon them in a given place at a given time.

One might also claim that in describing such activity one would necessarily write about the parts or kinds of furniture, the materials of which it is made, the manufacturing operations, the place or the time of production, or about complexes of any two or more of these. If this is so, a classification which is to reflect knowledge accurately would need to allow for these categories. Colon Classification follows such a pattern, each of its main classes being considered to have five compulsory facets corresponding with the five fundamental groups. It is debatable whether this pattern can be traced through the natural sciences, without postulating a "quarry" of entities upon which man works by study or analysis, to produce the "personalities" of the various pure sciences.

This is fundamentally the same idea as occurs in the work of Mortimer Taube in the United States. He writes of coordinate classifications in Jesse Shera's and Margaret Egan's *Bibliographic Organisation.* 'It is the idea that specific subjects can be broken down into simpler terms, which are susceptible of more detailed indexing, and which themselves fall into various categories.

Depth-classification, which is the name given by Ranganathan to the very minute kind of classification needed for documentary work, often demands subsidiary divisions in any given category in addition to those normally provided. Hence we find Colon Classification allowing "optional" facets for documentation, in addition to the compulsory ones provided for book-level classification. Thus an effort is made to meet the special librarian's needs by placing the development of any class or subject in his hands. In the major schemes, the special librarian finds the subdivision far too minute everywhere except in his own field; there it is never sufficiently minute. Colon Classification seeks to provide a general scheme which can be developed by the user at any point and to any degree desired. In this way its author aims to match the exact requirements of every library for close classification.

Indeed, the major contribution of Colon to classification science is its demonstration that the autonomy which Decimal Classification and the

Bibliographic Classification give in their tables of geographic constants can be extended to other areas of subject division, via the faceting method of construction. Such a method demands a notation which matches it in flexibility, and this, too, is provided. The research of Ranganafhan in this connection has been considerable.

Apart from the recognition of internal relations between the parts of subjects, Colon provides ample means for taking into account external relations between different branches of knowledge. These Ranganathan calls "phase-relations," and he is at present pursuing inquiries into their different kinds, and into methods of controlling the records of them. They form an increasing part of monograph literature in an age of rapidly expanding knowledge, for more and more we find the research in one field of human activity throwing light on work in a hitherto unrelated field.

There is no pretense on the part of Ranganathan and his followers that classification ever can represent knowledge wholly and in all its complexity. The multidimensional nature of it cannot be fixed, because we can only cope with it item by item—that is to say, in a unidirectional manner. The problem of classification is, therefore, to reduce many dimensions to one, and yet to make any part of each truly accessible. The trelliswork of Colon imposes a pattern on knowledge, just as any other scheme does; but the pattern is a communicable one, not the private process of one mind. Once the scheme has been learned, the day-to-day classifier takes on the constructive function of the maker, and can build a plan for his own private area of interest which will use the same type of notation and same mode of construction as the general one. This coordination with a general scheme frees the "local man" from the task of having to devise properly helpful numbers ranging over the whole field of knowledge for his fringe-topics, since the general plan is available to him as a quarry from which appropriate numbers can easily be drawn.

If Colon is not, in its present published form, ready for early adoption in the West, as some declare, it nevertheless has earned its passage by the light it has thrown on classification. No longer can the skeptical claim that classification theory is a few odd and unrelated pieces culled from ancient logic and modern makeshift. Today there is a well-reasoned hypothesis, which takes account of all the facts known, but which can be adjusted if experimentation and new facts throw it out of gear. Today there can truly be said to be a science of classifications on which research is proceeding in India, Britain, the United States, and possibly elsewhere.

In India, Ranganathan himself conducts the research work at Delhi University, aided by a group of enthusiastic young fellow countrymen. The results of his work reach us from time to time in tentative typescripts circulated among friends, and, later on, as published articles in *Abgila,* This periodical, published by the Indian Library Association, is an assemblage of research and news; and it is a goldmine for advanced classification students.

In Britain, too, there is some interest in such research, largely inspired by Ranganathan's work. Led by Vickery and A. J. Wells, a small group of librarians meets for occasional discussion and circulates papers. Perhaps it soon will get beyond the discussion stage and proceed to practical proposals.

In the United States, interest in classification is active. Certain names spring to mind in connection with the subject. There are Jesse Shera, of the School of Library Science, Western Reserve University; Maurice F. Tauber, of the School of Library Service at Columbia University; and Mortimer Taube, formerly of the U.S. Atomic Energy Commission, and now of Documentation, Incorporated. Doubtless there are others who are thinking and experimenting in classifications, but have not yet committed themselves to print. The challenge of advancing technical and scientific knowledge is probably felt more in America than any other country, with the possible exception of the U.S.S.R. Some of the papers presented at the institute held in June 1952 at Columbia University give an excellent reflection of the interest this subject is provoking in the United States.

Colon, however, is not the only scheme which now uses faceting as a means for achieving a closer relationship between classification and knowledge. As has been mentioned earlier, Universal Decimal Classification has introduced the principle into its Metallurgy schedules, published in 1949. Here there are two facets provided for, Metals and Processes. In Ranganathan's terminology these represent the Personality and Energy categories. It is highly probable that the introduction of this method of division was quite independent of Colon. The idea of "categories" is in the air.

Recognition of the advantages of faceting is likely to grow in the coming years. Within a week of the present writing, a review of a new classification in a specialised field had appeared in the *Library Journal.* Examination of the scheme shows that its schedules fall quite clearly into the five fundamental categories enunciated by Ranganathan, although at first this is obscured by the notation. The main divisions are given alphabetical symbols, and divide into three distinct groups, the second and third of which correspond with Energy and Personality. The author has obviously been influenced by Ranganathan's ideas, even if he has not followed his practice. His preface indicates his indebtedness.

Wherein lies the peculiar advantage of a faceted classification? Possibly it is in the fact that the enumeration is restricted to more fundamental and, therefore, possibly more permanent concepts than the complexes of activities and things that make up specific subjects. In Packaging, for example, the Material facet lists kinds of materials used, and the Energy facet lists operations, unrelated to any particular material; thus at no time are the lists out of date, because no subject gets a number until the library has some material about it, and, equally, the number drops out of existence when the subject ceases to attract literature.

We come now to consideration of a new phenomenon in the field of research: the introduction of coding devices to make possible the use of punched card and other searching machinery. Basically, the idea is to represent a piece of information by the position of a hole punched in a card, the card being endorsed with that information. A machine which "feels" a series of cards and picks out those with a given punching recaptures the recorded information at will. Accurate and sensitive mechanisms enable the searching to be done at very high speed, as indeed is essential, since the whole series of cards has to be gone over for each inquiry. There are also electronic devices, but fundamentally the process is the same storing and rapid finding by some coding device.

Now if an enumerative scheme of classification is employed for coding purposes, it registers information only under its dominant facet, and provides no automatic method of selecting further data scattered under distributed facets. An example might make this clearer.

In Agriculture, Propagation Methods is a focus in the Energy facet, while Potatoes, Tomatoes, and Onions are foci in the Personality facet. A general work on propagation methods offers no problem in classification, for it goes with the Energy facet numbers; but works on methods of propagating potatoes, methods of propagating tomatoes and methods of propagating onions all offer two possible placings under the crop concerned, or under the operation. Good practice would put these under the crop; but this results in distributing some specialised material about propagation methods up and down the crop schedules. Equally, placing under propagation methods would result in scattering all except the most general information about any crop up and down the farming operation schedules. In either case, an enumerative scheme cannot exhaustively provide for all such distributed facets, and if it does not provide for them it cannot exhaustively code them. What is not coded in the searching machinery cannot be selected by the machine, so that whichever way an enumerative plan displays its information, its distributed facets get obscured. The faceted type of classification, however, being built upon the principle of separate facets bound together in a predetermined manner, is able to code the foci of each facet separately. Thereafter, no matter where a focus turns up, it can be found by the searching apparatus, because its design meets the needs of such apparatus. Here is an example of a distributed facet drawn from the index of the *British National Bibliography.*

Timber: Building construction	694
Building materials	691.1
Forestry	634.98
Manufactures	674
Manufactures: Economics	338.47674
Trade: Management	658.974

This gathers under Timber all the works scattered in various parts of the classification by the more dominant subject relation. Only a faceted scheme gives the fullest facility to an index for doing this, and the same facility is required for coding. A monograph on classification and coding for search has been published by UNESCO. Colon comes out of it better than all the other devices. This was not intended when the essay was planned, but it undoubtedly reflects the writer's outlook. It is not suggested that Colon is a finished scheme ready to go into action at the drop of a hat; no one is more aware of its inadequacies than its author. Nevertheless, its enormous value in making possible an advance in critical understanding of classification, and of revealing ways of improving even existing schemes would alone justify its existence. This, however, is not its only recommendation; it definitely goes much nearer to the control of recorded knowledge than anything yet. The western world has not paid enough attention to the analytico-synthetic kind of classification, of which Colon is the prototype, and we still get systematic tabulations of specific subjects offered as classifications.

Perhaps the most useful valedictory for a paper of this nature is to urge that the groups working on classification in the various countries should come closer together. An international circulation of the many unpublished papers, which at present are exchanged among friends, might be organised. Possibly, when we are all a little further advanced and know more clearly where we are going, we might even get some personal contacts on an international basis. Would it be too much to hope that an American specialist in classification should come to Britain on a Fulbright scholarship when the rime is ripe? One of the most valuable products of the Anglo-American library alliance was the *Rules for Author and Title Entry.* This standardised practice throughout the English-speaking world. It is time we pooled our resources in classification theory.

Reclassification and Recataloguing

Reclassification has existed in some form since the beginning of cataloguing and classification itself. However, the term as we use it today means the complete reorganisation of a book collection from one scheme of classification to another. Such change of classification systems has taken place in all kinds of libraries public, school, special, government, college and university but in the last it has predominated. In the past thirty years many institutions have made conversions, and for the most part this has meant a shift from the Dewey Decimal or Cutter to the Library of Congress Classifications.

Professional literature tells little about the efforts of early libraries to find a desirable classification. Because collections were small, the librarians possibly were not confronted with the difficulties facing us today, and the classification in use was one that sufficed. However, by the early 1920's, when the national library in Washington made available in printed form its classification schedules, many librarians began to see the adaptability of that system for large, fast-growing collections, and the wave of reclassification began.

Some of the libraries that became interested in this change in the twenties and early thirties have seen the job through to completion. Others began but were unable to carry out their programs because of discouragement and insufficient funds. However, in the last ten years a new surge of interest has developed, and more libraries are feeling the need for an expansive system of classification, as necessitated by the changing nature of society and the new developments in most areas of learning. This not only has meant the influx of large quantities of new materials, but also great growth of knowledge, especially in the fields of science and technology. Productive research in social science and the humanities likewise has increased book collections, to the extent that the problems of organisation and management have become acute.

The enhanced interest in reclassification has become especially apparent in colleges and universities. In the following institutions libraries now are changing from the Dewey Decimal Classification to that of the Library of Congress, the dates being those at which they began the process: Washington University, St. Louis, 1946; the University of Tennessee, March 1950; the State University of Iowa, September 1950; the University of Miami, March 1952; and the University of Mississippi, September 1952. Another, that at Alabama Polytechnic Institute, is considering such a move, as recommended by a survey made in 1948-49. There are undoubtedly other libraries, including special and public, in the process of conversion. The literature cites only a few, but contributions by K. A. Baer, Rosamond Danielson, and Dora Pearson attest that libraries other than college and university are reorganising their book collections. There is also evidence of the reclassification of special collections, resulting in the modifications of some standard classification schemes. Because of the growing interest in reclassification, there is need for a review of the recent trends in libraries with particular reference to the organisation and functioning of such projects. Many libraries have suffered during the period of conversion, either because needed infirmation has not been available in the literature or through misunderstanding of the problems evolving from the change. Until recent years, when N. L. Kilpatrick and Anna O'Donnell published their article on the special reclassification project at the State University of Iowa, little has been written on this subject since the important contributions of Maurice Tauber " in the early forties.

Since reclassification usually implies recataloguing, the terms are used here somewhat synonymously. In most libraries a lack of uniformity in records has developed through the years, and the mere purchase of new Library of Congress printed cards to replace the old and soiled ones means recataloguing in a broader sense. In reclassification the opportunity exists to weed the card catalogue of needless and outdated cross references, to eliminate the extra analytics rendered unnecessary by the accessibility of printed bibliographies, and to accept a more logical system of bibliographical organisation. All of this means recataloguing in one sense of the word, and therefore any reference to reclassification means recataloguing as well.

Many reasons for reclassification of book collections are given in the literature. Tauber, as a result of his doctoral research at the University of Chicago, has summarised them in his writings. Twenty-five years ago R. H. Gjelsness expressed the following philosophy, which still applies today:

> The perfect classification, even to meet all contemporary requirements, has never been devised; it is much less to be hoped that any one scheme of arrangement will find acceptance in its entirety, over a long period of time. Books remain in libraries, materially unchanged, for centuries, but readers' use of them, and attitude toward them, changes, as external aspects of human activities change from one generation to the next. This shift in the relation of books and readers recurs more frequently in a rapidly moving age such as the present, and in library service, is met more promptly in a country such as ours where the emphasis is on the use of books. To some degree, this explains the extent of reclassification now under way in American libraries.

Some of the obvious reasons for the current trend toward reclassification are:

1. Recent publication in the fields of science and technology has forced many libraries to use a broader, more expansive, and up-to-date system of classification. This is especially true when the librarian understands that "the watertight compartments, into which scientific knowledge used to be divided, have broken down completely, and now the different branches of science and technology are inseparably intermingled."
2. The trend today is to get books and users together, and hence there is an emphasis on "wide-open" libraries. This is evident in the growth and use of divisional libraries, such as those at the universities of Colorado and Nebraska; in the special undergraduate collections

designed for a specific clientele, such as Harvard's Lamont Library and the Undergraduate Library at the University of Illinois; and in the unique experiment at Iowa, where books are arranged by historical divisions and where the whole collection is open to direct student use. If library users are to browse and live with books, there is definite need for a fairly logical arrangement that will allocate literature adequately.

3. Economy in processing materials may be promoted by reclassification. Most libraries today use the Library of Congress printed cards, in buying which they are subscribing to a service backed by some of the best professionally trained personnel and specialists in subject areas. Furthermore, most large libraries are using the L.C. *Rules for Descriptive Cataloguing* and the L.C. *List of Subject Headings.* An acceptance of such work already performed materially lessens the time spent on cataloguing and classification. A change to the Library of Congress system seems to be the nearest libraries can attain to centralised cataloguing and classification as it is available today.
4. The appearance of the fifteenth edition of the Dewey Decimal Classification has prompted some libraries to consider reclassification under a system which is constantly being revised and kept up to date. Too, large libraries using the fourteenth edition of Dewey with the modified expansions have found that much reclassification would be necessary if the fifteenth edition were to be used.
5. An increasing number of faculty and research members of institutions throughout the country have become familiar with and have recognised the merits of the Library of Congress Classification. Their interest in the arrangement of books has developed through study in other research libraries. Tauber, speaking before a group of faculty members at the University of Tennessee in 1949 on the subject "Book Classification in University Libraries," found this concern in such a group to be amazing. As a result, the faculty became interested in the problems of book organisation and a thorough study was made, with the resulting decision to reclassify the library's holdings.

The University of Mississippi exemplifies further the interest in book organisation by members of an institution's administration and faculty. As part of a planned liberal arts development program partially financed by one of the foundations, a sum of $45,000 was set aside to reclassify the university library over a period of three years, beginning in 1952. This proposal came first from the administration, particularly the dean of the College of Liberal Arts, and from different department heads in the College, and not from the librarians on the campus. Further, there had been a collection of some twenty thousand volumes in the library that was classified only by the broad classes in Dewey. This group of books bad been weeded by representatives of the various departments, and the remaining volumes were to be assimilated into the collection. Most of the periodicals had never been classified and were arranged alphabetically by title, and hence caused constant irritation to members of the faculty doing research in subject areas. The chairman of the Library Council, who was head of the Department of Psychology, was much interested in having the journals in his field grouped with the books. Because of these factors, the decision was made in the late spring of 1952 to reclassify the book collection according to the Library of Congress system.

The following excerpt of a letter from A, L. McNeal, Director of the University of Miami libraries, further reveals interest in reclassification by an administrator of an institution of higher education:

> When the Vice President raised the question of reclassification, I was not unprepared to discuss it. His reaction was to the effect "If it is desirable and is something we will eventually come to, let's begin on it now." I pointed out the difficulties involved, the expense, and the handicaps to service. On the other hand, as a result of the purchase of a major library about two years prior to my coming here, there was a backlog of 20,000 to 30,000 volumes to be catalogued. It seemed to me an opportune time to undertake reclassification, even though no extra funds were available for it either from foundations or from our own institution.

After a decision has been made to reclassify a collection, a careful study of methods and organisation is extremely important. The literature on reclassification reveals most of the problems. However, it takes a careful analysis to select the answers most applicable to an individual situation. Some help can be found in studies of the literature and of current practices that have not yet found a way into print. Too little has been written on the solutions individual libraries have found to the problems. The general process of reclassification is, in its essentials, much the same for all libraries. It is rather the details of organisational procedure that vary.

The preliminary phases of a reclassification program involve existing administrative relationships, especially in a college or university. Institutional officers to whom the librarian is responsible should understand the problems and needs and give approval of the project. The faculty as a whole should be informed of the contemplated undertaking, and their cooperation should be solicited. The library committee should be in sympathy with the change and give its approval. Heads of departments and faculty members having charge of office or departmental collections should be consulted, as books in these collections have to be called in for reclassification. Students, especially graduate students, should be informed.

Frequent consultations should enlist the close cooperation and coordination of all departments in the library. "Reclassification and recataloguing are not isolated intellectual or clerical processes carried out by a few specially trained workers in the confines of the Cataloguing Department." Department heads and assistants throughout the library system must have an understanding of the problems and the part each may be expected to play. Cooperative planning well in advance of the actual beginning of the work can do much to insure the efficient functioning of the operation as a unit in which all are involved and to which all may contribute in one way or another.

Libraries that have carried through reclassification programs have found some preliminary activities most useful. An inventory of holdings, by locating lost books, setting the stacks in order, and clearing the records, saves time later. Because of size or lack of adequate personnel, some libraries do not find it practical to maintain systematic inventories. Others have established inventory processes as a regular routine that goes on continually. Such a practice can be carried out quite well in conjunction with reclassification. Special collections or sections of the stacks can be covered in units ahead of the reclassification project. If the catalogue department makes the inventory, it is least complicated to have it completed before reclassification begins.

A program of weeding the collection can be staggered ahead of reclassification, since it is not the responsibility of the catalogue department. The possible procedures vary. The Providence Public Library began systematic weeding over a year before starting reclassification, with an experienced reference assistant recommending titles for withdrawal. The prevailing practice seems to be for staff members thoroughly familiar with the collection, local conditions, and the use and demands upon the library, to do the preliminary work, with such aid as they may require from the librarian and from faculty members or specialists in the field, and with an adequate group of bibliographical tools to consult. A series of time studies on costs of discarding reported from the State Teachers College, Milwaukee, Wisconsin, is applicable where one may be considering the cost of reclassifying.

Reclassification gives an added impetus to the current trend of using storage space or reservoir libraries for little-used titles and duplicates. Old editions, duplicate copies, serial sets rarely used, and other items may well be put in storage without reclassification. The Providence Public Library reported in 1949 that "Quantities of infrequently called-for books and old files of bound periodicals have been cleared from the central library shelves but remain within reach of the occasional reader and research worker." Not only is time saved by not reclassifying storage collections, or in deferring it to a later date, but also additional shelving space, which may be needed in reclassification, is provided.

The period before beginning reclassification is an appropriate time for critical examination of circulation procedures and the routines of technical processes. Unnecessary and cumbersome details in circulation can hinder the progress of the work immeasurably. Some librarians have found after starting that they could have proceeded much more efficiently had this problem been presented to the head of the circulation department for careful consideration. An overall view of technical processes needs likewise to be taken. Some routines may need to be changed or eliminated. In reclassifying, careful organisation and strict economy are imperative. If any necessary reorganisation is effected before the operation begins, arrears can be more nearly brought under control or eliminated, and the department prepared for the accelerated program usually necessary in making the change.

Any major revision in library procedures calls for examination of the physical and financial resources, and of the personnel to accomplish the change. The size and arrangement of the main building, the number of outlying collections and their distance from the main library, and the plan of the stacks cause variations in procedure. One can scarcely overemphasize the necessity for a careful survey of the entire situation, since weaknesses in the physical arrangement are bound to be intensified in a reclassifying project, where a rapid flow of work is desired. Tauber reports three recent surveys that were "general examinations of all facilities and services of the libraries involved. In all three instances, reclassification or reorganisation of the materials was presented as a major consideration." The State University of Iowa made a "detailed study of the cataloguing practices currently in use" in its preliminary study prior to reclassification. The Chemists Club Library in New York preceded reclassification by a survey of the library. Such preliminary studies are incalculable aids in establishing policies that will not have to be changed later, and in avoiding mistakes that could make the end-product of reclassification of questionable value.

The amount of reclassification and the speed with which the project operates is in most cases determined by the funds available for the purpose. Some libraries have been the recipients of special grants. Columbia University was given special appropriations by the Board of Trustees at different times. The State University of Iowa, which reclassified a part of its collection in 1950/51, was allowed a special budget of $27,000, William and Mary College received a grant from the General Education Board in 1943-45 to continue its project.

Some libraries have begun a reclassification program without additional money by carrying the expenses on the library budget, the work being performed by the regular staff. The Indianapolis Public Library used a special fund for part of its juvenile collection in order to make the change more rapidly, but the adult books were done without an added appropriation. The District of Columbia Public Library did not request unusual finances. Its project was undertaken "without disruption of the library budget or additions to the library staff. This meant careful organisation and strict economy." The University of Tennessee is carrying on a reclassification program begun in 1950 without a special appropriation. Libraries have found that a survey of the processing department may increase efficiency and allow extra time and money for reclassification. This may mean at first little more than the processing of new material in the new classification. However, by planning the work carefully, a cataloguer may soon be devoting full time to reclassification. Saving can be effected by accepting the classifications number on the printed cards and making full use of the cataloguing entry as given. Additional time can be found by delaying the processing of some types of material, such as maps, films, and older less-used titles, although cataloguing should be kept up to date for current acquisitions and those in particular demand.

The rate at which the task proceeds is dependent on the number of personnel and of the professional and nonprofessional members that may be added. A staff that can hardly process current accessions or that has accumulated a large backlog of material should hesitate to undertake reclassification without additional help. Incumbents may contribute to the classification project by adding all new accessions, by reclassifying old editions when new ones are received, by reclassifying titles when extra copies or new volumes are added, and by reclassifying titles which also require recataloguing. However, work can go ahead much more rapidly and satisfactorily if there is a special staff. A large amount of routine duty must be performed by clerical or nontechnical workers, who must be closely supervised. A bead of processing who can coordinate all operations can secure a more efficient and uniform result.

Before beginning reclassification, some general policies must be formulated. The first question is the extent of the undertaking. Practices have varied with local conditions. Some collections have been completely reclassified while others have minor areas that will never be reclassified. Because of size, money available, or some special nature of the collection, some libraries have found partial reclassification feasible. This may be practical for sections badly in need of attention, such as science and technology or literature, groups most used, or open-shelf collections. In university and college libraries, special or departmental collections may be maintained very easily in classifications different from that used in the main library.

Libraries have found by experience that reclassification involves a considerable amount of recataloguing. Older libraries and libraries reclassifying several years ago found that problem most acute. The advent of Library of Congress cards and their widely accepted use has brought a marked improvement in card catalogues in recent years. Nevertheless, most libraries still have old cards with incorrect or incomplete entries, in outdated or improper forms, and with inconsistencies in added entries and subject headings. A catalogue badly in need of revision slows the process of reclassification and adds considerably to the cost. Some decision must be made as to the amount of recataloguing that will be done. Princeton adopted a policy of reclassifying with a minimum attention to the catalogue, but the results were not wholly satisfactory. The University of Michigan found that recataloguing needed as much attention as reclassifying. W. W. Bishop concludes from these experiences:

> Reclassification alone, with no recataloguing at all, is an impossibility. And unless the catalogue has been exceptionally well made, the recataloguing will be a much more serious job than the reclassification. The result, however, of the two processes should be a remarkable increase in efficiency of the library as a whole.

Every library arrives at its own decisions as to how much it will deviate from the Library of Congress Classification and descriptive cataloguing. Most libraries make some changes, but the general consensus seems to be expressed by Miss Pearson in describing the practices followed at the District of Columbia Public Library:

> An attempt is made to make the fullest possible use of printed cards and other aids commensurate with the requirements of good service. . . . They are not accepted blindly, but, with a minimum of checking and of changing, they prove, of course, to be thoroughly adequate in a large proportion of the cases. Their main entries, their subject headings, and the Dewey classification are adopted, with some corrections, some adjustments and some simplification, but with few variations from their established policies and practices. The basic assumption is that individual library variations are seldom necessary and that in a project such as this, their omission is a definite timesaver. In original cataloguing for titles without L.C. cards, the new A.L.A. Rules for Entry and the new L.C. Descriptive Cataloguing Rules are used, [and] the L.C. List of Subject Headings is the basic list. . . .

Library literature indicates a general accord on policy regarding acquisitions. It is to begin at a set date to put all incoming material in the new classification, except for those areas not to be reclassified at all. The decisions on where to start and the order of procedure vary somewhat, but the general trend is toward beginning with open-shelf and special collections, and then proceeding to the stacks by areas of subject matter, working from the shelf list. The Chemists Club Library in New York commenced with a general reading collection of eight hundred volumes. The University of Tennessee started with the branch libraries, proceeded to the reference collection, and then to the stacks. The Providence Public Library began with the open-shelf collection in the circulation department and moved then to specialised fields.

Decisions on methods of handling special types of material must be made by individual libraries on the basis of their own needs and interests. Probable methods were thoroughly investigated in the Tauber studies. Since that time scarcely anything in library literature indicates what libraries engaged in reclassifying actually are doing. The University of Tennessee did not reclassify fiction, preferring not to group it with literature, whereas a PZ arrangement in the L.C. scheme did not seem enough of an improvement over the F plan to warrant a change. The District of Columbia Public Library also did not reclassify fiction. Again, utilising L.C, biography at the University of Tennessee was placed with the subject, when possible, otherwise in CT; and collective biography went into CT. Bibliography was classified in Z, whereas the Chemists Club Library placed it with the subject. Periodicals in subject areas at the University of Tennessee were reclassified in the L.C. number, but many libraries, especially public and small college libraries, prefer an alphabetical arrangement, unclassified. Additional studies on the processing of all continuations, including government and United Nations documents, could well be made. The cost of handling, particularly in the duplication of records, is a problem many libraries have not worked out effectively.

Every library has minor groups of special materials. Juvenile collections, textbooks and courses of study in a university library, theses and archival material, and local history, present problems that could well be worked out by standard and uniform methods, if current practises were more fully presented in the literature. Changes in existing procedures come most logically at the time a regular reclassification project is under way.

Libraries may need to examine various forms of records and statistics in beginning reclassification. Some, such as that at William and Mary College, have formed a new catalogue in the process; others have interleaved the cards. Departmental catalogues often need to be made or old ones improved. Some libraries add shelf lists for departmental collections; others eliminate them. The use of temporary author cards does not seem to be widely recommended. If a routine is worked out by which cards are pulled and changed one day and returned to a preliminary tray for filing the next day, the time spent on temporary cards is largely wasted.

The value of a staff manual for reclassification is as debatable as that of one for regular use in a library. A few policies and practices must be formulated, and if deemed advisable they may be put in writing. The cost and time spent in devising a manual and in keeping it up to date, however, as well as the efficacy of its use, should be carefully explored before one is worked out.

In the final analysis, the success of any reclassification project depends on its organisation and administration. Properly organised, no library should suffer during transition. Some libraries have experienced a period of chaotic confusion; others have undergone only minor interruption of service. Harriet MacPherson, in reporting a study of some twenty libraries using the Library of Congress Classification, quotes as follows a reply received from one of the institutions in which reclassification has been going on for twenty-five years: "We believe that reclassification can be so organised that a so-called 'general upheaval' is not necessary." The increasing number of libraries that are reclassifying is some evidence that the change can be made smoothly and effectively.

In planning any program of reclassification proper attention should be given to the kind of equipment necessary and the additional supplies needed. The problem is not so great as it may appear, however, and the actual expenditure of funds for this phase of the program is negligible in relation to personnel costs. Too, the amount and kind of equipment and supplies necessary will depend largely on how the organisation is set up and the speed with which the project is carried on.

Extra typewriters will be needed, and hand erasers to remove old call numbers from the cards. Some system needs to be devised for expunging the call numbers from the books. The difficulty of this rests primarily on the kind of marking that has been done through the years, whether with white ink, electric stylus, or labels. Kilpatrick and Miss O'Donnell found that black automobile paint could be used in covering the old call number. Other libraries are employing electric machines, designed to run continuously, with flexible shafts into which eraser plugs can be inserted. This way of treating the call numbers seems to be the most desirable in removing old white ink and shellac. In the case of books marked with the electric stylus, the number is easily taken off by certain chemical solutions. Labels can be removed most effectively by moistening and scraping with a knife. Additional catalogue cases are unnecessary unless the decision is made to separate the card catalogue during the process, although space should be provided to allow for normal growth.

Card reproduction is unavoidable in most libraries, and this will be true especially during any reclassification program. Many of the present catalogue cards will need to be replaced because of soiled condition and poor cataloguing. If the Library of Congress printed cards are used, many titles will not be available or will be reported out of stock, with indication that they will not be reprinted. The multilith machine has grown in popularity for manifolding in recent years, although many libraries are still using mimeograph devices. Funds must be provided for the purchase of new Library of Congress printed cards and for plain catalogue cards needed in reproduction of entries. Many libraries carry these items along on the regular budget for supplies.

One main objection to reclassification in libraries has been the difficulty of maintaining the collections. Constant references are made in the literature to the excessive shifting of books and to the evil of having to look in two locations for materials desired. The problem of shelving depends first on space allotments within the library. The solution is not so difficult in a new building where one has room to begin expanding in the new classification while the older classification gradually diminishes in size. In libraries less fortunate, the old classification may be closed in and the new classification started in the space accumulated, If storage shelving is available the lesser-used volumes in the old classification may be put away, allowing space for growth of the new collection. The problem becomes less serious in a small library. An interesting experiment has been to place the volumes in the new classification on the same shelves from which the books came originally.

In a closed-stack collection, where access to material is by call number, the problem of arranging the book collection in two different places is not so great. Here graduate students and faculty members and others having direct access to materials soon learn that their books can be found in one of two places. If the dual arrangement exists on the same stack level, users may be willing to cooperate until the project is finished. In open-shelf collections the problem is somewhat more acute; however, it is those collections which are usually reclassified first, so that the period of time in which it is necessary to confront two different arrangements of the books is brief.

Results of reclassification depend somewhat on the reasons for reclassifying in the first place. The nature of the collection, new demands of the clientele, changing concepts of the organisation of library materials, the economy of processing and efficiency in servicing—these necessitate changes in the placing of materials to fit new needs and interests. There are those who believe that no classification plan can assure systematic arrangement of collections. However, until the thinking on proper bibliographical control and documentation brings fruitful, practical results, librarians need to house and service the vast quantity of material at their disposal.

DDC Online Project

In the Dewey Decimal Classification (DDC) Online Project, Karen Markey demonstrated the first implementation of a library classification scheme for end-user subject access, browsing, and display. Although many online catalogues provide call number browsing, few employ classification in the manner described by Elaine Svenonius or explored by Markey in her innovative use of the DDC in an experimental online catalogue which enabled users to search and browse online classification data.

Only recently, some ten years after Markey's pioneering research, is online classification data once again being seriously viewed as a tool for providing advanced browsing and retrieval capabilities in online systems. One factor that has contributed to the slow adoption of classification as a retrieval tool is that the DDC and the Library of Congress Classification (LCC) have only recently been converted into machine-readable form.

The computerisation of the DDC began with the production of DDC 19 from computer-based photocomposition tapes. This development and the Markey study prompted Forest Press, in 1984, to commission Inforonics to develop an online editorial support system (ESS) for the Dewey Classification. The resulting system and database was used to produce DDC 20, the first classification to be produced using an online editorial support system. A different path is being taken in the conversion of the LCC to machine-readable form. Recognising the benefits of online classification data for maintenance and distribution of LCC, the Library of Congress began developing the USMARC Format for Classification Data in 1987. The format was given provisional approval in 1990 and shortly afterward the Library of Congress began converting the forty six LCC schedules. The LCC database is expected to contain over 450,000 classification records when complete.

Electronic versions of the DDC and LCC make it possible to realise the potential of library classification to improve subject retrieval; however, much of the renewed interest in classification as an organising and retrieval device for information resources has been sparked by the growth in usage of the Internet and World Wide Web (WWW). Several WWW sites give users the ability to perform word or phrase searches to retrieve items of interest, with two popular sites, Yahoo and Infoseek, providing the additional capability of allowing users to navigate through a series of subject categories to discover potentially relevant documents.

Although, Yahoo and Infoseek use essentially the same input as the basis for their subject structures, the resulting categories displayed to users are quite different. The broad subject "Education" is found at the top level of both Yahoo and Infoseek, however, the next level under "Education" reveals a very different organisation of the topic in each system. Library classification schemes have long provided a similar organising tool for library materials. The subject categories found in the DDC and LCC are based largely on the topics expressed in monographic material in traditional book format.

For printed books, the Dewey Summaries and LC Classification Outline are the library community's functional equivalent to the subject categories of Yahoo and Infoseek. In fact, several noncommercial WWW sites are using DDC and LCC to provide subject access to Web-accessible documents. At a time when both Internet-based classification schemes and traditional library classification systems are being used to provide access to Internet resources it is appropriate to review the major characteristics of DDC and LCC and to assess whether the electronic versions of these schemes can be successfully extended to the Internet.

DDC vs. LCC

DDC and LCC are general classification systems. The purpose of the Dewey Decimal Classification is to arrange a general collection of materials. The DDC aims to classify books and other material on all subjects in all languages in every kind of library. Similarly, LCC is designed to provide order for a general collection, the collection of the Library of Congress. Although based on the collection of a single library, the LC Classification has been successfully adopted by a majority of U.S. academic and research libraries.

DDC and LCC have a hierarchical structure. Hierarchical relationships are the essence of all classification. Enumerative classifications systems provide a systematic arrangement of subjects according to set of principles based on an accepted philosophy of the organisation of knowledge, on patterns established on the basis of literary warrant, and frequently, on a combination of both. However, classified order is not self-evident. Some method or device is required to preserve the relationships among classes, subclasses, topics and subtopics.

In some classification systems, for example DDC, these relationships are preserved and may be manipulated through the hierarchical notation. LCC does not fit this pattern. Its notation preserves order but does not reflect hierarchy some other means must be found to preserve those relationships. In DDC, the sequence of subjects from general to specific, is indicated by the number of digits that form the DDC number. For example, when the DDC number 663.223 for the topic "making of red wine" is shown in the context of its Dewey hierarchy it can be seen that "White Wine," "Red Wine," and "Sparkling Wine" are at the same hierarchical level.

The DDC number 663.22 corresponding to the heading "Specific kinds of grape wine" is one digit shorter than those used to indicate exact kinds of wine and is considered to be broader or superordinate to those with longer numbers. Indentation is also used to indicate hierarchy.

Portals and Catalogues

The world's information resources are abundant, but time is a scarce commodity. The ideal discovery tool, therefore, is one which consults omnivorously, but which returns a selection of relevant results in rapid sequence. Searchers find what they need promptly without having to wade through a vast assortment of tangentially related, inaccurate, or otherwise deficient data. It costs little to build and operate, and it yields a high degree of user satisfaction because it delivers reliable information in a timely manner with relative ease. Such a tool is still imaginary, although it could become a reality in the near future if librarians organise themselves appropriately and commit the resources to dcsign it.

One precursor of this discovery tool is the library catalogue. Over the past century, the catalogue has achieved a reputation as a dependable starting point for people seeking particular kinds of information: published information appearing chiefly in books or journals that has undergone a formal review and editing process. Libraries have further filtered these publications through their selection practices, in which collection policies guide the acquisition of texts to meet the needs of a particular community. The titles chosen by bibliographers represent quality because they have been at least twice vetted, once by professional editors and once by library subject specialists. Once acquired, the volumes receive added value through their integration with other related materials held by the institution. Through the cataloguing of these chosen items, they gain in significance as trained experts distil their essence into a standard bibliographic description.

Subject headings and classification contribute further to the access of these materials. Widespread adoption of the Anglo-American Cataloguing Rules, Library of Congress Subject Headings, Library of Congress or Dewey Decimal Classification, and the MARC format has enabled the creation of virtual union catalogues with a number of superior attributes. The catalogue yields highly codified citations to quality publications in a predictable and dependable fashion. Names are usually authoritative and consistent. These features instill a strong degree of user confidence in the results of their searches. Libraries enhance this trust by ensuring that the materials cited are readily available for consultation, since titles catalogued are either locally held or obtainable through resource-sharing agreements.

Furthermore, the library's commitment to preserve the documents in its custody guarantees enduring access. Over the past few years, library management systems have matured and now present catalogue users with sophisticated online public access capabilities that include web access, improved keyword searching, relevance ranking, ability to limit searches by date or other fields, and reference linking.

Compounding the situation, there has been a rise in interest in other formats, such as films, recordings, photographs, manuscripts, maps, and, now, digital objects. At the same time that the aperture of scholarship has been widening, libraries have been diverting resources devoted to cataloguing to other functions, as ARL statistics reveal: the percentage of the total professional workforce in ARL libraries employed as cataloguers has dropped by 25% from 1990 through 1998. The declining role of the catalogue was highlighted in a New York Times article headlined "Choosing Quick Hits Over the Card (sic) Catalogue."

While conceding that "libraries are organised and easily navigated," the author reports "students prefer diving into the chaotic whirl of the Web to find information." More and more students and faculty turn to the Internet as their first point of contact for information. Even deans at top-ranked universities have confessed that they get satisfactory results from "Ask Jeeves," or that they question the need for physical libraries since they find all the references they require for their writing available online. Over the past five years, there has been a strong trend in many quarters of the university to prefer electronic resources because of the ease and speed of access.

More recently, the concept of portal has emerged as a unifying device for the wide variety of data made available on the web. The portal serves as a starting point for searching, and it usually offers an array of associated services such as news, related products, and reference tools, often clustered around a theme or discipline. Portals differ from the catalogue in a number of significant ways. They provide access to a wide range of materials, much of which would fall in the "unpublished" category. Harvesting of data occurs through the use of algorithmic programs, and there is little human cataloguing effort.

The largest catalogue departments process 250,000 volumes annually, while Google's search engine indexes millions of web pages weekly and claims to hold links to more than a billion URLs. To cope with the effect of large response sets, portals have moved to include relevance ranking. Still it is common to experience duplicates, false drops, and dead ends in many searches conducted with the discovery tools popular on the web. In addition, the free service they provide in locating information is often subsidised through advertising, which sometimes even affects placement in search results. Proprietary information, such as licensed databases to which libraries often subscribe, is inaccessible through most commonly used portals. Despite these deficiencies, portals offer many compelling features. They yield up-to-the-moment information, and they deliver a vast quantity and rich variety of resources, including full-text, images, and sound.

The web's ability to support linking enables the searcher to move with ease from document to document, and to capture material for his own use and facile manipulation. Customisation and even personalisation of searching and retrieval are other popular characteristics of search engines and portals. The enthusiasm with which people embrace the web, and the skepticism which many of these same digerati express about traditional libraries, has been sobering for some librarians. Information professionals note the flaws in search engines and in digital "library" content, which is often unstable, of dubious quality and authenticity, and incomplete. Their cautionary observations go unheeded among the hype and the reality of the flexibility of the web and the wealth of resources it encompasses. It is unlikely that the catalogue—in its present incarnation—can ever be the tool that provides the principal mode of access to information for students and scholars.

It would build on the collaborative strength of libraries to create a destination for scholars that would convey the traditional values of careful selection, expert organisation, skilled retrieval and delivery, interpretation, and endurance that have characterised libraries over the past century. The scholars portal has not yet come to fruition, but the energy and debate surrounding the proposal are healthy signs of the realisation that libraries must transform themselves and create new services in the near future. One area that is ripe for review is the proportion of time dedicated to the cataloguing of books and journals.

In the past decade and more, cataloguers have become increasingly productive, using copy cataloguing and automated workstations to lower the cost of cataloguing. Library administrators have seized resources previously devoted to cataloguing and reallocated them to other, higher priority areas, such as technology development. There is a chronic imbalance between the amount of work to be done and the resources available to do it, however, and in addition to backlogs of printed publications such as books and journals, the level of bibliographic control over sound recordings, photographs, films, and archival materials such as manuscripts remains poor. To this growing population of resources, which is increasingly considered important research territory, we now add endlessly proliferating electronic files. User expectations are expanding for timeliness, for in-depth access at the word or image level, for rapid retrieval, and for linkages. To serve their clients well, libraries must blend the features of the catalogue with the virtues of the portal. This will require the use of a sophisticated search engine to deliver the quantity of resources, the hyperlinks, the customisation and personalisation, and the instantaneous access that provides the user with convenience, flexibility, and immediacy.

Libraries can add value by promoting filtering and ranking which would prefer resources produced by universities, governments, and other sources that meet a set of established criteria, such as having a strong likelihood of authenticity, accuracy, or endorsement by others of standing. Added to the content retrieved by the search engine should be material contributed by libraries through a reengineered cataloguing process.

This reformed activity should favour timely access to a wide variety of formats. To achieve this, libraries will have to reallocate funds presently devoted to describing books and journals to materials that are proportionately underrepresented in today's catalogues, such as films, music, photographs, and digital objects. This cannot be accomplished by fine-tuning, but will rather require significant compromise and change. Although certain titles may still receive full bibliographic description and analysis such as is conducted today using the Anglo-American Cataloguing Rules and the Library of Congress Subject Headings, the need to increase greatly the number of resources of interest to scholars that can be located through the library's access tool will result in the application of a different standard to many materials.

For digital documents, it should be possible to derive key metadata using automation informed by and combined with human intelligence. The emphasis should be placed on identification of many new resources of value to the scholar and researcher, rather than on the cataloguing of only a few, relatively speaking, new items.

Communication Technology Access

Many parents and teachers feel that they are losing their authority in relations with members of younger generations. This is not only because they do not consider themselves qualified or because they are reluctant to change from traditional forms of the transmission of knowledge, but also because children have access to ever-greater quantities of knowledge through other interactions. Children can now access educational resources other than those adults traditionally believed to control. The concept of authority that parents exercise over their children is changing in Europe. The school has always been considered as one of the main points of entry to a democratic society, but one of the most important questions today concerns how such entry will be achieved in the none-too-distant future. The interaction the communications media and social groups are generating not only new youth cultures, but also, as has become increasingly evident, children's cultures.

The two are relatively independent, and often differ both from the culture of adults and from adults' expectations about cultural development in relation to the new generations. On the one hand, adolescents have always had the need to assert their own identity, and they frequently construct it with the aim of differentiating it from that of adults. Today, however, there are clear signs that in technologically advanced countries this normal psychosocial process is beginning at ever earlier ages, even before adolescence - especially when new technologies play a role in the relations between adults and children. We can observe that, as they grow, adolescents and teenagers tend to construct their own collective spaces, occupying physical spaces in our cities when adults are not present. This leads to the organisation of their own particular timetables, and to their occupying diverse social spaces in a symbolic way. In relation to the new audiovisual technologies it seems that teenagers are gradually becoming more active as social agents, and this is also the case for children.

On the other hand, certain new technologies are causing new problems of communication between parents and children. From the traditional perspective, children do not yet have the same skills and abilities as adults. Nevertheless, it is undeniable that at present many children are better prepared than a large proportion of adults to use new audiovisual technologies. These new social phenomena using only the old approaches. The need to adopt new ways of relating to children as citizens has often underlined. Nevertheless, we know that many adults do not accept that the children are not only our future but also citizens in the present, and that new forms of behaviour should be considered that promote processes of socialisation for responsible citizenship.

In our expansive and evermore rapidly changing society of information, relationships between minors and adults may well become more and more complex, at least when new technologies are involved. But what is really surprising and worrying is that, in this case, we can frequently observe a reluctance in some, even many adults to act as socialising agents in relation to the new information and communication technologies.

As shown by various studies, socialisation spaces outside the adult environment are continuously increasing in size. The new audiovisual, multimedia and other technologies are influencing our daily lives, our lifestyles and our forms of entertainment, as well as the way we relate to and communicate with one another. These technologies also stimulate some of our skills, and can potentially be used to promote and deal in a practical way with values that are of great importance for international understanding and co-operation. The new information and communication technologies (NICTs) are often presented as instruments to help improve our lives. Some European writers have recently been re-analysing and underlining how these new instruments will allow us to establish relationships in new ways. In fact, new types of relationships and communications with other people are already being established.

Nevertheless, these relationships are not only to be found in cyberspace, but are also being set up due to, or by means of or in the context of audiovisual media. Some recent research has explored how adults and children, specifically parents and their own children, communicate with one another when they refer to television and NICTs. Although activities with audiovisual media are frequently highly motivating for children, research results show that all too often communication about these subjects is nonexistent, and for a variety of reasons (including fears, lack of information, and feelings of incompetence on the part of adults). It has also been observed that the communication that actually does take place is frequently unsatisfactory for children and adolescents. Many of the children used audiovisual equipment in the homes of friends: 79.6% watched television there, 73.1% used computers and 71.7% used video consoles (boys more frequently than girls). The percentage of children using the Internet or educational CD-ROMs at their friends' homes was low, since they mainly played games there: 71.7% for video consoles and 69.3% for computers. In any case, girls used CD-ROMs more frequently in the homes of friends than boys.

Internet use at friends' homes increased with age. The use of games at friends' homes appears to reach its peak at age 13, decreasing sharply from then on. The use of audiovisual equipment at friends' homes does not appear to be related to the wealth of the location in which the children live, with the exception of Internet. Computers are the only audiovisual equipment that many children claimed to use at school: 72.9%. 47.9% of the children stated that they sometimes used television at school, while only 2.5% said that they played with video consoles at school.

Nevertheless, 22.4% had used computer games at school, 21.6% the Internet and 28.8% educational CD-ROMs. The use of television and Internet at school increases with age, while at the use of computer games decreases. The highest average number of hours per week spent watching television, playing video games and using educational CD-ROMs is found among 14-year-olds. For computer games and the Internet, the highest weekly average is found for those aged 15. The majority of both boys and girls believed to have had a high to very high degree of influence on the decision to buy them a computer. This contrasts with the low to medium influence they believed to have had in the purchase of a television set. When asked about video consoles, the majority of boys perceived a high to very high level of influence, while the majority of girls perceived a very low to medium influence. The majority of boys believed they had a high to very high influence over purchases of video games and video console games, while the majority of girls perceived a very low to medium influence in these decisions.

The children showed similar levels of perceived influence over the purchase of a television set in the different towns. In contrast, there were important differences with regard to computers and consoles and the applications related to them. Children in the wealthier towns had significantly different perceptions of their influence (lower for video consoles and higher for computers and the Internet) from those of their peers in the less wealthy towns. Age does not appear to be a factor related to the children's self-perceived influence, except in the purchase of games: the younger the child, the higher the influence s/he perceived to have had in the purchase of games for computers and console.

With regard to boredom or entertainment, children evaluated television as the most entertaining audiovisual medium and educational CD-ROMs as the most boring. However, the highest score corresponds to boys' evaluation of computer games. By age, the 16-year-olds appear to be the most enthusiastic when evaluating television, computers and the Internet.

Enthusiasm for the Internet clearly increases with the age. Enthusiasm for CD-ROMs is highest at the age of 12, gradually decreasing after that. As regards learning or not learning, children evaluate educational CD-ROMs as the best for learning, and console games as the least useful for learning. Computers also received a high score in terms of learning potential, to the extent that computer games were considered slightly more educational than video console games, particularly by girls. The only significant differences by age appear with respect to the Internet and CD-ROMs: the older the children, the more they think they can learn through the Internet and the less through educational CD-ROMs. In terms of wasting or making good use of time, the children evaluated educational CD-ROMs as the tool with which they could spend their time most usefully, and video console games as the biggest time-waster. Computers also scored highly in terms of use of time. In this case the differences between different audiovisual equipment and applications are less spectacular than in the semantic differential "learning - not learning". This reinforces the hypothesis of different perceptions by children and adults of the values related to the use of time.

The older they become, the more the children seem to consider the use of the computer and the Internet as a useful way of spending their time; meanwhile, the younger ones are those that are less likely to consider the use of television, computer and video games and CD-ROMs as a waste of time. By age, the usefulness of educational CD-ROMs was most highly rated at age 12. The usefulness of both consoles and computer games was rated highest by 13-year-olds, that of computers by those aged 14 and that of the Internet and television by 15-year-olds. From this age onwards, the expression of enthusiasm decreases with age in all cases, except for that of the Internet, for which enthusiasm grows until age 15, and educational CD-ROMs, for which enthusiasm already starts to diminish at age 12. Girls normally express more enthusiasm than boys about talking to friends of the same age about television and educational CD-ROMs. Boys tend to be more enthusiastic than girls when talking about games (for both computer and console).

The Internet seems to be an equally interesting activity for both boys and girls when it comes to talking to same-age friends. Both girls and boys display the lowest level of enthusiasm with reference to conversations with same-age friends about educational CD-ROMs, which represent the only multimedia application to score less than 3 points on average for both sexes. Television is the preferred medium when it comes to talking to siblings, with higher scores among girls. Boys expressed the highest mean preference when talking to brothers and sisters about using the console. As when talking to mothers, all audiovisual media, with the exception of the Internet, obtained the highest scores at the age of 12, scores diminishing gradually thereafter.

Talking to teachers about any audiovisual activity scored less than 2 points on average in all cases, with the exception of girls talking to them about CD-ROMs or computers, in which case scores still failed to exceed 2.3 on average. CD-ROMs appear to have their slightly more "special" moment as the subject of conversation with teachers at age 12, and computers at age 13, but in both cases the scores diminish rapidly with age. Talking to older friends about any audiovisual medium seems to be very interesting for boys, with the exception of CD-ROMs. The Internet is the only activity for which we do not observe gender differences with regard to enjoying talking to older friends. There are no differences according to age related to preferences when talking to older friends, with the exception of talking about what they have seen on television. On average, parents claim to be less interested in all audiovisual media than their own children.

They tend to attribute quite high levels of interest to children with reference to computers, a moderate-to-high interest in television and CD-ROMs, a moderate interest in the Internet and computer games, and a low-to-moderate interest in consoles. There are no significant differences between mothers and fathers, except when parents answered jointly about educational CD-ROMs. In this case they claim that their child has a significantly higher interest in such applications. The parents attribute a significantly higher interest in computers, the Internet and console and computer games when they refer to a male child. Furthermore, they perceive that the interest of the children for console and computer games, as well as educational CD-ROMs decreases gradually with age from 12 to 16. On average, parents also believe that their children are much better informed than they themselves are about all audiovisual media. They attribute to the children a moderate to high level of information about all audiovisual media, scoring only the Internet below 3 points on average. There is only one significant difference between fathers and mothers, with mothers tending to believe that their children are significantly better informed about the Internet.

Parents tend to believe that their child is better informed about games and the Internet when they are referring to a boy. Furthermore, they perceive their children to be progressively more and better informed about the Internet from the age of 12 up to 15. According to parents, their children enjoy talking to brothers and sisters above all about computer activities, in second place about television and in third place about games.

References

Pearson, Dora M.: Library Reclassifies Books. *Library Journal,* 74:919-923, June 15, 1949.

Sayeis, W. C. B.: An *Introduction to Library Classification.* 8th ed, London, Grafton and Co., 1950.

Tillett, Barbara B. "FRBR and Cataloguing for the Future," *Cataloguing & Classification Quarterly*, v. 39, no. 3/4, p. 205-216.

Universal Decimal Classification. Complete English ed. 4th international ed, BS 1000. 669 Metallurgy. London, British Standards Institute, 1949.

U.S. Library of Congress. Descriptive Cataloguing Division: *Rules for Descriptive Cataloguing in the Library of Congress.* Washington, D.C., 1949.

5

Preserving Digital Information

Today, information technologies that are increasingly powerful and easy to use, especially like those that support the World Wide Web, have unleashed the production and distribution of digital information. Such information is penetrating and transforming nearly every aspect of our culture. If we are effectively to preserve for future generations the portion of this rapidly expanding corpus of information in digital form that represents our cultural record, we need to understand the costs of doing so and we need to commit ourselves technically, legally, economically and organizationally to the full dimensions of the task.

Preserving or archiving digital information is not a new one and has been explored at a variety of levels over the last five decades. Archivists responsible for governmental and corporate records have been acutely aware of the difficulties entailed in trying to ensure that digital information survives for future generations. Far more than their library colleagues, who have continued to collect and organize published materials primarily in paper form, archivists have observed the materials for which they are responsible shift rapidly from paper objects produced on typewriters and other analog devices to include files created in word processor, spreadsheet and many other digital forms. Early attention to the difficulties in preserving digital information focused on the longevity of the physical media on which the information is stored. Even under the best storage conditions, however, digital media can be fragile and have limited shelf life. Moreover, new devices, processes and software are replacing the products and methods used to record, store, and retrieve digital information on breathtaking cycles of 2- to 5- years. Given such rates of technological change, even the most fragile media may well outlive the continued availability of readers for those media.

Efforts to Preserve Digital Media

Efforts to preserve physical media thus provide only a short-term, partial solution to the general problem of preserving digital information. Indeed, technological obsolescence represents a far greater threat to information in digital form than the inherent physical fragility of many digital media. In the face of rapid technological obsolescence and to overcome the problem of media fragility, archivists have adopted the technique of "refreshing" digital information by copying it onto new media. Copying from medium to medium, however, also suffers limitations as a means of digital preservation. Refreshing digital information by copying will work as an effective preservation technique only as long as the information is encoded in a format that is independent of the particular hardware and software needed to use it and as long as there exists software to manipulate the format in current use. Otherwise, copying depends either on the compatibility of present and past versions of software and generations of hardware or the ability of competing hardware and software product lines to interoperate.

In respect of these factors- backward compatibility and interoperability- the rate of technological change exacts a serious toll on efforts to ensure the longevity of digital information. Digital information today is produced in highly varying degrees of dependence on particular hardware and software.

Moreover, it is costly and difficult for vendors to assure that their products are either "backwardly compatible" with previous versions or that they can interoperate with competing products. Jeff Rothenberg, for example, has recently suggested that there may be sufficient demand for entrepreneurs to create and archive emulators of software and operating systems that would allow the contents of digital information to be carried forward and used in its original format. Refreshing digital information by copying it from medium to medium and the possibility of maintaining a complex set of emulators describe two distinct points on a continuum of approaches to preserving digital information. However, neither refreshing nor emulation sufficiently describes the full range of options needed and available for digital preservation.

Instead, a better and more general concept to describe these options is migration. Migration is the periodic transfer of digital materials from one hardware/software configuration to another, or from one generation of computer technology to a subsequent generation. The purpose of migration is to preserve the integrity of digital objects and to retain the ability for clients to retrieve, display, and otherwise use them in the face of constantly changing technology. Migration includes refreshing as a means of digital preservation but differs from it in the sense that it is not always possible to make an exact digital copy or replica of a database or other information object as hardware and software change and still maintain the compatibility of the object with the new generation of technology. Even for information that is encoded in a contemporary standard form, forward migration of the information to a new standard or application program is, as anyone knows who has witnessed or participated in such a process, time-consuming, costly and much more complex than simple refreshing. Compounding the technical challenges of migrating digital information is the problem of managing the process in a legal and organizational environment that is in flux as it moves to accommodate rapidly changing digital technologies.

Consider, for example, the barriers to decisive preservation action caused by widespread uncertainty about legal and organizational requirements for managing the intellectual property that digital information represents. Addressing and resolving the legal and practical questions of migrating intellectual property in digital form necessarily involves a complex set of interested parties, including the creators and owners of intellectual property, managers of digital archives, representatives of the public interest, and actual and potential users of intellectual property.

In addition, the parties who represent, for example, owners and users of different kinds of intellectual property (e.g., text and other document-like objects, photographs, film, software, multimedia objects) each operate under very different organizational regimes, with different experiences and expectations. Adding to these complexities is the deep uncertainty that these groups face in confronting an increasingly digital world. Owners of intellectual property are unsure about how to price access to their information and worry, given the ease of copying, that the first digital copy of a work they sell may be the only copy they sell. Users of intellectual property are unsure about what rights are conveyed with the use of a particular digital information object and about how much such use is worth. Government representatives seek in the public interest to manage the powerful changes that accompany digital technologies, but are unsure about what levels of influence are available to them and how to generate appropriate public policy. The state of the copyright law, which was generated and developed in an analog world but is applied in an increasingly digital universe, is itself confusing and uncertain.

And all of these concerns are exacerbated by the fact that bits know no borders. The costs and the technical, legal and organizational complexities of moving digital information forward into the future raise our greatest fear about the life of information in the digital future: namely, that owners or custodians who can no longer bear the expense and difficulty will deliberately or inadvertently, through a simple failure to act, destroy the objects without regard for future use. Repeated anecdotes about the loss of land use information, satellite imagery or census data, even when false or misleading, feed our general anxiety about the future of the cultural record we are accumulating in digital form.

And uncertainty and lack of confidence about our will and ability to carry digital information forward into the future exert a major inhibiting force in our disposition to fully exploit the digital medium to generate, publish and disseminate information. But how well does the evidence really support our fears, anxieties and inhibitions regarding digital information? Even after more than forty years of growth, the digital world of information technology and communication is still relatively young and immature in relation to the larger information universe, parts of which have been under development for centuries. Viewed developmentally, the problem of preserving digital information for the future is not only, or even primarily, a problem of fine tuning a narrow set of technical variables. It is not a clearly defined problem like preserving the embrittled books that are self-destructing from the acid in the paper on which they were printed. Rather, it is a grander problem of organizing ourselves over time and as a society to manoeuvre effectively in a digital landscape. It is a problem of building-almost from scratch-the various systematic supports, or deep infrastructure, that will enable us to tame anxieties and move our cultural records naturally and confidently into the future.

For digital preservation, the organizational effort-the process of building deep infrastructure-necessarily involves multiple, interrelated factors, many of which are either unknown or poorly defined. One of the biggest unknowns is the full impact on traditional information handling functions of distributed computing over electronic networks. The effort to meet the cultural imperative of digital preservation thus requires a complex iteration and reiteration of exploration, development and solution as the relevant factors and their interrelationships emerge and become clearer and more tractable.

And the first task in the effort is not to posit answers, but to frame questions and issues in such a way as to engage the many parties already working in various ways with digital information so that they can help us understand the relevant issues and, within the context of their work, help us identify, define and incorporate solutions that contribute to the larger, common goal of preserving our cultural heritage. Digital archives are distinct from digital libraries in the sense that digital libraries are repositories that collect and provide access to digital information, but may or may not provide for the long-term storage and access of that information. Digital libraries thus may or may not be, in functional terms, digital archives and, in fact, much of the recent work on digital libraries is notably silent on the archival issues of ensuring long-term storage and access. Conversely, digital archives necessarily embrace digital library functions to the extent that they must select, obtain, store, and provide access to digital information. Many of the functional requirements for digital archives defined and thus overlap those for digital libraries.

Processes of Preserving Digital Information

Digital technologies increasingly serve to integrate information resources. Text, numeric data, images, voice, and video have heretofore resided in print or other analog media for storage and transmission. When they are encoded digitally, either by conversion or at the point of creation, these various kinds of resources share layers of technology-a common means of storage and transmission- that allows them to be brought together and used in both old and new ways. Multimedia and hyperlinked objects on the World Wide Web represent some of the new kinds of information and new ways of knowing in the digital realm that bring together the traditional forms of information and transform their use. The application of computer hardware and software has also generated other new kinds of information objects, including the products of simulation, remote sensing, computer-aided design (CAD) and geographic information (GIS) systems. These objects come into being and exist as creatures of the digital environment; if nurtured well, digital technologies will certainly beget still other kinds of information objects, which we can now only anticipate.

The processes of preserving digital information will vary significantly with the different kinds of objects-textual, numeric, image, video, sound, multimedia, simulation and so on-being preserved. Whatever preservation method is applied, however, the central goal must be to preserve information integrity; that is, to define and preserve those features of an information object that distinguish it as a whole and singular work. In the digital environment, the features that determine information integrity and deserve special attention for archival purposes include the following: content, fixity, reference, provenance, and context.

What digital archives are trying to preserve after all is the intellectual substance contained in information objects. The notion of content, however, is itself a complex idea that operates at several different levels of abstraction. To preserve the integrity of objects in their charge, digital archives must decide at which level, or levels, of abstraction they are defining information content. At the lowest level of abstraction, all digital information objects consist of simple bitstreams of 0s and 1s. One can distinguish objects from one another merely by distinguishing the configuration of bits.

Preserving the integrity of an information object in this sense means preserving the bit configuration that uniquely defines the object. There are various well-established techniques, such as checksums and digests, for tracking the bit-level equivalence of digital objects and ensuring that a preserved object is identical to the original. Defining content as a collection of bits, however, is often too limited and simplistic to be useful. In the digital environment, as we have seen, ideas are typically embedded in particular formats and structures that are dependent on hardware and software technologies subject to rapid change.

Conceived at this higher level of abstraction-that is, in terms of format and structure-the definition of content poses considerable difficulties for managing information integrity in an archival context, and we are just beginning to come to terms with the expression of these problems in the digital environment. Text today is generally covered by a formal, international ASCII standard for representing character formats. Standard extensions exist for encoding diacritic characters in romance languages other than English and a new standard is slowly emerging to incorporate scripted languages under a new common encoding scheme (UNICODE).

Alternative encoding methods, however, abound. IBM maintains its own EBCDIC character encoding scheme and Apple and Intel-based personal computers differ in the ways that they support extended ASCII character sets. For documents in which any of these character codes can adequately represent the contents, the differences in encoding schemes may matter little and digital archives can manage object integrity by mapping character sets from one to the other. However, for works involving multiple languages or complex equations and formula, where character mapping is imperfect or not possible, character set format takes on considerably more significance over the long-term as a matter of content integrity.

In addition to character set issues, digital archives must also grapple with the means of representing and preserving textual content embedded in layout and structure. Markup systems, such as implementations of TeX and the Standard Generalized Markup Language (SGML), do exist as platform-independent mechanisms for identifying and tagging for subsequent layout and retrieval detailed structural elements of documents. The use of TeX and its variants, for example, is relatively common among scholars in some scientific disciplines such as mathematics and computer science, and the federal government and scholarly publishers are increasingly employing the SGML standard in documents that they produce and distribute electronically.

Beyond these relatively specialized segments, however, word processing and desktop publishing systems still dominate the market for the creation of documents with complex structure and layout, and the software for such use typically models and stores document structure and layout in proprietary terms. Although software may provide mechanisms for converting documents to common interchange formats, use of such mechanisms often results in the loss or inadequate rendering of content such as page structures and the layout of headers, footers and section headings.

The preservation of images comprises another example of the ways in which content, defined in terms of structure and format, poses integrity problems for digital archives. Image resolution, accuracy of color representation and compression for storage all require attention, but the interaction of these structural factors tends to pit judgments about the quality of content against the need for its efficient archival storage and use. In general, one can express the tradeoffs as follows: the higher the resolution and the richer the color register, the larger the file size and more costly the storage.

The use of compression technologies further complicates the equation because the application of some algorithms to reduce space needs may involve an irreversible loss of data. The popular JPEG algorithm, for example, supports "lossy" compression, whereby the greatest degree of compression requires the maximum settings for allowable loss. At the highest level of abstraction, digital archives define content in a way that transcends the limits of the hardware and software systems needed for reading and interpreting the bits of an information object and for rendering it for use in a specific format and structural representation; that is, they define content in terms of the knowledge or ideas the object contains.

Expressed in this way, the preservation challenge for digital archives is to migrate (or to enable the user to migrate) intellectual content using standard interchange algorithms and other appropriate migration strategies so that the ideas available in the end are identical to those contained in the original object. The measure of integrity in the preservation process thus turns, at least in part, on informed and skillful judgments about the appropriate definition of the content of an digital information object-about the extent to which content depends on its configuration of bits, on the structure and format of its representation, and on the ideas it contains-and for what purposes.

The process of identifying and preserving a digital information object as a whole and singular work goes well beyond considerations of content. It also depends, for instance, on the way that the content is fixed as a discrete object. If an object is not fixed, and the content is subject to change or withdrawal without notice, then its integrity may be compromised and its value as a cultural record would be severely diminished. Outside the digital landscape, business practices, editorial policies, and legal constraints, have created disciplines for fixing information in discrete objects. The acts of production and broadcast establish radio and television programs as discrete objects.

And the act of publication marks a specific version or edition of a literary work. In each of these cases, it is virtually impossible to change or withdraw the cultural record that the release of an information object establishes. On the digital landscape, by contrast, it is still relatively easy for a creator to alter or retract previously released information. Such actions can eliminate or overlay significant content and thereby corrupt the record. It is also relatively easy in an on-line environment-and equally confusing for purposes of preserving information integrity-for an author (or user) to make available concurrently multiple representations of what he or she considers to be the same work, providing no definition of a canonical version and viewing all representations as having equal quality and validity.

To address these problems, a wide range of cryptographic techniques, such as watermarking, already exist for various kinds of digital information objects. These could serve well to mark and identify specific, canonical versions and editions of textual, audio and visual works, and to establish trusted, protected channels of distribution for those objects. However, the standards and infrastructure and the policies and practices for applying such techniques to the creation of fixed versions of digital information objects still need considerable development. Absent such development and the fixity of information that would result, digital archives face considerable challenges in trying to preserve the integrity of digital objects.

Some kinds of digital objects present the problem of fixity of information in yet another way. An increasing number of networked information resources are better modeled, not in terms of versions or editions of works, but as continuously updated databases. The Human Genome Project supports such a database, which serves as a vehicle and record for a worldwide collaborative effort. The financial communities also depend on large, continuously updated databases. There is no natural way to fix these resources at the database level, no natural set of publication points for the objects as a whole. Their integrity, or singularity, as databases resides in the coherence of the database as a whole and in the continuousness of the updates.

To preserve the integrity of such information resources, the complete record of changes has to be built into the design of the database and fixed at the record level. Technology exists for constructing databases that maintain all previous versions of the records in the database as well as details about when new information is added or logically deleted. A database designed to a so-called time-travel specification, however, is expensive to construct and operate. In the absence of such a preservation-oriented design, digital archives may have no choice but to fix the database artificially in time and capture a series of snapshots of its state at periodic intervals as a way of preserving its integrity.

A third aspect of information integrity that bears crucially on the preservation process is that information objects must have a consistent means of reference. Information objects come into being and acquire their distinctiveness in relation to various other objects in an information space. For an object to maintain its integrity, its wholeness and singularity, one must be able to locate it definitively and reliably over time among other objects. Systems of citation, description and classification provide the necessary means of reference so that one can consistently discover, identify and retrieve relevant objects.

Such systems traditionally include bibliographies, catalogues, indices, data dictionaries, directory systems, finding aids and the like, all of which collect, assemble and organize references to bodies of work. Creators of these resources are already extending them with such innovations, for example, as the use of the 856 field in bibliographic records, to incorporate reference to digital objects. Moreover, in the electronic environment, there are also emerging sophisticated tools for automatically gathering and presenting in new kinds of products referential information from textual, image, sound, video and other kinds of digital objects.

To meet the test of consistent reference, however, citations to digital objects from these various manually and automatically generated sources must over time reliably identify the works to which they refer. One way of establishing confidence in a reference system is to generate citations in the first place- either manually or automatically-from the self-referential information that a work itself carries with it, perhaps in a header, a digital envelope or some other distinct part of the digital object. Unfortunately, except for documents marked up to the standard of the Text Encoding Initiative, few digital objects today contain self-referential information that meets conventional citation quality.

Matching citation and digital work to meet the test of consistent reference thus is difficult. Moreover, reliably identifying multiple versions and editions of works in electronic form remains a persistent reference problem. Part of the general problem of identifying and consistently referring to variant digital works is the specific problem of resolving names and locations for them. Coordinated by such groups as the Internet Engineering Task Force (IETF), active research and development has led to an emerging consensus that several factors contribute to the unique identification of digital information objects.

Two of the most important factors are the Uniform Resource Name (URN) and the Uniform Resource Locator (URL). The URL refers to the specific place where a digital object resides and is currently the dominant method of object location on the World Wide Web. The weakness of the URL, however, is that it may frequently change, especially as an object migrates from one machine to the next. By contrast, a name, the URN, is supposed to apply uniquely and permanently to a distinct object and to designate it independently of its particular location at any point in time.

URNs today exist more in concept than in practice. Thus, resolving the name and location for variant digital works and thereby providing consistent reference to them means moving from a conceptual design of the relation between names and locations to an operational reality through the implementation of naming authorities, which assign URNs, and and the development of digital services that translate names into currently valid URLs. In order to provide a consistent means of reference for digital objects, systems of citation, description and classification will need to dispense more than name and location information.

The IETF framework provides a general category for additional reference information in what it calls Uniform Resource Characteristics (URCs). Among the kinds of information that a reference system might provide under this general category is information about the intellectual property rights governing the use of a particular object and its cost. For archival purposes, however, there are two other qualities of digital information objects that a reference system must take into account. These are the features of provenance and context.

Provenance

Provenance has become one of the central organizing concepts of modern archival science. The assumption underlying the principle of provenance is that the integrity of an information object is partly embodied in tracing from where it came. To preserve the integrity of an information object, digital archives must preserve a record of its origin and chain of custody. For some information objects, the formal process of publication creates a trusted channel of distribution and serves to establish a sophisticated record of provenance, at least from the creator through the point of release.

In the digital environment, the problems of documenting provenance through a record of publication are bound up with the problems of fixity. Outside the path of publication, however, there are several other channels of information creation and distribution, including tracing the path of migration within their own organization, that digital archives need to document in order to preserve the integrity of digital objects in their custody.

First, there is a chain of provenance from individuals, a trail which has comprised a traditional concern of archivists. In the digital environment, as in other domains, individuals produce and accrete much information that relates to their private lives and to their public roles and responsibilities, including their means of livelihood. Among the kinds of information objects that may count as personal records in digital form are electronic mail, notes, manuscripts, journals, photographs or videos, and databases of personal finances. For objects of these kinds, which make their way into digital archives and which the custodian deems worth keeping as part of the historical record, the archival responsibility in establishing provenance is to establish, as unambiguously as possible, the identity of the individuals who are the source of the objects and to trace the chain of custody to arrival in the archives.

A second kind of digital information flow that requires special attention with respect to provenance are those mediated or governed by corporate information systems. The digital products of such systems may include databases of employment and financial records, contracts and other legal records, planning documents, FDA filings, technical reports and so on. The distinctive feature of such objects is that they are all best viewed not as the result of individual works but as proceeding from the business, governmental or other social practices that the information system organizes and instantiates. The archival challenge for establishing the provenance of such objects is to find ways to preserve an understanding of the corporate policies and processes and roles and responsibilities thus represented in the information system and its products.

Third, there is the chain of provenance that traces information, particularly scientific data, to a source in electronic instrumentation. In some cases, the instrumentation produces data in the service of individual experiments or of clinical practice; in other cases, remote sensors gather streams of observational data about physical systems in space or on earth. Of course, one ultimately accounts for the origin of the resulting data in the design and conduct of the experiment or clinical service, or in the character of the remote sensing program. However, the use of the instrumentation creates a special requirement to trace the provenance of the data to the design characteristics of the instrument itself. The data are a direct product of and derive their meaning and usefulness from the calibration, units of measure, sampling rate, conditions of recording and other relevant features embedded in the technology of the instrument.

Finally, a concern for provenance in preserving the integrity of digital information means that digital archives must document what happens to the information within their own organizations. They must keep a record of migration activity, and particularly of the transformations they make to keep information objects current with new technologies for use. In the end, the investment that digital archives make in establishing the provenance of objects in their care serves to preserve the integrity of digital information in two distinct ways. First, a tracing of chain of custody from the point of creation helps to create the presumption that an object is authentic, that it is what it purports to be and that its content, however defined, has not been manipulated, altered or falsified. The second effect of establishing provenance through a chain of custody is to document, at least in part, the particular uses of the object by the custodians. In thus creating a record of use, the archival concern with provenance is intimately related to the notion of context as a matter of information integrity.

The fifth attribute of information integrity that bears on the preservation of digital information objects is their context, the ways in which they interact with elements in the wider digital environment. The context of digital information includes a technical dimension, a dimension of linkage to other objects, a communication dimension, and a wider social dimension. Digital archives must be attentive to the ways in which each of these contextual dimensions affects the integrity of the objects in their care. First, to specify the technical context of digital information is to specify its hardware and software dependencies. Digital objects, by nature, require the use of computer hardware and software to create and use them. In some cases, an object may be closely dependent on a configuration of technology. For example, a particular digital document may require a particular word processing program running on a machine with a special kind of computer processing chip and operating system. Other objects, such as an image file, may be readable using a variety of software programs, but may be stored on disk in a format that is readable only with a special computer. For still other objects, like World Wide Web documents marked-up in HTML, the hardware and software dependencies may be specified in very general terms because they are readable with a software browser that is available on almost any hardware platform.

Challenges for Preserving the Integrity of Digital Information

The archival challenges for preserving the integrity of these various kinds of objects are, on the one hand, to represent faithfully the context of the objects in terms of their hardware and software dependencies and, on the other hand, to overcome, through appropriate migration efforts, those dependencies that threaten to hinder future use. On the World Wide Web, for example, the HyperText Markup Language (HTML) provides a way to place in one object references to various other objects. A click of a mouse key then enables one to move quickly from one linked object to another. If the integrity of these objects is seen as residing in the network of linkages among them, rather than in the individual objects, or nodes, on the network, then the archival challenge would be to preserve both the objects and the linkages, a task that would today be exceedingly complex. At present, there appears to be no good archiving solution; a possible stop-gap measure would be to treat the network in terms of its component parts and to take periodic snapshots of the individual WWW objects. The communications medium comprises a third dimension of the context of digital information.

The character and integrity of digital information objects depends, in part, on their mode of distribution. Material distributed on CD-ROM, for example, has a set of file format and other characteristics that set it apart from material distributed in, say, networked form. As digital materials increasingly come into being and subsist in an electronically networked environment, contextual features of the network, such as bandwidth and security, will account for characteristics of the digital objects. Increasing bandwidth, for example, will stimulate the production and dissemination of high-bandwidth digital materials such as full-motion video. Similarly, improved security on the network will encourage the conduct of a wide variety of confidential transactions. As network-based objects, such as video and records of confidential transactions, make their way into digital repositories, an archival account of their integrity must include an account of the features of the network context that supports their existence. Finally, the wider social environment plays a significant contextual role that contributes to the integrity of digital information objects. Networked information, for example, depends on specific policy and implementation decisions that address the bandwidth, security and other qualities of the network and related technical infrastructure.

Electronic mail is subject to a variety of social distinctions when, in some contexts, it is used to convey highly personal messages among friends and, in other contexts, is a vehicle for formal communication among academic or business colleagues. One might account for digital business records, too, in the social context of the political and organizational regime in which they were generated. Indeed, the social context of digital information objects is an expression of what one might characterize in other terms as the interests of stakeholders in those objects. Digital information objects acquire the qualities of content, fixity, reference, provenance and context-and thereby their integrity-as they move through a life cycle in a series of relationships with parties, or stakeholders, who have specific interests in their creation, management, dissemination, use or retention.

The initial stakeholder in a digital information object is, of course, the creator of its content. Following creation, a digital information object may pass through a series of gateways of increasingly public release and access. Some digital information objects may never be released beyond the initial creator; others will be limited to an immediate circle, which may or may not be physically co-located with the creator. Once a creator fixes a digital information object by releasing it, for either personal or wider use, the object invites various other kinds of stakeholder interests. Depending on the extent of the release and the nature of the object, users and other stakeholders may refer to it, index it or cite it. Still others may acquire, license or otherwise take custody of it to edit and publish it, to invoke it as evidence of a transaction or perhaps, as in the case of scientific data, to study, analyze and report it. And eventually during the course of its life, a digital information object may attract the interest of stakeholders, such as a digital libraries, which serve as collectors/disseminators of information objects. What unites all these various stakeholders, of course, is their particular interest in adding to or making use of the value of digital information objects.

However, the integrity of information objects in the digital environment is today so fragile that as stakeholders disseminate, use, reuse, recreate and re-disseminate various kinds of digital information, they can easily, even inadvertently, destroy valuable information, corrupt the cultural record, and ultimately thwart the pursuit of knowledge that is their common end. Against such a danger, a safety-net is needed to ensure that digital information objects with long-term cultural and intellectual value survive the expressions of stakeholder interest with their integrity intact. Among the stakeholders serving as collector/disseminators, those who perform archival functions provide just such a safety-net. Digital archives build and maintain reliable collections of well-defined digital information objects and they preserve the features-content, fixity, reference, provenance and context-that give those objects their integrity and enduring value. Such an archival network will establish a critical part of the foundation needed to support a burgeoning, but still fragile, national and international knowledge economy.

Within an archive, metadata accompanies and makes reference to each digital object and provides associated descriptive, structural, administrative, rights management, and other kinds of information. This metadata will also be maintained and will be migrated from format to format and standard to standard, independently of the base object it describes. But some of the metadata associated with an object is computationally bound to the specific object representation, creating another problem when objects and their metadata migrate asynchronously.

Key processes involved in the management of digital objects over time include the tracking of authenticity as part of provenance; maintaining the integrity of the digital object and ensuring the referential integrity of links to that object and understanding how reformatting impacts the integrity of the object. These involve both the digital object and its metadata.

Life of an Archived Digital Object

A digital object enters a repository as a set of sequences of bits; it is accompanied by a variety of metadata related to that object. With proper storage management, replication, and refreshing, this set of sequences of bits can be maintained indefinitely. In order to provide verification of the origin of the digital object, digital signature techniques may link it to a public key that is recorded in a public key infrastructure (PKI). Typically, at the point of deposit a hash of the object would be computed using an algorithm such as MD-5 or SHA-1, and that hash would then be signed using the private key of a public/private key pair.

The public key of the pair would be bound to an identity recorded in a certificate issued by a trusted certificate authority. This signed hash would form part of the provenance metadata for the object. At any point, the provenance could be verified by checking the certificate against the PKI, and then checking the signed hash against a new hash computed from the object itself, using the public key from the certificate. This is satisfactory until the object has to be reformatted.

Once format translation occurs, the object is represented by a different set of sequences of bits, and the signature no longer verifies. There are several unattractive alternatives. The original author can re-sign the reformatted object, but that author may no longer be available to generate a new signature, or may be unwilling to judge the suitability of the reformatted version of the object. If the original author (who originally signed the object and owns the certificate) is not involved, the repository must begin to establish a chain of provenance (and, potentially, a chain of liability) for the object. There are several possibilities. The repository can sign the reformatted object, and also create and sign a new piece of provenance metadata that links the original author's certificate with the reformatted object. We now have only the repository's testimony that the original author once made a verifiable authorship claim. Or, we can maintain the original signed authorship testimony and the original, unreformatted object permanently, even though it can no longer be interpreted for access purposes, but can only verify the original author's authorship claim. The original testimony can be supplemented with a metadata certification, signed by the repository, that the original object is a predecessor to the new reformatted object.

It will be common to use a hash in a metadata record or a link in order to ensure referential integrity. Once the object is reformatted, all of these hashes need to be recomputed and, where appropriate, links or metadata objects need to be re-signed since the hash has changed. Similar questions arise about who signs the new links. There is always the question of how much information is lost or corrupted in the course of reformatting. We want to be able to guarantee that for a given object the reformatted version is equivalent to the original version with regard to some specific set of object characteristics. While it would be best to prove general properties of the reformatting process, such a guarantee may be very complex or impossible to verify, particularly when the reformatting is done by proprietary software. In these cases, it would be useful to have some confidence about the effects of format translation on specific individual documents—in other words, to be able to verify that for a given document the relevant set of characteristics remains invariant when it moves from the old to the new format.

Archival Function in the System of Knowledge Creation

The digital world is too new for us to describe fully the life cycle of the information objects that do now or will in the future reside there, but what surely unites the community of actors in their various information-based activities is their common purpose in support of the pursuit of knowledge. The pursuit of knowledge is a process in which the emergence of new knowledge builds on and reconstructs the old. Knowledge cannot advance without consistent and reliable access to information sources, past and present.

It is the archival function in the system of knowledge creation and use that serves to identify and retain important sources of information and to ensure continuing access to them. How reliable the archival process proves to be in the emerging digital environment hinges on the trustworthy operation of digital archives and on their ability to maintain the integrity of the objects they are charged to preserve. For digital objects, no less than for objects of other kinds, knowing how operationally to preserve them depends, at least in part, on being able to discriminate the essential features of what needs to be preserved. Digital technologies increasingly serve to integrate information resources. Text, numeric data, images, voice, and video have heretofore resided in print or other analog media for storage and transmission. When they are encoded digitally, either by conversion or at the point of creation, these various kinds of resources share layers of technology-a common means of storage and transmission- that allows them to be brought together and used in both old and new ways.

Multimedia and hyperlinked objects on the World Wide Web represent some of the new kinds of information and new ways of knowing in the digital realm that bring together the traditional forms of information and transform their use. The application of computer hardware and software has also generated other new kinds of information objects, including the products of simulation, remote sensing, computer-aided design (CAD) and geographic information (GIS) systems. These objects come into being and exist as creatures of the digital environment; if nurtured well, digital technologies will certainly beget still other kinds of information objects, which we can now only anticipate. The processes of preserving digital information will vary significantly with the different kinds of objects-textual, numeric, image, video, sound, multimedia, simulation and so on-being preserved.

Whatever preservation method is applied, however, the central goal must be to preserve information integrity; that is, to define and preserve those features of an information object that distinguish it as a whole and singular work. In the digital environment, the features that determine information integrity and deserve special attention for archival purposes include the following: content, fixity, reference, provenance, and context. What digital archives are trying to preserve after all is the intellectual substance contained in information objects. The notion of content, however, is itself a complex idea that operates at several different levels of abstraction.

To preserve the integrity of objects in their charge, digital archives must decide at which level, or levels, of abstraction they are defining information content. At the lowest level of abstraction, all digital information objects consist of simple bitstreams of 0s and 1s. One can distinguish objects from one another merely by distinguishing the configuration of bits. Preserving the integrity of an information object in this sense means preserving the bit configuration that uniquely defines the object.

There are various well-established techniques, such as checksums and digests, for tracking the bit-level equivalence of digital objects and ensuring that a preserved object is identical to the original. Defining content as a collection of bits, however, is often too limited and simplistic to be useful. In the digital environment, ideas are typically embedded in particular formats and structures that are dependent on hardware and software technologies subject to rapid change. In addition to character set issues, digital archives must also grapple with the means of representing and preserving textual content embedded in layout and structure.

Markup systems, such as implementations of TeX and the Standard Generalized Markup Language (SGML), do exist as platform-independent mechanisms for identifying and tagging for subsequent layout and retrieval detailed structural elements of documents. The use of TeX and its variants, for example, is relatively common among scholars in some scientific disciplines such as mathematics and computer science, and the federal government and scholarly publishers are increasingly employing the SGML standard in documents that they produce and distribute electronically. Beyond these relatively specialized segments, however, word processing and desktop publishing systems still dominate the market for the creation of documents with complex structure and layout, and the software for such use typically models and stores document structure and layout in proprietary terms.

Although software may provide mechanisms for converting documents to common interchange formats, use of such mechanisms often results in the loss or inadequate rendering of content such as page structures and the layout of headers, footers and section headings. The preservation of images comprises another example of the ways in which content, defined in terms of structure and format, poses integrity problems for digital archives. Image resolution, accuracy of color representation and compression for storage all require attention, but the interaction of these structural factors tends to pit judgments about the quality of content against the need for its efficient archival storage and use. In general, one can express the tradeoffs as follows: the higher the resolution and the richer the color register, the larger the file size and more costly the storage.

At the highest level of abstraction, digital archives define content in a way that transcends the limits of the hardware and software systems needed for reading and interpreting the bits of an information object and for rendering it for use in a specific format and structural representation; that is, they define content in terms of the knowledge or ideas the object contains. The measure of integrity in the preservation process thus turns, at least in part, on informed and skillful judgments about the appropriate definition of the content of an digital information object-about the extent to which content depends on its configuration of bits, on the structure and format of its representation, and on the ideas it contains-and for what purposes.

The process of identifying and preserving a digital information object as a whole and singular work goes well beyond considerations of content. It also depends, for instance, on the way that the content is fixed as a discrete object. If an object is not fixed, and the content is subject to change or withdrawal without notice, then its integrity may be compromised and its value as a cultural record would be severely diminished. The acts of production and broadcast establish radio and television programs as discrete objects. And the act of publication marks a specific version or edition of a literary work. In each of these cases, it is virtually impossible to change or withdraw the cultural record that the release of an information object establishes. On the digital landscape, by contrast, it is still relatively easy for a creator to alter or retract previously released information. Such actions can eliminate or overlay significant content and thereby corrupt the record.

To address these problems, a wide range of cryptographic techniques, such as watermarking, already exist for various kinds of digital information objects. These could serve well to mark and identify specific, canonical versions and editions of textual, audio and visual works, and to establish trusted, protected channels of distribution for those objects. However, the standards and infrastructure and the policies and practices for applying such techniques to the creation of fixed versions of digital information objects still need considerable development. Absent such development and the fixity of information that would result, digital archives face considerable challenges in trying to preserve the integrity of digital objects. Some kinds of digital objects present the problem of fixity of information in yet another way. An increasing number of networked information resources are better modeled, not in terms of versions or editions of works, but as continuously updated databases.

The financial communities also depend on large, continuously updated databases. There is no natural way to fix these resources at the database level, no natural set of publication points for the objects as a whole. Their integrity, or singularity, as databases resides in the coherence of the database as a whole and in the continuousness of the updates. To preserve the integrity of such information resources, the complete record of changes has to be built into the design of the database and fixed at the record level. In the absence of such a preservation-oriented design, digital archives may have no choice but to fix the database artificially in time and capture a series of snapshots of its state at periodic intervals as a way of preserving its integrity. Information objects come into being and acquire their distinctiveness in relation to various other objects in an information space.

There are several factors contribute to the unique identification of digital information objects. Two of the most important factors are the Uniform Resource Name (URN) and the Uniform Resource Locator (URL). The URL refers to the specific place where a digital object resides and is currently the dominant method of object location on the World Wide Web. The weakness of the URL, however, is that it may frequently change, especially as an object migrates from one machine to the next.

By contrast, a name, the URN, is supposed to apply uniquely and permanently to a distinct object and to designate it independently of its particular location at any point in time. URNs today exist more in concept than in practice. Thus, resolving the name and location for variant digital works and thereby providing consistent reference to them means moving from a conceptual design of the relation between names and locations to an operational reality through the implementation of naming authorities, which assign URNs, and and the development of digital services that translate names into currently valid URLs.

For archival purposes, however, there are two other qualities of digital information objects that a reference system must take into account. Provenance has become one of the central organizing concepts of modern archival science. The assumption underlying the principle of provenance is that the integrity of an information object is partly embodied in tracing from where it came. To preserve the integrity of an information object, digital archives must preserve a record of its origin and chain of custody. For some information objects, the formal process of publication creates a trusted channel of distribution and serves to establish a sophisticated record of provenance, at least from the creator through the point of release. In the digital environment, as in other domains, individuals produce and accrete much information that relates to their private lives and to their public roles and responsibilities, including their means of livelihood. The archival challenge for establishing the provenance of such objects is to find ways to preserve an understanding of the corporate policies and processes and roles and responsibilities thus represented in the information system and its products.

In some cases, the instrumentation produces data in the service of individual experiments or of clinical practice; in other cases, remote sensors gather streams of observational data about physical systems in space or on earth. The investment that digital archives make in establishing the provenance of objects in their care serves to preserve the integrity of digital information in two distinct ways. First, a tracing of chain of custody from the point of creation helps to create the presumption that an object is authentic, that it is what it purports to be and that its content, however defined, has not been manipulated, altered or falsified. The second cffcct of establishing provenance through a chain of custody is to document, at least in part, the particular uses of the object by the custodians. In thus creating a record of use, the archival concern with provenance is intimately related to the notion of context as a matter of information integrity.

As network-based objects, such as video and records of confidential transactions, make their way into digital repositories, an archival account of their integrity must include an account of the features of the network context that supports their existence. Finally, the wider social environment plays a significant contextual role that contributes to the integrity of digital information objects. Networked information, for example, depends on specific policy and implementation decisions that address the bandwidth, security and other qualities of the network and related technical infrastructure.

Long-term Preservation

Different types of information involved in the long-term preservation of information in an Open Archival Information System (OAIS). Each of these types can be viewed as a complete Information Object in that it contains a data object and adequate Representation Information to understand the data. The Content Information is the set of information that is the original target of preservation by the OAIS. Deciding what is the Content Information may not be obvious and may need to be negotiated with the Producer. The Representation Information for a digital Content Data Object (both semantic and syntactic) is needed to fully transform the bits into the Content Information. In principal, this even extends to the inclusion of definitions (e.g., dictionary and grammar) of any natural language (e.g., English) used in expressing the Content Information. Over long time periods the meaning of natural language expressions can evolve significantly in both general and in specific discipline usage.

As a practical matter, the OAIS needs to have enough Representation Information associated with the bits of the Content Data Object in the Content Information that it feels confident that the members of the Designated Community can enter the Representation Network with enough knowledge to begin accurately interpreting the Representation Information. This is a significant risk area for an OAIS, particularly for those with an expert Designated Community, because jargon and apparently widely understood terms may be short-lived. In such cases extra care needs to be exercised to ensure that the natural evolution of the Designated Community Knowledge Base does not effectively cause information loss from the Content Information. For an Information Object in general, the Representation Information can also be viewed as being augmented by Access Software that supports the presentation of the Content Information to the Consumer. Examples of this type of software include word processors supporting complex document format representations of Content Information and scientific visualization systems supporting representations of Content Information as a time series or a multidimensional array. The software uses its knowledge of the underlying Representation Information to provide these services. Often required information will be embedded in the software packages used by the Designated Community to present and analyze the Content Information.

A reason for preserving working Access Software arises from a convenience factor. Even with a complete set of Representation Information, practical access to all or part of a digital Content Data Object requires the use of Access Software. Thus a software module that provides useful access to a digital Content Data Object may be preserved in a working state as a matter of convenience. This is not difficult to do as long as the environment, which supports the software module, is readily available.

This environment consists of some underlying hardware and an operating system, various utilities that effectively augment the operating system and storage and display devices and their drivers. A change to any of these may cause the software module to no longer function, to function incorrectly, or to be unable to present results to the application or human user. The complexity of these interactions is what traditionally makes the preservation of working software such an arduous task. In short, the use of Access Software to replace Representation Networks is attractive from the point of view of minimizing the resources needed to ingest data and provide current users with access to data. However the reliance on working software can provide major problems for Long-Term Preservation when that software ceases to function. Indefinite long-term information preservation requires a full and understandable description of the Representation Information.

An important function of the OAIS is deciding what parts of the Content Information are the Content Data Object and what parts are the Representation Information. In addition to Content Information, the Archival Information must include information that will allow the understanding of the Content Information over an indefinite period of time. The specific set of Information Objects, which are required for this function, is collectively called Preservation Description Information (PDI). The PDI must include information that is necessary to adequately preserve the particular Content Information with which it is associated. It is specifically focused on describing the past and present states of the Content Information, ensuring it is uniquely identifiable, and ensuring it has not been unknowingly altered. This information is typical for all types of archives and has been classified in the context of traditional archives. However, the class definitions must be extended for digital archives. The following definitions are preserving Digital Information:

— *Reference Information*: This information identifies, and if necessary describes, one or more mechanisms used to provide assigned identifiers for the Content Information. It also provides those identifiers that allow outside systems to refer, unambiguously, to this particular Content Information. Examples of these systems include taxonomic systems, reference systems and registration systems. In the OAIS Reference Model most if not all of this information is replicated in Package Descriptions, which enable Consumers to access Content Information of interest.

— *Context Information*: This information documents the relationships of the Content Information to its environment. This includes why the Content Information was created and how it relates to other Content Information objects existing elsewhere.

— *Provenance Information*: This information documents the history of the Content Information. This tells the origin or source of the Content Information, any changes that may have taken place since it was originated, and who has had custody of it since it was originated. This gives future users some assurance as to the likely reliability of the Content Information. Provenance can be viewed as a special type of context information.

— *Fixity Information*: This information provides the Data Integrity checks or Validation/Verification keys used to ensure that the particular Content Information object has not been altered in an undocumented manner. Fixity Information includes special encoding and error detection schemes that are specific to instances of Content Objects. Fixity Information does not include the integrity preserving mechanisms provided by the OAIS underlying services, error protection supplied by the media and device drivers used by Archival Storage. The OAIS needs to explicitly decide what the exact definition of Content Information is in order to be able to ensure that it also has the PDI needed to preserve the Content Information. Once the Content

Information has been determined, it is possible to assess the Preservation Description Information.

- *Packaging Information*: The Packaging Information is that information which, either actually or logically, binds or relates the components of the package into an identifiable entity on specific media. For example, if the Content Information and PDI are identified as being the content of specific files on a CD-ROM, then the Packaging Information may include the ISO 9660 volume/file structure on the CD-ROM. The Packaging Information does not necessarily need to be preserved by an OAIS since it does not contribute to the Content Information or the PDI. However, there are cases where the OAIS may be required to reproduce the original submission exactly. The OAIS should also avoid holding PDI or Content Information only in the naming conventions of directory or file name structures. These structures are most likely to be used as Packaging Information.
- *Descriptive Information:* To preserving information, the OAIS must provide adequate features to allow Consumers to locate information of potential interest, analyze that information, and order desired information. This is accomplished through a specialization of the Information Object called Descriptive Information, which contain the data that serves as the input to documents or applications called Access Aids.

A library is not a last resting place for the books contained there but a place where information and ideas live and breathe in new minds. The digital age brings, here as elsewhere, opportunities and challenges. The Library can now provide access to some objects without assuming any responsibility for preserving them. The acquisition of materials and their integration into a library's collections traditionally have implied a responsibility to preserve those items for use by future generations. Its preservation responsibilities using a variety of professionally accepted practices:

- Providing adequate storage conditions (e.g., proper environmental controls and appropriate binding and shelving);
- Reformatting materials from their original fragile formats and media to more stable media; and
- For a small percentage of rare and unique materials with intrinsic value in their original formats, restoring originals through conservation treatments.

Over the last two centuries, it has conducted research and led efforts in areas such as binding and shelving books, proper environmental conditions for storage, use of microfilm for preservation, and mass deacidification of paper. The Library faces challenges in digital preservation that are widely recognized and shared by many other libraries and archives. They include the following:

— *Fragile storage media*—Digital materials are especially vulnerable to loss and destruction because they are stored on fragile magnetic and optical media that deteriorate rapidly and that can fail suddenly from exposure to heat, humidity, airborne contaminants, faulty reading and writing devices, human error, and even sabotage.

— *Technology obsolescence*—Digital materials become unreadable and inaccessible if the playback devices necessary to retrieve information from the media become obsolete or if the software that translates digital information from machine- to human-readable form is no longer available.

— *Legal questions surrounding copying and access*—Libraries, archives, and other cultural institutions have limited and uncertain rights to copy digital information for preservation or backup purposes, to reformat information so that it remains accessible by current technology, and to provide public access.

All organizations with responsibilities for preserving digital information are seeking better technical solutions, model policies, best practices, and clearer guidelines regarding legal and intellectual property issues. In US, Library Congress (LC) providing leadership or contributing actively to solving critical problems of digital archiving and long-term preservation. Until now, LC seems to have assumed a wait-and-see attitude toward its role in preserving digital information created outside the walls of the Library itself; this was probably exacerbated by the absence of a director for the Preservation Directorate.

The Library's collecting policies and mechanisms with regard to born-digital materials are closely tied to its preservation capabilities. As long as traditional collecting mechanisms guarantee a steady stream of print, other analog materials, and tangible digital objects such as CD-ROMs into the Library's collections, there is an illusion that little significant content is being lost.

The absence of significant digital content in the Library's collections removes a sense of urgency about digital preservation, and the lack of organizational capacity to preserve many types of born-digital information discourages the Library from taking on responsibilities that it is not prepared to fulfill. The methods for doing this include traditional collecting and custodianship and developing relationships with publishers, other research libraries, other national libraries, bibliographic networks and utilities, government agencies, and archives.

Traditionally, the acquisition of materials through purchase, exchange, or deposit and their cataloguing into the Library's permanent collection entailed a commitment to preserve those materials. In the digital environment, libraries will assume a wider variety of roles and responsibilities with regard to preservation. One of the first steps that librareis needs to take in adapting its collecting practices to accommodate born-digital information is to delineate clearly its responsibilities for preserving digital information.

As libraries identifies the areas in which it will assume the lead responsibility for digital preservation, other organizations can adjust the scope of their digital collections accordingly. Just as the Library cannot ignore the problem of digital preservation, so also it cannot be expected to do it all. If libraries does not set clear boundaries around its digital preservation responsibilities, then many people may assume unrealistically that the Library will be the repository of last resort for everything worth keeping. In the paper world, each library that decided to provide its users with a given resource both obtained and conserved its own copy of the object. This replication in the paper world served as a powerful fail-safe mechanism, helping to ensure long-term accessibility through the uncoordinated but distributed maintenance of independent copies. In the digital environment, in which much content is distributed through the centralized services of a publisher, it is not clear where the preservation responsibility lies.

Library needs to articulate carefully a policy identifying the subset of digital materials for which it will assume long-term curatorial responsibility, taking into account the following:

— The burden of preserving digital collections is daunting and must be shared with other archiving institutions.

— The archiving and preservation of digital resources normally accessed over the Internet will not take place as a by-product of normal access but must be explicitly pursued. Simply assuming that preservation will be carried out somewhere across numerous replicated research collections will not be a solution for networked resources.

Both considerations argue for libraries to define the scope of their archiving roles, in order that responsibilities be distributed across the archiving libraries of the world. The archiving and preservation responsibility is a long-term one that will serve researchers in generations to come. One advantage of digital materials is the potential to distribute preservation responsibilities among a wide variety of partners so that each institution preserves only a designated portion of the global digital record.

With careful planning, coordination, cooperative agreements, and clearly articulated boundaries around its curatorial collection, the Library could assume long-term preservation responsibility for a much smaller portion of the digital corpus than it did for the paper one. Some redundancy is necessary for backup and security purposes, but less redundancy is needed for digital collections than was required in the past because access no longer requires physical proximity to materials.

Even if LC carefully defines its roles and responsibilities along the continuum from serving as a portal to acting as the primary custodian for digital materials, there is an urgent need for it to enhance its technical capacity and expertise in digital preservation. Such preservation will involve a wide range of activities, including the following:

— "Protecting the bits"—The making of backup copies, periodic recopying to new media, and regular checking of object coherence and validity are required to make certain that rarely accessed materials remain technically sound. Access will be enhanced to the extent that archived materials remain online rather than, say, being stored on media such as tapes, which must be mounted manually.

— Archiving appropriate copies—For many digital materials, the format most useful for current services (say, a PDF file or a GIF image) is not the most robust for long-term archiving (SGML, XML, or TIFF may serve better). A preservation program must encompass the selection and archiving of the appropriate formats for long-term use and then the derivation of current-use copies appropriate to the technological base of today's users. It must also work with users to help them undertake these tasks.

— Maintaining appropriate metadata—All preservation activities will depend on the completeness and quality of the metadata for the objects to be preserved. It will be critical for the Library to monitor developments in metadata standards and follow best practices for metadata as they develop.

— Migrating formats—Even the most careful selection of archiving formats cannot ensure that objects will be useful in the decades to come. It will be necessary to migrate objects periodically from one archival format to another. Such processes must be carefully designed and executed to ensure minimal loss of content (it is impossible to ensure that all such migrations will be loss-free). Some works, such as those that include active software (e.g., Java applets), may raise particularly difficult issues.

— Conducting research and development—Only a handful of institutions are likely to face digital preservation challenges on the scale or scope of those that LC faces in the coming years. This makes it unlikely that LC will be able to import models and solutions for all of its preservation needs. An active program of research and development in digital preservation is needed to solve immediate preservation problems--technical, legal, and economic—at LC and to provide guidance to other libraries and archives.

— Educating the relevant communities—Especially in this transitional period, when digital materials are new and preservation practices are still in flux, institutions and particular communities will need to be educated about digital preservation: What is the state of the art? What factors must be taken into account in planning for preservation? LC is well situated to participate in such efforts and possibly to take the lead.

A robust preservation program will employ curators and preservation staff with knowledge of the formats of materials in their collections and of appropriate metadata standards and practices and an understanding of the issues involved in migrating objects from one format to another. It will require well-developed production services for creating the specified metadata, sound and robust repository services, and periodic quality checking and copying of objects in the collection.

In the future, libraries will also need to make much more extensive use of digitization for preservation. Some professionals consider digital objects—whether born digital or turned digital—unacceptable as preservation masters because their longevity is uncertain. In some cases, however, digital conversion may offer the only viable means of salvaging and preserving certain materials, such as audio recordings in obsolete analog formats. The Library has used digitization to preserve severely damaged black-and-white negatives and some audio and video records on magnetic media.

Challenges of Digital Preservation

The main problem with digital preservation is that digital technology, in comparison to print, is an extremely fragile medium for the cultural memory of the world. The most commonly given example of this fragility is the 1960 United States Census, where raw data stored on magnetic tapes apparently became obsolete and, to all intents and purposes, unreadable by the late nineteen-seventies. Digital information has two main weaknesses:

1. *The storage medium* - digital storage media, whether magnetic or optical, are subject to relatively rapid decay: especially when compared with print.
2. *The hardware and software* - digital information is machine-dependent, and to be 'read' accurately it needs specific computer hardware and software. Unfortunately, hardware and software quickly become obsolescent or otherwise unusable.

Proposed solutions to these problems usually involve periodic 'refreshing' or recopying of the digital information onto new media and the occasional 'migration' of data into new formats. Assuming that some answer can be found to these problems, there remains the important issue of intellectual preservation.

The archives community has been addressing these issues for some time now. This has partly been led by the need for electronic records to be accepted in legal evidence but the fact that electronic records are increasingly created in a variety of important situations: government; health-care; business-transactions, etc., has resulted in a renewed interest in authentication and validation issues.

When the library and information community discuss metadata, the most common analogy given is the library catalogue record. Priscilla Caplan, for example, has defined metadata as a neutral term for cataloguing without the "excess baggage" of the Anglo-American Cataloguing Rules or the MARC formats. The most well-known metadata initiative, the Dubin Core Metadata Element Set, has the specific aim of supporting resource discovery in a network environment. The Internet has many virtues, but it was not designed specifically for information retrieval. The search technologies that evolved - Archie for anonymous ftp sites, Veronica for gopher and search engines for the Web - were developed as a response to perceived needs rather than as an integral part of the original concept. Search engines like Digital Equipment Corporation's Alta Vista construct indexes by means of robots which 'crawl' through the Web collecting indexing information.

This is a less than perfect solution as Web sites typically do not contain all the relevant information for automated indexing and if they do it is unlikely to be in a form identifiable to most robots. It is possible that if Dublin Core metadata is attached to or embedded in a large number of Web documents, a new generation of Web robots or harvesters could collect this metadata and make it available through improved search services. Search engines, however, are not the only solution to the Internet resource discovery problem. An alternative approach has been to get people to select resources according to agreed criteria and then make them available via a Web site, where they can be browsed or searched. Metadata formats come in a variety of shapes and sizes. Dublin Core is intended to be a simple structured record which can, if required, be enhanced or mapped to more complex records.

Dublin Core may have a role as a minimal metadata set in order to allow for interoperability between other, more complex, metadata formats. Library and information professionals with an interest in the Internet should be interested in the development of metadata for resource discovery. Clifford Lynch points out that if the Internet is to continue to thrive as a new means of communication, "something very much like traditional library services will be needed to organize, access and preserve networked information". Metadata does have an acknowledged role in the organisation of and access to networked information, but it could additionally be important in the general area of digital preservation. Society has vital interest in preserving materials that document issues, concerns, ideas, discourse and events. Custodians of the cultural record have always had to manage the inherent conflict between letting people use manuscripts, books, recordings or videos, and being sure that they are preserved for future use. For works printed on acidic wood pulp paper, as most books have been since 1850, they measure the remaining lifetime of those materials in decades, not centuries.

In 1993, forty-five percent of U.S. workers were using a computer; the number is surely larger now. Virtually all printing and a rapidly increasing amount of writing is accomplished with computers. Professional sound recording is digital, and digital video is on the verge of moving from experimental to practical applications.

As a means of recording and providing access to their cultural memory, digital technology has numerous advantages and may help relieve the traditional conflict between preservation and access. For materials stored digitally, users operate on exact images of the original works stored in their local computers. Separating usage from the original in this way, digital technology affords multiple, simultaneous uses from a single original in ways that are simply not possible for materials stored in any other form. Digital technology also yields additional, effective means of access. In full text documents, a reader can retrieve needed information by searching for words, combinations of words, phrases or ideas. Readers can also manipulate the display of digital materials by choosing whether to view digital materials on a screen, store them on their computer or external media, or to print them. Digital technology, however, poses new threats and problems as well as new opportunities. Its functionality comes with complexity. Anyone with a compass could theoretically set up or repair a sundial.

A digital watch is more useful and accurate for telling time than a sundial, but few people can repair it or even understand how it works. Reading and understanding information in digital form requires equipment and software, which is changing constantly and may not be available within a decade of its introduction. Who today has a punched card reader, a Dectape drive, or a working copy of FORTRAN II? Even newer technology such as 9-track tape is rapidly becoming obsolete. They cannot save the machines if there are no spare parts available, and they cannot save the software if no one is left who knows how to use it.

Rapid changes in the means of recording information, in the formats for storage, and in the technologies for use threaten to render the life of information in the digital age as, to borrow a phrase from Hobbes, "nasty, brutish and short." Some information no doubt deserves such a fate, but numerous examples illustrate the danger of losing valuable cultural memories that may appear in digital form. Even if the software had been retained, the hardware and operating system needed to run the software were no longer available.

Preservation of Audiovisual Heritage

The audiovisual heritage is an important element within the cultural heritage and has achieved prominence in the twentieth century, the first to have been recorded on audiovisual formats. Audiovisuals are not new but have become of increasing importance as art, entertainment and information carriers. In some cases the transmission of sound and visual data has greater value and impact than the printed document—where, for example, there is a literacy or language barrier.

Audiovisuals may also be the only suitable records for the oral or sonic transmission of culture and the arts, news and other current items. The spread and development of modern technologies mean an increase in the role of audiovisual data carriers for communication, information and culture. Today's radio and television rely heavily on archive material and it is estimated that more than 60% of radio and television programmes use archival or stock material for programming. The definitions are still being formulated, but audiovisual materials are to be understood as visual recordings and sound recordings irrespective of their physical base or recording process. The carrier usually requires a playback device. This definition is meant to cover the maximum number of forms and formats.

Audiovisual materials should not be confused with multimedia; the former provide source material for the latter, and multimedia as such are not archival material. Two features of audiovisual materials add an extra dimension to the principles of collection and preservation: a proliferation both of formats and of systems of production and playback. These cause incompatibility problems between formats and systems.

Archives have to maintain original playback devices and employ technical staff who know how to use and maintain the machinery. Audiovisual archives are storehouses for a large proportion of the social and cultural heritage of the twentieth century. An audiovisual archive is defined as an organization or department of an organization which is focused on collecting, managing, preserving and providing access to a collection of audiovisual media and the audiovisual heritage, applying archival principles.

Such archives contain huge treasures of unique material. Archives of audiovisual materials are relatively new, but they have proliferated in the past few decades. Television was originally recorded on film, but video has been the principal material since the later 1960s. Although audiovisual materials have appeared so recently, time is not on their side and the longer we delay in gathering, conserving and preserving the materials, the less we shall be able to retain. It is vital that steps are taken now to collect and manage audiovisual materials properly before their fragile nature takes a further toll.

Already much has been lost owing to ignorance, lack of awareness of the dangers and careless handling. Audiovisual archives vary in type, purpose and function, and until recently most of them were singlematerial archives: moving image, sound and still-image archives, the latter frequently housed in more conventional archives of print materials. As the technologies converge so do the archives, to unite effort and conserve resources. Some archives take responsibility for all recorded materials, others take smaller bites and combine one or two of the materials.

The larger archives cannot always combine materials in one department; the physical techniques required to deal with each material from the point of view of storage, handling and restoration need different expertise and materials are therefore separated by this parameter alone. Other functions of collection management can be applied to all the materials: documentation and information retrieval, and selection. Storage vaults may have to accommodate more than one material and the resulting environmental considerations will be different from those more stringently applied to individual materials.

Alternatively, an archive may decide that it must apply the optimum storage and environmental values which apply to each material: single-material archives are more fortunate in these cases. Academic archives also house audiovisual materials, many in universities for research, and latterly educational materials for distance learning. These may be small and specialized, or have substantial collections and preservation programmes.

Specialized or thematic archives concentrate on a particular format, subject-matter or locality, or relate to specific cultural groups. Many of these archives have developed within larger organizations. Film companies, broadcasting companies and record companies maintain archives primarily for use and exploitation by the parent company. Many of these preserve and restore their materials for re-use, but the archives' main obligation is to the parent organization rather than to preserving the cultural heritage. This may be left to a national archive, which obtains a selection of the production company's material by deposit.

Other institutions with archival responsibility include museums, cinematheques, videotheques and national libraries. Most of these are more concerned with maintaining stock for exhibition purposes, and originals may be deposited for long-term preservation in a national archive. There are also collections of last resort which attempt to conserve copies of material in usable condition, but seldom retain archival originals or masters. Audiovisual materials result from a huge level of investment.

Archives in organizations such as broadcast associations or film production companies have commercial backing and motivation, and meet costs from their revenue. Once that commercial motive is fulfilled, however, it is generally acknowledged that, as with other records of the national cultural creativity, the cost of maintaining the collection reverts to government and granting bodies.

Many valuable collections have disappeared for ever as a result of production company closures or changes in franchise when materials are not taken over by already overstretched archives. The basic tasks of an audiovisual archive are collection, preservation, documentation and access provision. Methods of collection and acquisition vary, and include the legal or voluntary deposit of collections or individual items, the deposit of in-house productions, donations, special agreements for copying nationally produced materials, and purchase.

Other archives collect their own materials in the form of oral or video history programmes, with the purpose of recording cultures, languages and music before they disappear. Closely allied to acquisition are evaluation, selection and appraisal. The audiovisual archive acquires materials according to a particular remit, balancing new acquisitions against existing stock and the purpose and function of the archive. Storage space and resources being what they are, archives have to select material for preservation on the basis of relevance, uniqueness and quality. Wherever possible an archive should be dealing with original materials, but originals are hard to come by.

There is strictly only one original film, video or master sound recording. Such originals seldom survive and there are various forms of tampering with the products—cut/uncut versions, director's/producer's cut, censored and unexpurgated versions. Owners of original material may be reluctant to deposit their master material in an archive until they have no further use for it, by which time the technical quality has deteriorated.

Three elements in audiovisual documents have to be considered in the selection process: the artefact or carrier, the information content and the aesthetic content, particularly with film and sound recordings. The artefact or carrier will designate the form of the audiovisual and influence selection for technical reasons.

Audiovisual archives, therefore, do not have a huge selection of material, but most of it has unique value, and such archives retain more material than many other archives. Some audiovisual collections will include several interpretations of the same work—for example, music recordings—or several records of the same event carried in different documents: a film, video or sound version. Guidelines for archival selection exist, but they are usually those of organizations with their own parameters. Selection of material is dependent upon the function of the archive, the quality of the material and the uniqueness or rarity of the content.

Audiovisual archives should concentrate on recordings of national origin. To avoid duplication of effort, material should be offered back to the country of original production or to archives with a more relevant collection remit. The main function of any archive is to preserve the heritage and the artefacts which make up that heritage.

Service providers perform specific functions on behalf of the archival system. In an "integrated responsibility" model, service providers are essentially subcontractors for the main archive. In the "distributed responsibility" model, service providers are trusted sources, as defined above. Service providers help scale up an archival system by spreading out responsibility for archival tasks. They can be useful when an archival function requires specialized expertise or resources. For instance, if a company provides low-cost, highly replicated reliable data storage, an archive might out-source backups to that company rather than maintain backups itself.

Or, if content is submitted or stored in a variety of protocols and formats, ingestion and migration of this content might be usefully parceled out to service providers, each specializing in a particular format or data provider, instead of trying to have one organization handle everything. Service providers often do not need to make the same sort of long-term commitments as archives themselves do, unless their service includes long term information storage.

However, they still need to be visible in the design and operations of an archiving system. Archive users may want to make sure they are certified for carrying out their service correctly. Publisher agreements may need to allow them to access copyrighted material, and publishers may want to be assured that they do not distribute or alter this material without authorization. The business model for the archive or archival system also needs to include some sort of compensation for the services of the providers.

Open Archives Metadata Harvesting Protocol

Size of the content varied greatly among journals. For example, PDFs for American Law and Economics Review, a semi-annual journal, took up little more than 2 MB of storage space per year, whereas PDFs for Brain, a monthly medical journal, took up closer to 100 MB of storage space per year. Articles in PDF form were generally easy to harvest, usually as one PDF file per article, although in some instances the PDFs were page-oriented instead and included content from multiple or adjacent items in the same file. Correctly harvesting HTML presentation forms was considerably more problematic.

Many of the HTML-formatted articles were clearly generated from source files and included numerous automatically generated links, some of which led to content that was important to the article, such as high-resolution versions of illustrations, while others led to related material that was not part of the article itself. Many of these HTML articles were produced by the same organization, Highwire Press.

Ingesting material into an archive, whether manually or automatically, is far from foolproof. When publishers manually send a journal issue to an archive they may accidentally leave out articles, send misformatted files, or even send the wrong files altogether. Occasionally, articles published on Web sites included mistakes. An early spot-check of one mathematics journal article revealed a PDF file in which the last pages could not be read as the file was initially posted. Human checks may turn up some of these errors but can be expensive to perform. The Open Archives Metadata Harvesting Protocol, an important new infrastructure component for supporting distributed networked information services. The Metadata Harvesting Protocol-a mechanism that enables data providers to expose their metadata-is seeing very rapid deployment, and enables a fascinating array of new services and system architectures for a diverse set of communities. There has been considerable confusion about the Open Archives Metadata Harvesting Protocol, mostly beginning with and stemming from its name.

The protocol no longer has much to do with archiving or archives, other than in terms of its heritage. The Open Archives Metadata Harvesting Protocol grew out of an effort to solve some of the problems that were emerging as e-print servers became more widely deployed; it originated in the community concerned with advancing the development of e-print archives. However, as work on the protocol advanced it became clear that it provided a very general-purpose mechanism that could address a surprisingly wide range of urgent needs and, in order to be useful in the widest variety of contexts, this mechanism had to be defined so that it was agnostic to assumptions about types of content, economic models, intellectual property constraints, or systems of information flow.

For better or worse, by that time the protocol was widely known as the Open Archives Protocol, and the program to develop it was widely known as the Open Archives Initiative, so the decision was made to maintain the popularly known terminology. The protocol is now often referred to as the Open Archives Metadata Harvesting Protocol in an attempt to reintroduce a bit more clarity. This Metadata Harvesting Protocol (MHP), is simply an interface that a networked server (not necessarily an e-print server) can employ to make metadata describing objects housed at that server available to external applications that wish to collect this metadata.

A server does not need to be part of an e-print program to use the protocol; indeed, it does not need to house journal papers at all. The server does not need to offer free access to the digital objects that it stores. The Metadata Harvesting Protocol can be implemented by servers housing commercial products available by subscription (like scientific journals) or available for transactional purchase, by libraries or museums offering access to digitized images, or by scientific data archives, to list only a few potential applications.

Many of the people who have been involved in the work on the MHP are also strong proponents of the broader program to open free public access to the scholarly journal literature, but they are usually careful to differentiate between the two; the MHP can certainly advance the deployment of e-print archives, but it is not limited to supporting that program. It is a much more general and more neutral technical-enabling mechanism. The term "Open Archives Initiative" is ambiguous; it refers both to a specific, organized, funded effort to advance the Metadata Harvesting Protocol, and to a separate, diffuse movement to promote the deployment and use of e-print archives involving a lot of the same people. The Open Archives Metadata Harvesting Initiative had its roots in work done by Herbert Van de Sompel working in collaboration with groups that included researchers and librarians at Los Alamos National Labs in the United States. In late 1999, a meeting was convened in Santa Fe, New Mexico to address a series of problems that he had been exploring in the e-print server world.

Fundamentally, the problem was that as disciplinary e-print servers proliferated, often with overlapping disciplinary coverage and geographical affinity, there was a need to develop services that permitted searching across papers housed at multiple repositories. Repositories also needed capabilities to automatically identify and copy papers that had been deposited in other repositories. Further complicating matters, institutional e-print archives were beginning to emerge that would house the intellectual output of specific campus communities; it was undesirable to require scholars to deposit their work in multiple repositories, and hence it would be necessary for disciplinary archives to be able to identify and replicate material from these institutional archives and for federated search services to be able to search across both institutional and disciplinary archives.

The Metadata Harvesting Protocol uses a very simple HTTP-based request-response transaction framework for communication between a harvester and a repository. A harvester can ask for metadata to be returned with optional restrictions based on when the metadata has been added or modified; it can also restrict metadata by server-defined "partitions".

The server returns a series of sets of metadata elements (in XML) plus identifiers (i.e., URLs) for the objects that the metadata describes. Supporting this core harvesting transaction are a few ancillary transactions: for example, to permit a harvester to obtain a list of the names of partitions that a server has defined and which can thus be used as restriction criteria in harvesting requests. Multiple metadata schemes are supported in the Open Archives Metadata Harvesting Protocol-this is really the key architectural change from the Santa Fe Convention. The protocol requires that all servers offer unqualified Dublin Core metadata (encoded in XML) as a lowest common denominator; however, each server is also free to offer metadata in one or more other schemes, and a harvester can request that metadata be provided in a scheme other than Dublin Core as part of the harvest request. There is also another auxiliary transaction that permits a harvester to obtain a list of the names of the metadata schemes that a given repository supports.

The underlying idea here is that we will see communities of practice evolve that define metadata schemes that are richer and more precise than unqualified Dublin Core; for example, the e-print archives community is already working on one that encodes various important data elements for e-prints, such as author affiliations, bibliographic information if the paper has been published in a journal, and even the paper's cited references in a structured form. These community-specific schemes could be handled as qualified Dublin Core, or as de novo schemes; the only requirement is that they be transportable in XML. This is a very powerful method of enabling communities with common metadata to work together while still ensuring some minimal level of interoperability for very broad federated search or other services based on unqualified Dublin Core.

It seems very likely that the MHP will drive development of community-specific metadata schemes. It will also be helpful in clarifying our understanding of the value of unqualified Dublin Core for lowest common denominator cross-domain resource discovery. Authentication and access management are not covered. A given repository can use a range of access-management mechanisms that are external to the protocol to decide which harvesters it will provide with metadata if it wishes to impose access control.

Independent of access control decisions about providing metadata, the server only includes a pointer-such as a URL or URN-to each object described by metadata that it makes available for harvest; access controls on this base object may or may not exist. In addition, any authentication that the harvester wants to conduct on the repository is handled by external mechanisms. The protocol does not address the very real issue of how harvesters will identify repositories that they wish to harvest, nor does it provide information to help determine when harvesting should occur, or how frequently. There will clearly be a need for some kind of registry of names for well-known community-specific metadata schemes.

The MHP does not address this, though it clearly must be part of the broader infrastructure associated with the protocol. The most obvious applications that are enabled by the Metadata Harvesting Protocol are those that helped to motivate the work at the initial Santa Fe meeting: repository synchronization and federated search.

For repository synchronization, one compares metadata from two or more repositories and decides what objects should be copied from one repository to another. The hard part here is in the application: deciding what repositories to examine, and determining the criteria for identifying what to copy. There is also a problem with the propagation of metadata from one repository to another; it's not clear how to determine the most comprehensive metadata set describing an object so that all of the relevant metadata can be copied over. Similarly, federated search using MHP is not hard in principle; one collects metadata from a number of sites, normalizes it, clusters it in some fashion to deal with duplicates as appropriate, and offers search services against the resulting database. In practice, all of the details are complex: what sites to harvest, how often to harvest them, how to normalize metadata (especially if one wants to do better than the lowest common denominator-unqualified Dublin Core-offered by each site), how to handle duplicate objects-these are all key design issues that need to be addressed.

MHP provides a very powerful framework for building union-catalog-type databases (in the broad sense; not just union bibliographic catalogues, but all sorts of union descriptive databases) for collections of resources by automating and standardizing the collection of contributions from the participating sites, which has traditionally been an operational headache in building and managing union catalogues. But there are many complex specifics that need to be coded into any actual implementation. A set of applications closely related to federated search deal with the potential enhancement of web search engines in at least two distinct dimensions. One is providing a more efficient way for web search engines to crawl static HTML pages, and also to obtain metadata associated with these pages (there are other methods of getting the metadata, such as in-line META tags, but the MHP provides a much more flexible way of doing this).

The second is being able to integrate various parts of what is sometimes called the "deep web" or the "invisible web" with the indexing of static web pages, including repositories of digital objects and databases that do not exist as retrievable and indexable static web pages, and also proprietary content, where the content owner may be willing to make metadata about the content available to facilitate finding it, but may be unwilling to permit arbitrary web-indexing programs to have direct access to the content in order to index it.

The Metadata Harvesting Protocol allows a server to enumerate the objects it houses and to provide metadata associated with these objects, no matter what the nature of these objects and the access constraints that might apply to them. Any application dealing with metadata created and stored on distributed sites faces issues about whether it can trust the metadata it is relying upon. This means, for example, that it is unlikely that the public web search engines will use an OAI interface to harvest arbitrary sites anytime soon; however, federated searching or customized indexing of sites that are selected in some fashion-by being part of an organizational intranet, or through some type of editorial policy that selects quality sites as part of a subject portal, for example-will likely make wide use of the protocol. These are the most obvious applications (and the ones that will probably be available soonest), in that they directly extend or enhance existing practices. Interesting and novel applications are likely to emerge as well. For example, one can easily imagine the rise of intermediary services (reminiscent of the brokerage services in the original Harvest system) that collect raw metadata from sets of sites, consolidate and enhance it, and then redistribute it as a single feed or as custom-selected subsets to still other sites for reuse.

Creative applications designers are at the very early stages of exploring the services that the MHP can enable, and we can expect some fascinating and unexpected developments in the next few years. While the Open Archives Metadata Harvesting Protocol solves one very important set of problems, it also focuses attention on a number of other issues that will have to be addressed as applications proliferate. Some of them will require progress in standards and/or other networked information infrastructure components; others are simply not well understood at this point and will require considerable research and experimentation to allow the development of a body of design knowledge and community practice. Many sites make metadata about their holdings publicly available today in the sense that they offer publicly accessible search services operating against that metadata, which can then result in the display of individual records. This is the case with most library catalogues; for example, they offer searching to anyone who wants to search the database, and some systems will even provide formatted displays of individual, full MARC records that are retrieved by such searches as an option. There is a great difference between this practice and simply making the entire catalog's contents, or major subsets, available for bulk downloading and re-incorporation into other databases and services. In a world of MHP-enabled network resources, metadata becomes migratory and recombinant.

Owners and operators of large databases and repositories will need to think through how comfortable they are in making their metadata generally available on this basis, and what limits, if any, they want to place on permissible reuse. In addition, this may focus new attention on metadata ownership; while nobody may much care about who reuses the odd individual bibliographic database record, copying an entire bibliographic database may be viewed quite differently. There is no real way to encode acceptable-use policies or restrictions on metadata harvesting within the MHP; while it would not be difficult to make reference to textual statements about such policies, encoding them in a machine-understandable way is a difficult problem that calls for collaboration between computer scientists, lawyers, and standards developers, among others.

Many applications will use manually-curated lists of sites to harvest, and, indeed, the editorial processes and selectivity that go into the development and maintenance of these lists will be part of the value of the application itself. As these services multiply, operators of new repositories will face the problem of bringing their site to the attention of the appropriate service operators so that their metadata can be harvested. If we look at the operation of the public web search engines, which seek to be comprehensive, we find much more complex methods of identifying sites to crawl (the details of which vary from search engine to search engine, and are viewed as representing proprietary advantage to these search engines).

They start with a base of websites that they have identified, or that site operators have submitted to the indexing services, but then they also dynamically discover new sites to index by analyzing links on sites that they visit. They also use a variety of techniques (both manual and automated) to determine how often to revisit sites looking for new material to index. Some applications performing metadata harvesting will want to do a similar dynamic discovery of sites that are available to be harvested. This could be done in a number of ways. Certainly, for systems that harvest static HTML pages, it would be possible to program their crawlers to also attempt to do an OAI query against each site to see if it offered metadata for harvesting.

It would be possible to establish a central registry of sites that offered metadata via the OAI secretariat; setting up a database that allowed sites to register themselves and interested parties to search the registry to identify harvestable sites is technically straightforward and not terribly resource intensive.

A prototype of this exists today on the Open Archives website; this is simply a list of MHP-compliant sites that have submitted their addresses to the OAI secretariat. The secretariat does some essentially mechanical validation of the sites by running a program periodically that issues OAI queries; it checks that the site is still there and provides syntactically well-formed responses to these queries.

This mechanical validation is very valuable in these early days of experimental implementations. But it is important to recognize the very limited value of such a registry. It does not address how one might classify sites (for example, by the nature of their content or their subject coverage) in order for applications to decide which sites should be harvested. Developing computer-based methods of doing this, at any level of generality, is a complex proposition. Many applications will likely be structured around the principle of offering in-depth access to high-quality information resources, which means that they will have to be concerned with the assessments of the quality of the metadata offered by the sites they choose to harvest.

It's difficult to see how this can be handled at this point other than by evaluation and/or trust decisions by the individual applications. Scaling these decisions past manual editorial management of lists of sites to harvest takes us quickly to research areas such as reputation management systems, further complicated by the fact that both the harvesting services and their end users may want to be able to make choices about trust and reputation in their use of metadata. In developing MHP interfaces to databases or repositories, a key design decision has to do with the granularity of the objects for which the site exposes metadata. For the original e-print-archive applications this was straightforward; the objects of interest were individual article e-prints and thus they made available metadata for each article e-print.

But as metadata harvesting is deployed in a wider range of contexts, the answers are less clear. For many repositories we have little or no metadata at the individual object level, and instead have various forms of collection-level description (such as the Electronic Archival Description, or

EAD, files); in other cases we may have both collection- and item-level records, each of which has value in its own right, but it is not clear how to link the two and it also isn't always clear that it is useful to make huge numbers of item-level records available. OAI-enabled service would use the MHP to pull metadata for all of the individual records in a database, and would then perform computations that allow it to provide some kind of summary metadata record for the entire database as output; these summary records could then be returned to the database owner or operator or could be made available to other resource discovery services.

The Metadata Harvesting Protocol is a means of making machine-processable metadata widely available for use. It will create tremendous pressure for standards programs that are now developing schemes to codify and represent such metadata, especially the Dublin Core Metadata Initiative. MHP specifies unqualified Dublin Core as the lowest-common-denominator mandatory metadata scheme for interoperability purposes.

It is certainly clear that almost any metadata scheme can be "downgraded" into unqualified Dublin Core, but the actual usefulness of such a coarse metadata scheme has been the subject of considerable debate and speculation. The Dublin Core Initiative is also codifying the notion of qualified Dublin Core-a series of extensions to the base Dublin Core elements that can provide much greater precision but that can be "interpreted down" to unqualified Dublin Core in a consistent fashion by applications that are not knowledgeable about specific extensions. At a broader level, the idea of community-based metadata schemes is central to the vision of the Metadata Harvesting Protocol. There has been a great deal of work in this area over the past few years, in part driven by the promise of XML and the growing interest in the interchange of computer-processable information using the Internet.

Fundamentally, the development of these standards is a social process within a community, though it calls upon a poorly-codified body of knowledge in data structuring, descriptive practices, classification, and other areas. It is still very slow, and very expensive, to develop these community standards, and it is hard to predict which ones will be successful in terms of broad adoption or in terms of effectively meeting community needs over reasonably long periods of time. The Research Libraries Group (RLG) manages one of the largest union library catalogues in the world.

REFERENCES

Godden, Irene P. ed. *Library technical services : operation and management*. 2nd ed. Sydney : Academic Press, 1991.

Kessler, Jack, *Internet digital libraries: the international dimension*, Boston and London: Artech House.

Liu, Ying, and Anita S. Coleman. "Communicating Digital Library Services to Scientific Communities." *LIBRES* 14, no. 1, 2004.

Michelle Q. Wang Baldonado and Steve B. Cousins. Addressing heterogeneity in the networked information environment. *New Review of Information Networking*, 2:83-102, 1996

Racine, Drew. ed. *Managing technical services in the 90's*. Sydney : The Howarth Press, 1991.

6

Online Collections and Access

Libraries are expanding the amount and variety of high-quality information resources that are directly available to academic and research users via the Web. They are also expanding the definition of collections to include "born-digital" content that is neither owned nor licensed by the library. The varied efforts toward this goal may be characterized as follows: changing collection development policies to emphasize the acquisition of electronic resources, engaging in digitizing and electronic publishing projects, and assuming responsibility for managing and servicing born-digital content that resides outside the domain of the library. Even in the electronic and networked environment, the economic model continues to feature the library as the central agency on campus that buys and/or manages information resources on behalf of the institution. Libraries have shifted the focus of their collection development policies to the acquisition of more electronic content, much of it via consortia. While aggregate data documenting the quantity of e-resources currently being made available by libraries has proven elusive, there is data on the spending trends.

Many libraries have adopted a policy of adding the e-version of journals when available and are showcasing titles of e-journals available to users via the Web by making this a staff priority and by applying software management tools for titles included in aggregated electronic databases. The processes for selecting, budgeting, and acquiring electronic materials are continually changing and greatly differ from those for the selection and management of print. The print process is orderly: discrete amounts of money are allocated by discipline, the marketplace is fairly predictable, and materials are selected and ordered using established procedures. By contrast, the processes for selection and management of electronic resources are chaotic. The migration from print to electronic varies in speed and extent by discipline; electronic products are interdisciplinary and expensive, giving rise to selection by committee; projections for future funding are guesswork; and archiving and content control are problematic. Legal and negotiation skills are now mandatory. To complicate matters, decisions are often made through a consortium. The process for acquiring electronic resources turns the traditional acquisitions and user service model topsy-turvy.

In building electronic collections, libraries must also constantly respond to changing publisher behavior. The most profound influence on a library's collection management and access strategies has been the extraordinary price increases for scholarly journals, combined with publishers' use of licensing to define the terms under which a library may make the content available and to whom. It is reasonable to speculate that these phenomena, driven by some of the larger publishers but now employed widely, make up one of the forces that prompted libraries to blend the previously distinct operations of collection management and access. Some libraries have fully embraced initiatives stimulated or endorsed by SPARC (the Scholarly Publishing and Academic Resources Coalition) and other affordable publishing venues and are using acquisitions funds as investments in the future of scholarly communication. These libraries focus acquisitions on publications from scholarly societies and less expensive publishers, nonprofit and for-profit, that provide high-quality titles at affordable prices. These less expensive titles tend to be the most highly ranked by faculty but labor intensive to obtain, since each publisher has only a few titles and often lacks sales and technical staff. These libraries try to consistently view collection expenditures as investments, and to seek out publishers likely to contribute to a sustainable future for scholarly information.

Libraries are also supporting open access projects that experiment with alternatives to the current subscription-based funding model or the current journals-based publishing model for scholarly communication. These approaches are seen as those of a good citizen, especially in an institution whose needs for funding include many urgent priorities in addition to library needs. These libraries are investing in initiatives that may help solve the long-term problem of high prices for journals.

ADVANTAGES OF ONLINE CATALOGUES

It is clear that the role of the online catalogue has changed. That catalogue has become one of many databases available to users; libraries are linking to and from the catalogue to integrate all of these resources. In recognition of this broader role for the library catalogue, some libraries are considering modifying cataloguing to favor timely access to a wider variety of formats. One proposal called for reallocating funds that are devoted to describing books and journals to materials that are proportionately underrepresented in today's catalogues, such as films, music, photographs, and digital objects.

Libraries are also reconsidering their current efforts to collect and catalogue free Web resources, concluding that these labor-intensive activities can be avoided by perfecting nascent machine harvesting and cataloguing techniques. A small number of libraries and library organizations are participating in experiments funded by The Mellon Foundation to test the application of harvesting and search engine technologies. Using the recently developed OAI metadata harvesting protocol, these libraries are delivering information from the "hidden Web" not normally found by Internet search engines and from databases with retrieval formats that present special processing or presentation problems.

For example, several libraries are working with vendors to adapt existing portal software into multifunctional products with features and services desired by users in research communities. Other examples of library involvement in development of software applications are ILL management systems, instructional tutorials, management of content and services for digital libraries, and institutional repositories. Although where information resides matters less to the user, the library as place—the physical entity—remains more important than ever and performs a host of functions vital to learning and research. Much research library space is busier than ever before. Library facilities are being reconfigured to provide space for collaborative learning and research. There are classrooms and media labs where faculty and librarians may interact in providing student learning experiences, group study spaces, and community spaces where students can meet to discuss ideas. The transformation of library space has also become an opportunity to attract new academic collaborations such as writing studios and academic skills tutoring. Library space is now seen as learning space on an equal footing with classrooms and laboratories.

Libraries are being renovated to expand e-access and foster community by providing electronic classrooms, wireless data networks, offering laptops, and expanding library hours. Libraries are establishing spaces called "information commons" where library reference services are offered jointly with information technology support. At the same time, libraries are responding to decreasing use of in-person reference service by combining service points and shifting resources to online reference service and online tutorials. To make the best use of prime real estate, libraries are adopting new approaches to managing large print collections by using storage centers with delivery services for less frequently used materials and engaging in cooperative approaches to long-term preservation copy retention.

The branch or departmental library remains valuable but its role too is changing. While access to information and library services is far less geographically based, branch and departmental libraries still play a role in development of community and serve as sites for collaboration. Yet, in the Internet world there are opportunities to rethink the role of multiple libraries and their configuration within an institution. One library reported establishing a program to replicate the opportunities for personalized services and contacts that characterize branch library service without the cost of creating additional branches.

Some of the same opportunities for reorganization may present themselves when libraries work in collaboration with other libraries outside their institutional boundaries. Libraries are active participants in building awareness among researchers, faculty, and students of uses of high-quality content and information technology in teaching and research. Curriculum review and changing expectations for teaching faculty present opportunities for libraries to contribute expertise and resources.

Libraries provide classrooms; training and consulting in finding and evaluating information; and assistance with creating electronic theses and dissertations, displaying and visualizing data, publishing journals on the Web, and using geographic information systems (GIS) and remote sensing. Recognizing that disciplines are adopting new technology at different rates, librarians are:

- Working with faculty to integrate information literacy skills and digital content into the course curricula
- Expanding the number of people reached by offering basic information literacy and fluency training through online tutorials

— Assisting researchers in acquiring, accessing, displaying, and visualizing spatial and numeric data by providing training in use of software and partnering with faculty to provide classroom instruction in its use

— Developing systems and instructional tools for pedagogical use of digital resources, including images

— Managing campus instructional technology initiatives

— Making Organizational Changes within the Library to Innovate and Improve Services

Libraries are embracing change—being willing to change what libraries do and how it is done—and, as a result, are reorganizing their operations and re-deploying staff to respond to the new environment. Examples of recent organizational change in ARL libraries include:

— Many libraries report having instituted an integrated approach to collection management, bringing together the activities of building, maintaining, and providing access to library resources in all formats, both in-house and remote, both acquired and locally created.

— Many libraries also report taking interdisciplinary approaches, training library staff to perform across traditional roles and to build bridges between the culture of the library and that of the faculty and information technology. An example is the creation of information commons jointly staffed by the library and information technology, often developing services in collaboration with faculty.

— Others report organizational redesigns to achieve a system-wide view of services to coordinate communications with all library users and to deploy staff more flexibly.

— Libraries are experimenting rigorously with organizational transformation reflecting strategies for team-based decision making, learning organizations, and quality management.

Communication Issues

Libraries are assuming leadership within their institutions to advocate for enduring institution-wide knowledge management policies and programs that contribute to a robust system of scholarly communication. Some libraries are accomplishing this goal by:

— Sponsoring scholarly communication seminars to broaden faculty and graduate student awareness of trends that threaten the long-term sustainability of the current system of scholarly communication

— Advocating for institution-wide intellectual property policies that balance the rights of copyright owners and those of users and libraries in educational settings, including the development of principles that guide the licensing of electronic resources for the institution

— Promoting individual behavior and building institutional support that contributes to the long-term health and viability of scholarly communication channels, including developing infrastructure for such alternative publishing practices as publishing open access journals or creating institutional repositories

All research libraries are innovating and adapting to the changing needs of their patrons, as well as to the changing requirements of their institutions. There is no clear evidence to suggest definitive trends in change based on the size of the library collection.

There are specific types of innovation, however, that seem to be related to library or institution size. There is anecdotal evidence that library size has been influential in the development of digital library programs; libraries with more mature digital library programs tend to be libraries with larger collections and more staff members. On the other hand, smaller institutional settings may encourage innovative collaborative activities, either because of the financial necessity to join forces to make something happen or because of the potential in smaller communities for more interaction across campus units. There is also anecdotal evidence that the institutional climate for change and the active support of groups and key individuals within the institution play a central role in the library's orientation and opportunities to innovate; to the extent that the size of the institution impacts this climate, size may be a contributing—if not driving—factor.

Research libraries' ability and desire to collaborate with other research libraries, with non-university libraries, or with other organizations and industries will determine the success of many library programs. Motivations for collaborations vary greatly and include leadership, political support, the lure of available funding, and the desire to transform the library, to move it into the digital age. An increasingly important collaboration is consortial buying of print and electronic content and services. Consortial buying and licensing for access to electronic resources have become central in every research library's arsenal of strategies for acquiring information more economically than could be accomplished by acting alone. Many libraries find user-initiated consortial borrowing combined with rapid delivery a successful avenue for making their users' access to books as easy as access to electronic resources. There is evidence that fast delivery of books within a consortium has increased book use, especially by undergraduates. Consortia also offer accompanying services that greatly expedite the discovery and delivery of non-book content for users affiliated with libraries participating in the consortium; some consortia are centrally managing image data banks, electronic theses and dissertations, and other digital materials.

Consortial structures vary and reflect the political framework of the state or region in which they operate and the institutions they represent. In some cases, a state legislature appropriates funds centrally to support consortial activities on behalf of libraries; in others, individual libraries pay to a common fund. External funding facilitates the process of individual institutions' making the adjustments and compromises that consortia require and tends to support consortial relationships among libraries of varying sizes and characteristics. Consortia funded solely by the participating libraries tend to be formed of libraries of similar size and characteristics. Consortia are on the front line of controversies between libraries and publishers about pricing, the terms of use defined by licenses, and publisher practices that make it difficult for a library to cost-effectively tailor its purchases from the publishers' lists or to reduce the total amount of money spent with that publisher. The tendency of consortia to acquire or license electronic resources from the larger, commercial publishers raises concerns that content from scholarly societies or other smaller publishers will be overlooked.

Research library staff are actively working with their partners in consortia to assess the benefits and challenges of consortial licensing and to influence publisher behavior in favor of scholarly communication needs. A closely related factor to collaboration is the degree to which the organizations involved in a joint effort are willing to share control, at both the intra- and the inter-institutional levels. This sharing of control has implications for many activities such as archiving; consortial buying; expanding online resources; collaborative efforts with faculty, information technology groups, instructional technology centers; and cooperative publishing projects. Libraries are promoting team operations to advance collaborative projects and to encourage a convergence of different organizational cultures where control is truly shared. Many research libraries are willing to establish new partnerships and share control in order to innovate.

Research libraries' ability to recognize their strengths and their willingness to leverage those strengths influences the success of library integration into the research institution. Libraries have a special kind of space on campus, space that is seen as politically neutral and representative of the intellectual commons--public-good space. This nature of space gives libraries leverage to attract and nurture collaboration with other parts of the institution. Libraries also have human talent they may deploy for the institution. Research library staffs have a wide range of expertise that can support new approaches to meeting user and institutional needs.

Many libraries are leveraging their space and human resources to the advantage of the institution, for example, in creating an information commons, establishing an institutional repository, or providing campus management of copyright clearances. A major factor in innovation is the degree to which research libraries and their institutions are willing and able to embrace change. The willingness of the library leadership (at all levels) to change its vision of what a library is and does, and to transform library operations to reflect that vision, obviously influences innovation. However, the culture of the institution itself also influences how the library engages and supports change. Many research libraries find themselves in the impossible position of being expected by some disciplines to implement systemic change while continuing to be responsive to the needs of other disciplines that have slower rates of adoption of new technology.19 During this period of transition, this is a major factor influencing how libraries implement change and how that change is received within the institution.

The degree to which people in the institution exhibit "interdisciplinarity" or demonstrate effectiveness in working with the various cultures of the institution—library, faculty, and information technology cultures—is another important factor in innovation. Success in collaboration depends on some degree of convergence of these cultures. Convergence or integration of cultures is being approached in several different ways. Examples include convergence of cultures in shared space; convergence of technical and bibliographic expertise; and convergence of human capital to consolidate efforts, encourage cooperation, and provide institution-wide access to the latest equipment, software, and support as well as a wide and deep collection of high-quality content.

Experience reported in the task force survey suggests there is a need to support greater cultural integration. Some libraries pursue this goal by establishing cross-cultural task forces, developing cross-training and mentoring programs for effective performance across and outside traditional roles, adopting position classification schemes that reflect the changes required of staff, providing opportunities for staff to cross boundaries, and by giving people time to work through the process of cultural convergence.

Converting existing collections and new acquisitions from paper to electronic-only is currently inhibited by the nascent state of strategies for preserving digital content. Internationally, publishers are working with national libraries (or their proxies) for them to assume the role of the publishers' archives for digitized texts; the reliability and terms of use of these archives are still being determined. When library, publisher, and technology communities reach consensus on how best to manage the preservation of digital resources, the transformation of library collections to largely electronic will accelerate.

In this rapidly changing environment, there are many opportunities for entrepreneurial activities, which often require the financial risk of investing resources in new activities even as budget pressures tighten. Entrepreneurship may also create new activities that bypass or challenge the standards, rules, and policies that are part of library operations. Success depends on the library's ability to reach informed judgments, usually with less than complete information, on the strategic importance of an opportunity and whether it warrants the financial and other risks that accompany change.

Research Library Collections

Responding to user expectations for easy searching and convenient access to an expanding array of information sources, libraries are spending increasing amounts of their materials budgets on electronic resources. While up to now many libraries have actually also maintained the print, where dual versions exist, recent budget and space constraints have led many to make a choice of the format they collect. The nascent state of strategies for preserving digital content makes some libraries reluctant to relinquish print editions. However, seeing that these preservation issues are now being addressed, and given the significant advantages of the electronic editions, many libraries have decided to collect electronic-only.

Libraries are also offering printing services to meet users' expressed need for print. As professional print-on-demand technologies become more cost effective, this option may offer, for users who require it, a way to generate high-quality bound printed editions from electronic information resources. At the same time, libraries have not abandoned print. They continue to acquire print in disciplines that are not moving as quickly into the digital world as others and in formats, such as monographs, that are still published primarily in printed form. Thus, integrating print and electronic resources and making print resources almost as easy to access as electronic content are challenges facing libraries in this hybrid environment.

Portal software is being designed to enable users to search library catalogues simultaneously with both open and licensed databases to find content regardless of format, thereby building a bridge between the library's print and digital collections. Timely, self-service resource sharing and other user-initiated services such as book renewals and book- and article-delivery are also making access to print resources much easier. In the future more information will be created, stored, delivered, and preserved digitally, but print—because of its physicality, flexibility, perceived reliability, ease of reading and sharing—will be used for reading and editing for some time to come. Even as print retains importance, the library's physical space has increasing value for other activities, especially collaborative learning and research. Thus, to free up prime real estate, libraries are moving lesser-used print collections to storage centers (with rapid delivery service) and are exploring cooperative approaches to long-term preservation copy retention. For now, research libraries' print collections continue to play a critical role for users even as that role and how users gain access to the material are changing.

Given the rapidly changing environment, however, libraries are carefully monitoring the information-seeking and reading habits of their users to see how their use of print and digital resources changes or does not change over time. Institutional repositories—digital collections capturing and preserving the intellectual output of a single or multi-university community—provide a compelling response to two strategic issues facing academic institutions. Such repositories:

— Provide a critical component in reforming the system of scholarly communication--a component that expands access to research, reasserts control over scholarship by the academy, increases competition and reduces the monopoly power of journals, and brings economic relief and heightened relevance to the institutions and libraries that support them; and

— Have the potential to serve as tangible indicators of a university's quality and to demonstrate the scientific, societal, and economic relevance of its research activities, thus increasing the institution's visibility, status, and public value.

Institutional repositories represent the logical convergence of faculty-driven self-archiving initiatives, library dissatisfaction with the monopolistic effects of the traditional and still-pervasive journal publishing system, and the availability of digital networks and publishing technologies. This convergence manifests itself in several ways:

— *Attitudinally*: Institutional repositories build on a growing grassroots faculty practice of posting research online, most often on personal web sites, but also on departmental sites or in disciplinary repositories.

— *Economically*: While the variety of institutional contexts and potential implementations make it difficult to project institutional repository development and operational costs with any precision, the evidence so far suggests that the resources required would represent but a fraction of the journal costs that libraries now incur and over which they have little control.

— *Technically*: Digital publishing technologies, ever-expanding global networking, and enabling interoperability protocols and metadata standards are coalescing to provide practical technical solutions that can be implemented now.

The rationale for universities and colleges implementing institutional repositories rests on two interrelated propositions: one that supports a broad, pan-institutional effort and another that offers direct and immediate benefits to each institution that implements a repository. While institutional repositories centralize, preserve, and make accessible an institution's intellectual capital, at the same time they will form part of a global system of distributed, interoperable repositories that provides the foundation for a new disaggregated model of scholarly publishing. This model unbundles the principal functions of scholarly communication, thus presenting the potential to realize market efficiencies previously hidden by the vertically integrated publishing model that now characterizes academic journal publishing.

Altering the structure of the scholarly publishing model will be neither simple nor immediate. The stakes are high for all the well-entrenched participants in the system--faculty, librarians, and publishers--and the inertia of the traditional publishing paradigm is immense. In the near-term, large journal publishers have both the power and the incentive to maintain the status quo: the prestigious journals they control appear integral to the very structure of academic professional advancement. However, digital publishing and networking technologies, harnessed by an increasingly dissatisfied library market—as well as by authors themselves--are now driving fundamental changes to this publishing model at an accelerating pace.

And new communications paradigms, especially when constructed by the scholars themselves, can eliminate seemingly insurmountable publisher advantages in relatively short order. Institutional repositories, by capturing, preserving, and disseminating a university's collective intellectual capital, serve as meaningful indicators of an institution's academic quality. Under the current system of scholarly communication, much of the intellectual output and value of an institution's intellectual property is diffused through thousands of scholarly journals.

While faculty publication in these journals reflects positively on the host university, an institutional repository concentrates the intellectual product created by a university's researchers, making it easier to demonstrate its scientific, social and financial value. Thus, institutional repositories complement existing metrics for gauging institutional productivity and prestige. The current system of scholarly communication limits, rather than expands, the readership and availability of most scholarly research (while also obscuring its institutional origins).

Rounds of journal price increases and subsequent subscription cancellations act to reduce the audience further. The role of alternative scholarly publishing models, such as institutional repositories, in breaking the monopolies of publishers and increasing the awareness of university intellectual output grows increasingly clear. Further, institutional repositories can serve this function whether they are implemented on individual campuses or in collaborative consortial projects.

Digital Institutional Repository

Stated broadly, a digital institutional repository can be any collection of digital material hosted, owned or controlled, or disseminated by a college or university, irrespective of purpose or provenance. A particular type of institutional repository—a digital archive of the intellectual product created by the faculty, research staff, and students of an institution and accessible to end users both within and outside of the institution, with few if any barriers to access. In other words, the content of an institutional repository is:

— Institutionally defined;

— Scholarly;

— Cumulative and perpetual; and

— Open and interoperable.

Institutional repositories can assume many forms and serve a variety of purposes. Indeed, the technical and administrative infrastructures developed by academic institutions for existing digital library initiatives might often be modified or repurposed to serve the requirements of an institutional repository. The institutional repository might form a component of a more comprehensive institutional initiative, one encompassing virtually all of an institution's digital assets.

In contrast to discipline-specific repositories and subject-oriented or thematic digital libraries, institutional repositories capture the original research and other intellectual property generated by an institution's constituent population active in many fields. Defined in this way, institutional repositories represent an historical and tangible embodiment of the intellectual life and output of an institution. And, to the extent that institutional affiliation itself serves as the primary qualitative filter, this repository becomes a significant indicator of the institution's academic quality. Depending on the university, an institutional repository may complement or compete with the role served by the university archives. University archives often serve two purposes:

1) to manage administrative records to satisfy legally mandated retention requirements, and

2) to preserve materials pertaining to the institution's history and to the activities and achievements of its officers, faculty, staff, students, and alumni.

Compared to institutional repositories, which aim to preserve the entire intellectual output of the institution, university archivists exercise broad discretion in determining which papers and other digital objects to collect and store. Developing institutional repositories does not require that each institution act entirely on its own. For many colleges and universities, existing state or regional institutional or library consortia will provide a logical infrastructure for implementing institutional repositories via collective development. Such cooperation could deliver economies of scale and help institutions avoid the needless replication of technical systems.

Indeed, consortia might well prove the fastest path to proliferating institutional repositories and attaining a critical mass of open access content. Depending on the goals established by each institution, an institutional repository could contain any work product generated by the institution's students, faculty, non-faculty researchers, and staff. This material might include student electronic portfolios, classroom teaching materials, the institution's annual reports, video recordings, computer programs, data sets, photographs, and art works—virtually any digital material that the institution wishes to preserve. This content may include pre-prints and other works-in-progress, peer-reviewed articles, monographs, enduring teaching materials, data sets and other ancillary research material, conference papers, electronic theses and dissertations, and gray literature.

To control and manage the accession of this content requires appropriate policies and mechanisms, including content management and document version control systems. The repository policy framework and technical infrastructure must provide institutional managers the flexibility to control who can contribute, approve, access, and update the digital content coming from a variety of institutional communities and interest groups (including academic departments, libraries, research centers and labs, and individual authors). Several of the institutional repository infrastructure systems currently being developed have the technical capacity to embargo or sequester access to submissions until the content has been approved by a designated reviewer. The nature and extent of this review will reflect the policies and needs of each individual institution, possibly of each participating institutional community. Essential to the institutional repository's role both within the university and within the larger structure of scholarly communication is that the content collected is both cumulative and maintained in perpetuity. This has two implications.

First, whatever the content submission criteria for a repository, items once submitted cannot be withdrawn--except in presumably rare cases involving allegations of libel, plagiarism, copyright infringement, or “bad science.” This removal would be the functional equivalent of revoking the registration initially granted to the contribution on accession into the repository. This does not necessarily mean that all content will be universally accessible in perpetuity. Institutions must develop criteria and policies--and implement rights management systems--for allowing access to a repository’s content, both inside the institution and from outside, that balance the goal of the broadest available access with the reality of encouraging faculty participation. The cumulative nature of institutional repositories also implies that the repository’s infrastructure is scaleable. While initial processing and storage requirements might prove modest, institutional repository systems must be able to accommodate thousands of submissions per year, and eventually must be able to preserve millions of digital objects and many terabytes of data.

Second, institutional repositories aim to preserve and make accessible digital content on a long-term basis. Digital preservation and long-term access are inextricably linked: each being largely meaningless without the other. Providing long-term access to digital objects in the repository requires considerable planning and resource commitments. The institution needs to balance the desire to accept the farrago of file formats popular with various disciplines, in order to simplify content submission and encourage faculty participation, with the complications that migrating some of those formats or media might present as new standards evolve.

While it is possible for an institution to dictate digital formatting standards for students—in the submission of electronic theses and dissertations, for example—prescribing such formats for faculty, for both attitudinal and practical reasons, proves far more problematic. The goals motivating an institution to create and maintain a digital repository—whether pan-institutional, as a component in the changing structure of scholarly communication, or institution-centric--require that users beyond the institution’s community gain access to the content. For the repository to provide access to the broader research community, users outside the university must be able to find and retrieve information from the repository.

Therefore, institutional repository systems must be able to support interoperability in order to provide access via multiple search engines and other discovery tools. An institution does not necessarily need to implement searching and indexing functionality to satisfy this demand: it could simply maintain and expose metadata, allowing other services to harvest and search the content. This simplicity lowers the barrier to repository operation for many institutions, as it only requires a file system to hold the content and the ability to create and share metadata with external systems. Given the disparate publishing practices amongst academic disciplines, an institution's content accession and access policies need to accommodate legitimate researcher concerns about access to pre-publication material deposited in the repository.

Open Access

The advent of the Internet, the World Wide Web, and digital technologies has revolutionized scholarly communication. Creative applications of these technologies are leading to innovations in the conduct of research as well as in the conveyance of ideas to readers. And the growing availability and application of these technologies has dramatically altered how readers may discover, gain access to, and use information. As positive and liberating as these developments are for many researchers, authors, and readers, they have also accelerated the commodification of information and drives by some content industries to make their channels of information distribution more secure.

As a result, changes are taking place in copyright, license/contract, and related laws that govern the management and use of intellectual property. For the most part, the changes result in more limited access and more restrictive uses for copyrighted material. It is no surprise then that, as the laws change to secure content for publishers, there is a negative impact on those in the educational and research communities where the creation, dissemination, and use of intellectual property is expected and, in fact, forms the very core of learning and research.

Historically, the library and academic communities looked to copyright law as the policy framework for balancing competing interests of creators, publishers, and users of copyrighted works. To achieve its constitutional purpose to promote the progress of science and the useful arts, copyright law provides a copyright owner with a private monopoly to reproduce, distribute, perform, display, and revise a work, while simultaneously providing exceptions for the special circumstances of education and libraries.

This balance has been significantly eroded as copyright and other laws have been revised to apply in the digital and networked environment.

Changes in the laws have come from many directions but are largely driven by players who are part of a large and diverse commercial marketplace seeking changes in the legal framework in order to maximize their profits from e-commerce in publishing and entertainment. The rules promoted by these players to govern a sizeable, general marketplace of users do not lend themselves well to the educational and research communities because, with a few notable exceptions, they do not provide for the special qualities and needs of education and scholarship.

Even in licensing, where libraries have made some progress in negotiating broad uses for their communities, efforts to legitimize mass-market licenses could eliminate fair use and erode the willingness of providers to negotiate at all. In the U.S. and Canada as well as other parts of the world, the library community has been actively engaged in policy debates as laws have been revised, consistently advocating the need to retain a balance among the interests of creators, owners, and users. Our involvement has been significant but these efforts have not been able to stop the economic and political forces of the marketplace that now so clearly dominate society.

It is critical that library community advocacy activities be sustained so there is no further erosion of the balance of interests among creators, copyright owners, and users. At the same time, it is essential for the community to step back, assess the current reality, and consider additional strategies for achieving our commitment to "promote equitable access to and effective use of recorded knowledge in support of teaching, research, scholarship, and community service." The current environment clearly favors commercial interests and thus mitigates against effective use of intellectual property for purposes of education and research.

After many years of the library community's struggle to retain the balance in copyright law, scientists and scholars have cast a new light on the debate. Researchers have come to depend on new technologies for rapid peer-to-peer communications and sophisticated searching and manipulation of data. They have begun to insist that publishers support articles with large datasets, image files, and simulations. And, as the original authors, they are demanding open, easy access to the literature as soon after publication as possible.

Some publishers have been resistant to open access, fearing loss of revenues and loss of control over their content. To date, librarians have exhibited mixed responses to open-access initiatives. Some librarians, like their scientific and scholarly colleagues, see open access as an opportunity to exploit technology more fully in support of research and teaching; others express concern, particularly with the Public Library of Science, that some libraries will cancel journal subscriptions thereby motivating publishers to raise subscription prices and increasing the overall cost of access. Now is the time for librarians to fully embrace the goal of open access, and join with scholars, scientists, and their institutions in working toward this goal.

Search Engines and Bibliographic Display

Most of the current American Memory collections have a set of item-level bibliographic records which can be searched. The search engine in use is INQUERY, the text search toolkit from the Center for Intelligent Information Retrieval. A ranked list of "hits" is returned. INQUERY's flexible query commands have been used to list the hits for queries of two or more terms in four sublists:

1. items that contain the entered query as an exact phrase;
2. items that have all the search words within 20 words of each other;
3. items containing all the words, but not close to each other;
4. items with one or more of the entered words, but not all.

A full bibliographic record display, which has a link to the item. For images, the link in the bibliographic display is a thumbnail version of the image. Each subject term displayed in a retrieved bibliographic record is also a link that invokes a search for items on the same topic. Names of authors, photographers, and other creators are links to searches for other works by the same person or organization. Many of the presentation details, including the division of the hit list into sections, have been modified after user feedback.

An informal study in the Prints and Photographs reading room involved ten users performing two pre-selected image retrieval tasks using an earlier version of the American Memory interface. The searchers were encouraged to talk as they searched; reference librarians logged their comments and the difficulties they were observed to have. Several users were very concerned when searches returned many results that were not close matches to their query; two explicitly requested that the system indicate if there were no items that matched all the entered terms.

In the future, browsable finding aid documents will probably be used as the primary access aid for many collections where item- level cataloguing is not feasible. Once the Library begins to use the Encoded Archival Description format for finding aids to digitized collections, finding aids will also be indexed for searching. Another access path is provided through the Library's main on-line catalogue, which has collection-level descriptive records. These catalogue records indicate that the collection is available on the World Wide Web.

Each record contains a pointer (in field 856 of the MARC format) to the collection by its assigned logical name, ready for future implementation of direct links. Because records from the Library of Congress catalogue are distributed widely as the basis for other libraries' catalogues, the Library is hesitant to add location-dependent identifiers, such as URLs that will change over the years, to its catalogue records. The combination of navigational tools supports a variety of approaches to identifying collections and browsing or searching for individual items. However, it is clear that as the archive grows, new approaches will be needed. Today it is possible to scan the list of collections in a few minutes; an hour or two gives time to dip into each collection and form an impression of its content. But collection identification through browsing a list with brief descriptions, although appealing to users, will not scale up as the number of collections increases and digitized historical collections at many institutions are incorporated into a truly national, distributed digital library. Better methods for quickly identifying the collections that are most likely to be of interest will be needed.

In US, the User Interface Team from the National Digital Library Program is currently working with the Human Computer Interaction Laboratory at the University of Maryland to explore new approaches for the user interface. The challenge of guiding the selection of collections has at least two aspects: determining the characteristics that best describe and distinguish the collections; and finding ways to present those characteristics in a fashion that lets the user select relevant collections easily. As an alternative or supplement to the traditional text-based searching of catalogue records, the User Interface Team plans to explore the use of direct manipulation and rapid feedback during the selection of collections through browsing and filtering operations. To support these operations in a prototype interface, the team will build an independent set of descriptive (but non-MARC) records for the collections using a format that is easily modified and indexed by INQUERY, but not intended for viewing by users.

After the experimental stage, during which the choice and format of attributes will be refined, the Library expects to integrate the content of these records into any standard architecture for collection-level metadata that emerges through broader digital library efforts. Guiding users to relevant collections is not the only navigational challenge for the user interface. When most items in the digital archive have individual bibliographic records, a search across all items is straightforward. The level of description is roughly comparable and cataloguers take considerable effort to be consistent (although consistency is more common within collections than across different collections).

The granularity of the chunks of text indexed are also comparable. However, the historical collections will soon provide a more complex structure. Some items will be described only through section headings and very brief descriptions in a structured finding aid. Textual items will be fully indexed by the words they contain. It is easy to pour all this text into an indexing engine. It is more difficult to structure search options and present results in a way that is both efficient and comprehensible to users. Another dimension of the challenge in building access tools is that a single interface is unlikely to satisfy the entire range of users.

Users will be engaged in very different tasks, from the detailed study of a period in the history of photography to picking one photograph to illustrate a high-school paper on the Civil War. As part of its educational outreach, the National Digital Library Program has already developed materials and tips aimed particularly at teachers. The initial search interface for American Memory's historical collections was made as simple as possible. Experienced searchers have requested the ability to formulate more precise searches. More complex query forms involving Boolean logic and searching for terms in specific fields are under test in other projects using INQUERY at the Library. The ability to specify queries more precisely will address some searching problems, but mis-matches in terminology also prevent users finding relevant items. Researchers making extensive use of the Library's traditional collections soon learn the subject headings that relate to their field of interest. However, casual users do not naturally use the terms from controlled vocabularies. Topical subject headings for bibliographic records are chosen from controlled vocabularies, such as the Library of Congress Subject Headings (LCSH) and the Thesaurus for Graphic Materials (TGM).

A search for photographs using the term "state house" retrieves 50 pictures for which the exact phrase occurs in the bibliographic description. However, the TGM specifies the synonym "capitols" as the appropriate subject index term and a search on "capitols" retrieves 256 photographs. In many contexts for information retrieval (for example, scientists accessing current literature in their field), the primary users can be assumed to be familiar with the terms in the documents themselves. For historical texts, that is not necessarily the case, especially for occasional users. Usage changes over time. "Teacher training" is unlikely to appear in a nineteenth century document, but teachers were certainly trained and the collections currently mounted have much to say about this topic, particularly for women and Afro-Americans. Finding the right level of specificity for search terms is also a problem for users. Teachers might be looking for materials to support their treatment of broad concepts and movements covered in the K-12 curriculum, such as "mass transportation," "leisure activities," "urbanization," or "economy of the South."

Cataloguing guidelines usually recommend the application of the most specific terms, with an emphasis on the concrete. One potential approach is to integrate thesauri into the interface, by providing a browsable hierarchy of terms to assist selection, or by mapping commonly used terms into formal subject headings or to synonyms actually found in text documents. The Library will be exploring possibilities in this area in at least two ways. Firstly, the approach used currently for automatically expanding a search query to search for plurals and other word variants can be extended to incorporate synonyms. Secondly, the Library is working with Project Management Enterprises, Inc., the developers of LEXICO/2, a thesaurus management system used by several divisions in the Library to manage thesauri, such as the Thesaurus for Graphical Materials and the Legislative Indexing Vocabulary.

Metadata—Tool for Finding Information on Internet

A number of Internet search tools are commonly used by the library community. Many libraries, maintain their own Web pages of selected Internet resources. This approach presents filtered and arranged information geared to a specific user community, but usually offers poor user interface and limited search options, may require surfing hyperlinks page after page, and segregates Internet resources from the library's catalog. Furthermore, since the creation and maintenance of these web pages depend entirely on scarce and expensive human resources, the databases produced by this approach are seldom comprehensive. Another prominent tool is the robot-based search engine, such as Lycos or Harvest. These engines automatically navigate through Web spaces, searching for hyperlinks, retrieving relevant documents, indexing them, and creating a database out of them.

An advantage of this type of search is quantitative recall. One of the drawbacks is lack of precision. With the size of the Internet expanding exponentially, it will become more and more difficult to sift through these massive indiscriminate search results. At the same time, the databases created by these search engines could potentially become bigger than the Internet resources themselves. Furthermore, none of these search engines adequately address the issue of indexing non-textual files such as executable, image, compressed, sound, or moving image files. Such problems lead us to conclude that using metadata—data about data—is an important long-term approach for finding information on the Internet.

Metadata

Metadata refers to a set of data elements that can be used to describe and represent information objects. At MIT, mapped data elements for the electronic publication City of Bits into TEI Header, Dublin Core, and URC metadata standards. Their flexibility in creating new data elements, compatibility with USMARC records, comprehensiveness in the representation of electronic objects, their reliability for retrieval, and the sophistication of their data structure with that of USMARC. This comparison helped us to determine the feasibility of using AACR2 and USMARC to access information on the Internet.

The Text Encoding Initiative (TEI), uses SGML as the basis for encoding and interchange of machine-readable texts among research communities. The TEI header, whether directly attached to a TEI-conformant text or not, consists of:

1) a file description, which describes the electronic object and its sources,
2) an encoding description which shows how the text was encoded along with editorial decisions made during the markup of the document,

3) a profile description which includes contextual nonbibliographic information, and
4) a revision description which documents each change made to the electronic text.

The encoding scheme of the TEI header is flexible. Its only mandatory data elements are the title statement, publication statement, and source description statement, which are the components of the file description. The header's descriptive elements can be defined and added to locally with the modification of SGML DTD. Encoders can decide which information to be included according to their local needs. The header can either be directly attached to the document it describes or be freestanding. Since the data elements are labeled intuitively, the encoding procedure requires less training than USMARC.

The reliability of TEI headers for information retrieval is variable. When the header is attached to a TEI encoded text, the user can search not only the full text but the SGML tags as well. However, TEI records may be unreliable for retrieval because of TEI's flexibility in encoding. This will affect data exchange among cooperating cataloging institutions unless there is agreement among them regarding the form and content of specific data elements. The TEI header's data structure is looser and less compact than USMARC. In the Publication Statement, for instance, a descriptive label is required for each separate data element, e.g., publication place, publisher, and date of publication, while USMARC uses tag 260, and three subfields to represent the same amount of information. USMARC carries data very concisely and efficiently, so a TEI header may be longer than a USMARC record for the same electronic object.

The only relationship between bibliographic entities directly recorded in the TEI header is the source description statement, which contains a bibliographic record for the original text. Discovered no provision in the standard to connect the electronic text to other related works. USMARC records, on the other hand, can document complex and sophisticated relations among bibliographic entities.

TEI header and USMARC can both be used to describe electronic text. Encoding in both formats is time consuming and labor-intensive. TEI header can describe electronic objects more vividly than USMARC. But USMARC strongly supports bibliographic data sharing and distribution. Libraries will be able to use TEI headers for describing Internet resources provided that:

1) the encoding forms and specifications are standardized as strictly as USMARC, and
2) library systems can accommodate automatic mapping from TEI headers to USMARC records.

The Dublin Core is a recently proposed metadata standard for describing networked resources and assisting in their discovery and retrieval. It is a simple set of thirteen data elements. The Core's flexibility allows these elements to be modified and expanded. It is so intuitive in design that information providers themselves may encode their own documents at the point of creation. Indeed, this is one of the developers major goals.

The core elements are designed to assist machine harvesting and indexing in the networked environment. Another goal of the developers is to accommodate mapping the core into USMARC records or other standards, such as TEI. The thirteen elements originally identified emphasize access versus description. But since the source data is so uncontrolled, its reliability for retrieval is questionable. The data structure of the Dublin Core is simple and unrefined, geared toward supplying a small number of generally applicable elements. Dublin Core represents an advance over unaided machine indexing and searching. Author-supplied metadata will be better than no metadata, but it still is not the same thing as a professionally prepared catalog record.

Information objects on the Internet with attached meta-information like Dublin Core's will facilitate great improvements in machine indexing. However, whether the Dublin Core will provide reliable retrieval depends largely on how information providers implement it. The Core's encoding forms and specifications will never be standardized as strictly as USMARC, but it is conceivable that library systems could adapt elements of the Dublin Core for import and expansion into full USMARC records.

Unlike the other standards evaluated, the URC focuses overwhelmingly on guaranteeing machine retrieval of electronic resources. Here are some definitions that helped us to understand the alphabet soup surrounding the URC. URN stands for Uniform Resource Name, a proposal for assigning persistent, unique, location-independent identifiers to networked information objects, similar to the ISBN in the publishing world. URL stands for Uniform Resource Locator and is the electronic address for a networked resource. URC stands for Uniform Resource Characteristic, and has been proposed to serve as a connection between URNs and URLs. If a URL changes, authorized users can go into the URC service to modify the URL associated with the URN. The URN stays the same even though the URL may change.

The URC may contain meta-information such as author, title, publisher, subject, and so on, which could assist in resource discovery and retrieval. It may also include other data elements, such as electronic signature and review information to ensure the veracity of the resource, an access element for usage restrictions, and a version element for revision history. In the future, it may be possible to connect to a variety of URC servers, along with some dedicated sites such as OCLC and the Library of Congress.

Both URC and USMARC can be used to document electronic objects. But the meta-information proposed for the URC is far more sketchy than in USMARC. As with the Dublin Core and TEI header, consistency will be required among cooperating servers regarding which metadata elements should be included in URC records. The URC uniquely guarantees retrieval of a resource if its name is known by mapping URNs to URLs; and it accommodates resource validation via digital signatures and seals of approval. Thus URC can assist librarians in cataloging and archiving quality information.

USMARC is actually a complex set of standards for the description, storage, exchange, manipulation, and retrieval of machine-readable bibliographic data. It is highly developed and refined, with individual data elements defined at a granular level. Originally developed in the 1960s for the description of printed books, USMARC is still being adapted to provide description, access and location information for networked resources. With the introduction of the 856 field, which allows a hyperlink between the MARC record and the electronic text it describes, USMARC has become a feasible standard for the discovery and retrieval of networked resources.

The standard is strictly controlled; changes or additions to USMARC take years and painstaking coordination among institutions, industry, and utilities. USMARC allows for rich analysis of the content of information objects. It strongly supports both access and description. This is especially true for full level encoding as it requires professional encoders to strictly follow standard cataloging code such as Anglo-American Cataloging Rules, 2nd ed. Rev. (AACR2R), controlled thesaurus such as Library of Congress Subject Headings (LCSH), and standard classification scheme such as Library of Congress Classification (LCC), etc. Although these cataloging tools can also be applied to the newer standards, none of them have the intention to implement the tools as strictly and fully as USMARC records. Unlike the newer metadata standards, USMARC includes an authorities format which facilitates successful retrieval.

Professional involvement in data creation, USMARC's strict encoding guidelines, and the sophistication of well-developed library systems further enhance access control. Library automated systems use USMARC to exchange data between systems. Most recently developed library systems such as Web-based OPACs or some window-based OPACs permit hyperlinks from the Electronic Location and Access field to its primary information which resides on the internet. With full Z39.50 connections added to this kind of interfaces, users can not only do the traditional searches such as keywords, Boolean, etc., but also use the new features such as simultaneous searches of multiple databases with a merged or de-duplicated search results from both print and electronic resources.

USMARC's data structure is compact and economical, but still allows for the encoding of complex and sophisticated relationships among information objects. For instance, it allows encoders to document sequential relationship, referencing relationship, etc., among bibliographic entities. Thus, users can relate one information object to all its related objects by following the bibliographic links within the record. None of the newer metadata standards support such detailed and complete bibliographic relation tracing.

Internet search engines and library Web pages can provide access, more or less successfully, to items on the net. But libraries are about more than this. They are value-added information centers where information in every format should be carefully selected, organized, preserved, and disseminated. If a networked resource is of high quality, of interest to users, and relevant to collections, it belongs in catalog. In this way, present users with a more accurate and complete picture of the information available in a given subject area. The fact that USMARC is labor-intensive, time-consuming, expensive, and sometimes misused does not prevent it from being useful for providing access information on the internet. USMARC offers us an immediately available tool for integrating important, relevant, high-quality networked resources into catalogs.

The emerging standards function differently than USMARC. Dublin Core and URC are still in the proposal stage. Even when they are fully implemented, they'll only serve as a basis for full catalog records. The TEI header's data elements are particularly suited for use with networked resources, but the standard lacks a provision for authority control, and this has negative implications for data exchange. USMARC is such a ubiquitous metadata standard that publishers, vendors, suppliers of automated systems, and indeed every aspect of library operation depend upon it. Although it is to modify the standard, must continue the legacy represented by millions of USMARC records that are the heart of library service itself. USMARC was originally developed for print resources, but it must be updatable on a constant basis to accommodate information in emerging formats. Cataloging approaches must be adaptable as well. During exercise in data element and data structure mapping, envisioned a future where selected internet resources that meet the criteria of a certain user community will still be cataloged with USMARC. But also look forward to a time when automated systems capable of unassisted metadata conversion from one standard to the other.

Dublin Core Descriptive Metadata Programme

The potential applications of the Dublin Core descriptive metadata program for libraries, museums, and other networked information providers. It includes a brief summary of the current thinking that has emerged from the Dublin Core initiative, including the broader metadata framework captured by the Warwick Framework, and also some consideration of the relationship with the Resource Description Framework under development by the World Wide Web Consortium, but the central focus is on applications scenarios for Dublin Core metadata.

The approach is strategic rather than technical; readers interested in the precise definitions of the individual Dublin Core data elements will need to consult the actual Dublin Core documents or other articles. It will be helpful to library administrators and technology managers who are trying to understand and evaluate the implications of the Dublin Core both for access to existing resources and for practices of description that will be used to create, maintain and provide access to new resources.

Metadata is literally "data about data," information that qualifies other information. Bibliographic description is a form of metadata, so also is information about intellectual property rights and terms of use, formats of electronic information, reviews, errata, abstracts and summaries, provenance information, and a host of other data.

Some metadata can be derived mechanically from objects; other metadata has independent standing as intellectual creation in its own right. It should be clear that the set of metadata associated with an information object is unbounded. The division between data and metadata is somewhat arbitrary and highly situational; information will be used as data in one setting and metadata in another.

There are certainly types of metadata that have been developed for various specific purposes and which it is now proving possible to repurpose, particularly in the digital environment-indeed, creative repurposing and reuse of metadata is emerging as a key idea in the development of sophisticated information organization, retrieval, and management systems.

But the point is that metadata is created and takes on importance through its ability to support activities; for example, the point is not to describe but to support discovery and other processes. The basic motivation for the work on the Dublin Core was to develop a set of simple data elements that could be used to describe document-like networked information objects in support of discovery (searching) activities.

It rapidly became clear that there were any number of legitimate, important requirements for types of metadata that went beyond the scope of the Dublin Core; the problem was that because the Dublin Core was an active effort, and also because it was not clear how to use the DC in conjunction with other sets of metadata, there was considerable pressure to extend the scope of the actual DC effort almost without boundaries.

This threatened the effectiveness of the Dublin Core program. To address this problem, an architecture called the Warwick Framework was developed that described how various sets of metadata for different purposes might be defined and maintained by appropriate communities of expertise. Collections of data elements from these diverse sets of metadata would be assembled into "packages".

The framework describes container structures whereby a digital object and a collection of such packages can be linked together. Each package is independent of all of the others, and software systems that understand specific metadata sets can extract packages that are based on those sets and examine them, bypassing other packages based on unfamiliar sets. Individual packages can even be encrypted independently.

Containers can also refer to remote packages stored independently on the network, and are recursive: a container can include other containers, allowing for the construction of complex composite objects. In designing the Warwick Framework, there was a recognition that division of the universe of metadata into packages would be imperfect; there would be some overlap between packages, and the content of one package might, in some cases, be derived computationally from another.

The importance of the Warwick Framework is twofold. First, it provides a broad architectural framework for defining and using metadata of various types. Second, it allows developers of metadata sets that have specific purposes to limit and focus their work by appealing to the Warwick Framework as an overarching context within which other groups interested in metadata can independently make progress on their own needs.

What is Dublin Core?

The Dublin Core is a set of fifteen data elements-each of which is both optional and repeatable-that was designed to be used as metadata to describe a broad class of information objects. The description applied to objects through the Dublin Core data elements is not intended to be comprehensive or exhaustive; it does not seek to capture everything that can be asserted about an object.

In particular, the DC is designed to support discovery of information objects of interest using search tools and systems; it is not designed to provide comprehensive support for access, management, use, or assessment of networked information. To give just one example of this distinction, the Dublin Core includes a data element for terms and conditions.

This is provided primarily because some limited information on terms and conditions of use-for example, that an object is not copyrighted, or that it can be used without restriction in educational settings-is actually important in finding objects of interest.

There is work underway to develop very complex codings to express terms and conditions that might be used in conjunction with electronic rights management systems; this data would be essential for use and management applications, but is probably too detailed and specialized to be of much use in the discovery process, particularly given the current immature state of both standards and conceptual understanding in rights management specifications.

The Dublin Core is not intended to carry this kind of very specific functional rights management terms and conditions metadata. The DC was developed to describe what have been called, for want of a better term, document-like objects. These have the characteristics of being relatively fixed, although they need not be textual. They may have internal sub-structure-for example, an object with component objects-but the main focus of the DC to date has been to describe objects as opposed to collections of objects.

The primary concern has been to ensure that the DC is serviceable for a rather broad range of common information objects-for example, a workshop was held with the specific focus and outcome of extending and validating the DC as a means of describing a large class of visual resources-rather than drawing precise boundaries for what is out of scope. The DC clearly can be usefully applied to collections or to very complex dynamic objects or information services, but it probably does not do a completely adequate job of describing such objects and services to support discovery.

The development of the DC has had a very strong theme of codifying practice rather than research: methods for satisfactorily describing these complex new classes of dynamic digital objects and network services is still. Further, while there is a great deal of consistency across the class of document-like objects that were the objective of the DC, there seems to be tremendous variation in the kinds of description needed for the still evolving menagerie of new digital resources.

And, at least today, there are a lot more document-like objects than anything else on the network; they are the rule rather than the exception. The fifteen Dublin Core data elements are: title; creator (author); subject and keywords; description; publisher; other contributer; date; resource type; format; resource identifier; source; language; relation; coverage; and rights management.

It should be clear from an inspection of this list that the DC is designed to serve as a sort of lowest common denominator form of description. It does not, at least directly, accommodate discipline-specialized description; indeed, some of the data elements, such as "date" are so vague that they are of limited utility without some further scoping. The DC was designed so that data element values for an object could reasonably be defined by its author, or by a site manager, rather than by a trained specialist cataloguer or indexer.

DC relies very heavily on natural language, and retrieval systems for the DC will have to rely heavily on heuristics and language parsing; not only does the basic DC framework ignore specialized thesauri and subject classification, for example, but it does not even make assumptions about the format that would be used to list dates or personal names.

One of the ongoing tensions and controversies in the development of the DC has been its lack of precision. The most basic version of the DC-called the Unqualified Dublin Core-doesn't carry any information about the format of the data element values, their source or context, or the specifics of their semantics beyond the very broad definitions of the basic data elements.

To address this need various qualifiers have been proposed to serve such functions as indicating the language or syntax in which the data element values are expressed, or to constrain the semantics of the data elements. Obviously, use of qualifiers will tend to reduce interoperability, because participating systems will need to understand much more than just the fifteen basic data elements in order to interpret the semantics properly.

To address this problem, a basic rule has been established for all types of qualifiers: if one ignores the qualifier, the data element value must be consistent with the basic definition of the data element's semantics in the DC. Thus, qualifiers can only constrain or refine the semantics of the DC data elements; they cannot be used to alter their meanings so that they are inconsistent with the original definitions.

Definition of the data elements which should under normal practice be qualified, and what the appropriate values of these qualifiers should be, is a subject of ongoing work within the DC community; in a sense, this can be viewed as a discussion about how to extend the DC beyond the original fifteen elements in practice without destabilizing the original definitions, although some qualification really has a different and less semantically significant character. It remains to be seen how the use of qualifiers will evolve within the various communities of DC users.

Another controversial issue in the definition of the Dublin Core has been how use of the DC elements should interact with the surrogates that are so commonplace in the digital environment. For a document that was created as a digital object, matters are simple: the DC data elements describe the document. The creator of the document is the person who authored it.

The three groups of DC metadata would be connected through the "relation" data element. This has the advantage of being conceptually simple, albeit a bit verbose, for those creating metadata (though this can clearly be mitigated by a well-designed data entry system for DC metadata). It also places a considerable burden on the design of retrieval systems to behave intelligently: to many users, the conceptual distinction between painting, photo, and digitized image is at best murky, and an end-user query will often ask for the painting when what the user really wants is a digitized image of the painting. Retrieval systems will need to be able to retrieve clusters of groups of DC data elements and present them to the user in a comprehensible fashion.

To date, the DC has been developed informally by a loose international consortium of interested parties through a series of five workshops: Dublin, Ohio (from which the core takes its name); Warwick, England; Dublin, Ohio again; Canberra, Australia; and Helsinki, Finland.

Note should also be made of the work of the World Wide Web Consortium, which is working on a program they call the Resource Description Format (RDF). While this work is not directly driven by the DC, and in fact has some of its roots in extending earlier Consortium efforts to develop PICS (the Platform for Internet Content Selection) for rating and content filtering applications, the group working on RDF includes heavy representation from the DC community.

The goals of the RDF effort include the definition of general mechanisms for attaching metadata of all kinds to web pages composed using the new Extended Markup Language (XML) defined by the Consortium, including DC metadata, the development of schema definitions for metadata sets, and query facilities for metadata. This work will likely be central to facilitating the large scale use of DC within the Web.

At one level, the Dublin Core is a conceptual construct; it captures the idea that there are pieces of text that can be associated with an information object with agreed-upon semantics such as those of "creator" or "relation." In order to make this conceptual construct concrete and to apply it in the networked information environment-which is characterized by the cooperation of large numbers of autonomous machines and agencies, and the sharing of information among them-there is need for a variety of supporting machinery.

This machinery is codified in supporting standards and practices. It's important to recognize that, in a sense, the Dublin Core transcends specific machinery, and that many different mechanisms can legitimately be developed within different communities of practice and implementation to meet these requirements. It is likely that over time new mechanisms will continue to develop as a result of the overall evolution of architectures and standards for the networked information environment.

The three major classes of mechanisms are: encoding and transfer syntaxes; methods of associating or attaching groups of Dublin Core data elements with the information objects that they describe; and, more generally, methods of retrieving or querying Dublin Core data associated with objects or groups of objects.

Several methods have been proposed for encoding groups of DC data elements for storage and inter-system exchange: these include the use of HTML META tags in today's HTML-based web pages; the use of XML structures as specified by the World Wide Web Consortium's Resource Description Framework (RDF) as part of future XML-based web pages; and the incorporation in SGML.

Several of these proposals also address the problem of associating DC elements with objects in a very direct way: in the Web setting, they are simply incorporated as part of web pages. There is also a way of requesting DC information for an object via HTTP; this mechanism can also be used to query third-party metadata servers for DC metadata.

One of the key deployment scenarios envisioned for the Dublin Core is that web pages will increasingly incorporate DC data elements as part of the pages-using either direct coding in META tags for current HTML pages or the new RDF structures for pages in the newly defined XML format-and that the familiar web indexing programs will be upgraded to capture this metadata and incorporate it into their web indexes.

The retrieval of an object from such a database-accomplished through an interactive forms-oriented query interface or an inter-system query protocol like Z39.50-might cause the retrieved object to be encoded as a well-known, common format, such as a page that included XML tags for the relevant DC elements.

Similarly, one might want to associate DC elements with an entire website or database; here one would need a mechanism (perhaps akin to some of those used in the Harvest system) that could be used by network resource indexing systems that build site or database directories.

At present, query facilities for Dublin Core data elements are very diverse. There are a number of interactive query systems that offer DC data elements as access points to specific databases or other information collections. Several Z39.50 attribute sets-notably GILS and BIB-1-are incorporating the DC elements as access points that can be used in query construction, and, as part of the migration to the new Z39.50 attribute architecture, it is likely that a separate Z39.50 attribute set will be defined. Part of the RDF work program includes the definition of query facilities for metadata; however, work on this is only at the earliest stages.

The Dublin Core has two different basic applications for libraries. The first is in permitting library databases to become part of broader network search services, or to allow libraries to provide their patrons with consistent views of both library and non-library databases. The second is in describing new resources that cannot be cost-effectively supported through traditional cataloguing approaches.

One of the key notions in networked information discovery and retrieval is that of federating disparate, independently maintained databases scattered about the network. Users should be able to search such constellations of databases as if they were a single, consistent, unified information resource. In order to do that, it is necessary to provide a common semantic view of the various databases involved, even though they may have radically different access points and data structures, and may be accessed through different search protocols or other query mechanisms.

Because the Dublin Core is designed as a lowest common denominator descriptive approach, it offers a very flexible and general context to support federation. Traditional library catalogues or abstracting and indexing databases can clearly support queries constructed using Dublin Core data elements (albeit with some reduction in the precision that queries can express as compared to queries formulated using the database's native search language, unless qualifiers are used extensively); thus it is possible to build a software layer that permits such databases to participate in federations that use the Dublin Core data elements.

These interfaces will use mappings or crosswalks to translate from Dublin Core data elements to the actual access points in the database.

Mappings have already been developed from DC to MARC fields. Conversely, because the Dublin Core is applicable to so many information resources, a library might develop a search interface and distributed search service that offered patrons a federated view of a very diverse set of databases, including not only traditional library databases, but also databases from other sources, such as government databases, databases produced by the next generation of web indexing services, or special purpose scholarly databases.

While such a search service would not eliminate the need for much more precise and capable domain-specific and database-specific search facilities, it would be very useful to some users both in identifying databases of interest which they might then search directly for more comprehensive and precise results, or in doing very broad searches across a wide range of resources.

In this connection, it is interesting to note that the Instructional Management System (IMS) being developed by Educom's National Learning Infrastructure Initiative (NLII) is using a descriptive scheme based in part on the Dublin Core for instructional media; this is a good example of a possible new resource that libraries may want to bring under the umbrella of a search system that also covers their catalogue and abstracting and indexing databases.

The Dublin Core-perhaps supplemented by additional metadata packages defined within the Warwick Framework-will be used to describe content where traditional cataloguing approaches are too costly, or where there is a need to create metadata for content that is not well served by current cataloguing practices. The NLII IMS is a good example: many of the key things that users need to know in searching for instructional media can only be captured by traditional cataloguing in unstructured textual notes.

The IMS supplements the DC elements with an additional descriptive package designed specifically for instructional media. For digitized images or other materials, whether created directly in digital form or digitized from other media (e.g., special collections), full bibliographic cataloguing is particularly expensive because most of these items are unique, and libraries cannot use the system of shared copy cataloguing to control and distribute costs.

It's important to note that, while the Dublin Core was designed to be simple and thus much less expensive to apply than traditional AACR-2 based original cataloguing, there is relatively little experience with it, particularly when the DC is supplemented with additional metadata packages.

The use of the DC and the Warwick Framework gives libraries the ability to design supplementary metadata sets -descriptive and otherwise-to characterize materials that either require more depth or precision of description than the Dublin Core alone can offer, or need not only descriptive but also other types of metadata associated with them in order to support processes that go beyond discovery (e.g., management, use and reuse, or rights clearance).

Instructional media objects are a good example of such a category of materials; statistical datasets are another. Museums will likely make substantial use of the DC plus additional metadata packages.

Network-based Library Information System

User-friendliness of library information systems is important, because they are used not only by professional librarians but also by novice users. Advanced hardware and software technologies have brought us new concepts to build user-friendly library information systems such as GUIs, multimedia user interfaces, collaboration support tools, etc.

The digital library will provide us with an intellectual environment where users can interactively retrieve and read documents, books, audio-visual materials, etc. However, from a practical point of view, we cannot build such environments in one day, because not all libraries can afford high-performance computing and network facilities.

Since library information systems are data-centered, it is not easy to modify data-dependent functions or to add new information to an existing database in order to create new functions and user interfaces. These points imply that we need to build toward the digital library gradually, starting from existing library information systems.

OPAC

OPAC has been the most common tool for library users and librarians, and it will be also commonly used in digital libraries. It is obvious that well-designed GUI improves user-friendliness especially for novice users. OPAC with a bookshelf-like browser of bibliographical data would be useful from a practical point of view, even if the bookshelf on a display does not look like a physical bookshelf. The advantages of the bookshelf-like interface are:

1) users can find not only a book retrieved via retrieval commands but also from a glance at other books placed on the same bookshelf,
2) the structure of bookshelves is semantically organizable, and
3) the display order of books is modifiable as needed.

HOPAC[hopac] has a bookshelf-like interface organization based on the Dewey Classification System. Its hierarchical structure helps a user move his/her viewpoint in the space of books and documents. The Book Shelf window of HOPAC does not look like a physical bookshelf. In addition to the text-based presentation, the authors consider that images of books and bookshelves would help users find books. The number of book images displayable on a display at a same time is obviously smaller than the number of book title texts. This fact looks disadvantageous, but too much information on a display is not friendly to users. The image-oriented bookshelf has the advantage that users can immediately see the size of a book without reading detailed bibliographic information. In addition, we can embed icons into a book image which represent such information as the book being checked-out, having duplications, one of series books, and so on.

Collaboration by Library Users and Librarian

The librarian is an important information resource in a library, and we cannot fully take advantage of a library without his/her help. A digital library will not necessarily be a fully automated librarian-less library, but will have to provide intelligent collaborative services of librarians.

Yamamoto mentioned the roles of librarians in the era of digital libraries as follows:

— Gateway between users and digital library networks,
— Reference via networks,
— Read-aloud via networks, and
  Intermediary as an information creator, editor, and publisher.

He also mentioned the types of reference services via network as follows:

— *Network Navigation:* support to find and approach information sources,
— *Cooperative Search:* support to search information,
— *Cooperative Translation:* multi-linguistic support to access foreign information, and

— *Instruction of Information Tools*: support to learn what tools users should use and how they should use the tools.

In addition to the collaborative services of librarians, the digital library will have to provide environments for group work. For example, researchers sometimes use a conference room in a library for research meetings using journals and other materials in the library. They store their new knowledge and information which are got from their discussion into the library. This means that the digital library should provide a virtual conference room where users can hold discussions through the same displays where library materials such as electronic journals and digitized images are shown.

Thus, collaboration support is one of the important features that should be explored in order to build the digital library. Reference services could be carried out using conventional media such as telephone, facsimile and email. However, these media do not offer the face-to-face communication that is quite important both for librarians and users; librarians must be able to correctly understand questions and needs of users, and users would be able to appropriately express their questions in their conversation with librarians.

SOPAC

SOPAC has been implemented based on the client-server model on a unix workstation which has the Motif GUI environment. The database of SOPAC is identical to the database used by XOPAC, which has 110,000 titles.

Users communicate with SOPAC via multiple windows. A SOPAC GUI includes the following windows:

— *Retrieval Command Window*: accepts retrieval commands as well as set operations AND, OR, and DIFF for intersection, union, and difference operations on retrieved data.

— *Result Window*: displays retrieved data. Users can get detailed bibliographic data of a member of the list on the Detailed Information Sub-window.

— *Memopad Window*: for user annotation.

— *Bookshelf Window*: browse a portion of bookshelf by designating a book on a result window. A bookshelf image of the designated book and its neighboring books is displayed. The order of the book images is primarily determined by the identification numbers of the books.

— *Detailed Information Sub-window*: all of the bibliographic information of a book which is selected on a result window or a bookshelf window.

Bookshelf Window

SOPAC displays a bookshelf with the book highlighted on the Retrieval Window and placed in the center. The order of books is the same as that on a physical bookshelf. The order is determined by the unique identification number given to each book, and users can scroll the bookshelf horizontally.

Each book image is a push-button to request detailed bibliographic information, which is displayed on a Detailed Information Sub-window attached below the bookshelf window. The shape of a book image is determined by the bibliographic description of the book, i.e., height and number of pages. The book title is presented from top to bottom and can be vertically scrolled.

It is not easy to re-create an OPAC database or to modify the scheme of its records. SOPAC has been developed on the XOPAC database. It would be better for bookshelf-like browsers to be able to show physical images of books, i.e., covers and title pages. However, it was not practical to scan in the physical image of every holding and to add it to an existing OPAC database, so the SOPAC book image is created only from existing data.

Books are displayed vertically in order to enhance realism. This means that title texts on the images are drawn vertically. This is convenient for titles in Japanese.

Several issues remain unsolved in the current SOPAC system:

— Bookshelf reorganization: functions to re-organize bookshelves in accordance with semantical requests from users,

— Browsing Support Tools based on Semantical Structure of Bookshelves: tools to show classification hierarchy and thesauri, and

— Active Information Tools: icons to show active information such as "checked out", "in bindery", etc.

Modeling Reference Work as Librarian's Desk

The principal components of reference work in conventional libraries are as follows:

— a librarian,

— a library user,

— library materials, which include primary information sources in a library such as books, journals, etc., and secondary information sources such as OPACs, thesauri, dictionaries, and encyclopedias,

— user's materials such as books and memos, and

— a librarian's desk.

The library user and librarian are modeled as the participants in a conversation carried out via the system. Library materials and user materials, which may or may not be in digital form, are modeled as objects to be displayed on the terminals in front of the participants. The librarian's desk is modeled as a display screen in front of each participant where the participants can see their partners and view the same materials.

It is natural to design a library collaboration support system based on the librarian's desk metaphor. We can find memo pads, a computer terminal, a telephone, a copy machine, and so on in addition to the library materials on/around a librarian's desk. These things should be modeled as system components visible to the participants.

System Structure

The CSS has been developed on two workstations of the ULIS campus LAN. The graphical environment of the workstation is OSF/Motif on X-window.

The following paragraphs are brief descriptions of the components.

— *Control Tool*: The control tool manages initiation and termination of a session between a user and a librarian.

— *TV-phone*: The TV-phone displays real time video pictures taken by a video camera placed at and digitized by the workstation. The captured image is digitized and transferred through the LAN. Sound communication is half-duplex, requiring a talk control panel to switch talking direction.

— *Shared Virtual Display (SVD):* SVD is a window which realizes a virtual display where multiple windows are displayed and input/output operations are performed on them. The participants share the virtual display where the user can see every operation by the librarian, and vice versa. This feature is crucial in order to enhance the quality of communication between the participants; that is, a participant needs to view all operations performed on the terminal of the other participant, for example mouse movement, mouse clicking, etc.

— *White Board*: The participants can input character text and draw images on the board which is equally accessible to both participants. The participants can use the white board to explain things which are difficult to express on the TV-phone.

— *Image Tool:* The participants can input images using a color image scanner. The input images are shown on both workstations.

Web Archiving

The Web is the largest document ever written, with more than 4 billion public pages and an additional 550 billion connect-ed documents on call in the "deep" Web. The Web is written in 220 languages (although 78 percent of it is in English) by authors from every nation.

Ninety-five percent of Web pages are publicly accessible, a collection 50 times larger than the texts collected in the Library of Congress (LC), making the Web the information source of first resort for millions of readers. Nonetheless, the Web is still less than 10 years old, and the economic, social, and intellectual innovation it is causing is just beginning. The Web is growing quickly, adding more than 7 million pages daily. At the same time, it is continuously disappearing.

The average life span of a Web page is only 44 days, and 44 percent of the Web sites found in 1998 could not be found in 1999. Web pages disappear every day as their authors revise them or servers are taken out of service, but users become aware of this only when they enter a Universal Resource Locator (URL) and receive a "404-Site Not Found" message.

As ubiquitous as the Web seems to be, it is also ephemeral, and much of today's Web will have disappeared by tomorrow. The implication is clear: if we do not act to preserve today's Web, it will disappear. In the past, important parts of our cultural heritage have been lost because they were not archived-in part because past generations did not, or could not, recognize their historic value.

This is a cultural problem. In addition, past generations did not address the technical problem of preserving storage media-nitrate film, videotape, vinyl recordings-or the equipment to play them. They did not solve the economic problem of finding a business model to support new media archives, for in times of innovation the focus is on building new markets and better technologies.

Finally, they did not solve the legal problem of creating laws and agreements to protect copyrighted material yet at the same time allow for its archival preservation. The very pace of technical change makes it difficult to preserve digital media. How many people can retrieve documents from old word processing diskettes or even find yesterday's e-mail?

All documents follow a life cycle from valuable to outdated, but then, perhaps, some become historically important. Archivists often rescue boxes of documents as they are being transported from the attic on their way to the dump. But the Web is not stored in attics; it just disappears. For this reason, conscious efforts at preservation are urgent. The hard questions are how much to save, what to save, and how to save it.

Every new technology takes a few generations to become stable, so we do not think to preserve the hardware and software necessary to read old documents. Digital documents are particularly vulnerable, since the very pace of technical progress continuously makes the hardware and software that contain them outmoded.

A Web archive must solve the technical problems facing all digital documents as well as its own unique problems. First, information must be continuously collected, since it is so ephemeral. Second, information on the Web is not discrete; it is linked. Consequently, the boundaries of the object to be preserved are ambiguous.

Who has the responsibility for collecting and preserving the Web and the resources to do so? The economic problem is acute for all archives. Since their mission is to preserve primary documents for centuries, the return on investment is very slow to emerge, and it may be intangible hence hard to measure.

Archives serve the public interest in the very long run, with immediate benefits for only a few scholars. For this reason, they tend to be small and specialized. However, a Web archive will require a large initial investment for technology, research and development, and training-and must be built to a fairly large scale if it is continuously to save the entire Web.

New intellectual property laws concerning digital documents have been optimized to develop a digital economy, thus the rights of intellectual property holders are emphasized. Copyright holders have reason for caution, because the technology is so new and the long-term implications of new laws are unknown.

Although the Web is popularly regarded as a public domain resource, it is copyrighted; thus, archivists have no legal right to copy the Web. And yet it is not preservation that poses an economic threat, it is access to archives that might damage new markets.

Finding a balance between preservation and access is the most urgent problem to be solved, because if today's Web is not saved it will not exist in the future. Access is a political as well as a legal problem. The answer to the access problem, like the answers to all political problems, lies in establishing a process of negotiation among interested parties. Who are the stakeholders, and what are the stakes, in building a Web archive?

— For librarians and archivists, the key issue is to ensure that historically important parts of the documentary record are preserved for future generations.

— For owners of intellectual property rights, the problem is how to develop new digital information products and to create sustainable markets without losing control of their investments in an Internet that has been optimized for access.

— The constitutional interest is twofold: the innovation policy derived from Article I, Section 8 of the U.S. Constitution ("progress in the useful arts and sciences"), and the First Amendment.

— The citizen's interest is in access to high-quality, authentic documents, through markets, libraries, and archives.

— Schools and libraries have an interest in educating the next generation of creators of information and knowledge by providing them with access to the documentary record; this means access based on the need to learn rather than on the ability to pay.

In sum, the policy problem is to find a process for balancing these interests in the long run, including finding a means through which each of the parties can conduct and evaluate significant experiments and reach solutions that strike a balance among legitimate contending interests.

Howard Besser has identified five key technical problems necessary for digital preservation:

1. The viewing problem is the maintenance of an infrastructure and the technical expertise necessary to make digital documents readable.
2. The scrambling problem is decoding any compression or technical protection service software protecting the Web page.

3. The interrelation problem is preserving the contexts that give information meaning, such as links to other Web pages.
4. The custodial problem is defining the standards, best practices, and collection policies that define the boundary of the work and its provenance and authenticity.
5. The translation problem concerns the way in which the experience and meaning of the Web page are changed by migrating it into new delivery devices.

When one is building a Web archive these problems translate into three questions: What should be collected? How do we preserve its authenticity? How do we preserve or build the technology needed to access and preserve it?

Ultimately, the scope and scale of a Web archive will be determined by the definition of the digital object to be collected-the "Web page." This is not a simple matter. From a user's point of view, a Web page is the image called forth by placing a URL address into a Web reader.

This operational definition is necessary but not sufficient, for an archive also must be sure that the document is translated in an authentic manner. In this case, authenticity means that the document must both include the context and evoke the experience of the original. The average Web page contains 15 links to other pages or objects and five sourced objects, such as sounds or images. For this reason, the boundaries of the digital object are ambiguous.

If a Web page is the answer to a user's query, a set of linked Web pages sufficient to provide an answer must be preserved. From this perspective, the Web is like a reference library; that is, it is the totality of the reference materials in which a user might search for an answer. If so, the object to be preserved might include everything on the Web on a given subject at a given point in time, for example, the 2000 election or the World Trade Center terrorist attack.

None of these possibilities would be easy to realize, for the Web is not a fixed collection of artifacts. Today, the "surface" Web contains all of the static hypertext markup language (HTML) pages that can be accessed by URLs. Some of the surface Web, especially in the commercial sector, requires passwords or encryption keys; this area might be called the "private" Web.

To archive these Web pages would require permission of the owners. The private Web is often encased in security protection services that make copying and preservation doubly difficult. Beyond these problems, surface Web pages are often generated on the fly, customized on demand from databases in the "deep" or "dark" Web.

The deep Web is estimated to be 500 times larger than the surface Web. It includes huge data sources and software code that provides information services for surface Web pages on the fly. The deep Web is the information architecture that produces what we read on the surface; the surface itself exists only as long as a reader is using it.

This deep Web cannot easily be archived, since the data are guarded by technical protection services. It is also potentially protected by privacy concerns, since if Amazon.com owns a profile of one's use of information, it is not necessarily available for archiving without his/her consent. Here there are not only tensions between markets and archives but also conflicts between privacy concerns and the interest of history.

The ambiguous boundaries of Web objects are also problematic because they are compounds of design elements, including texts, pictures, graphics, digital sound, movies, and code-the list expands as innovation continues. Each of these elements has intellectual property rights attached to it, although they are rarely marked and sometimes impossible to trace.

Yet, at least in principle, a digital archive would have to have permission from each of these rights holders. In the words of the US National Research Council's report, The Digital Dilemma: Intellectual Property in the Information Age, "for the digital world, one must sort out and clear rights, even of ephemera".

Even if the Web page could be copied technically and we knew what we wanted to preserve, Web pages are protected by copyright law. Even now there are sophisticated debates about how a Web archive should collect data: Should the default be that copyrighted information is collected and the owner has to opt out; or should it not be collected or disclosed unless the owner actively gives permission ("opts in")? This is a question that may be resolved by legislation or the courts.

It is important to remember that the Web is a global document; consequently, there are likely to be many jurisdictions making laws and rules, and enforcement across national borders will be difficult without treaty agreements.

Defining the boundaries of the object to be collected also requires decisions about authenticity and provenance. These decisions must be recorded as part of the archive; the preservation community calls this kind of information "metadata," or information about information, and often builds records of what is in the collection using these metadata.

A standard way of recording the metadata must be created to record the historical and technical context in which the document(s) were found. Among many other facts, metadata might record answers to the following questions:

— What is the name of the work? When was it created, and when has it been changed? Who created, changed, or reformatted it?

— Are there unique identifiers and links to organizations or files or databases that have more extensive descriptive metadata about this record?

— What technical environment is needed to view the work, including applications and version numbers, decompression schemes, and other files? If the Web page is generated on the fly, what database generated it, and what is known about its provenance?

— What technical protection devices and services surround it, if any?

— If the Web page contains more than text, what applications generated the sound, video, or graphics?

— What copyright information is there about each of the elements of the Web page, and what is the contact information for them?

— Work to define standard answers to these and other questions is ongoing through the Dublin Core metadata project.

— What Technologies Are Needed to Preserve the Web Collection?

Technologies to reproduce the Web object-however defined-must be preserved, including the hardware and software necessary to access the information in an authentic context or to recreate it. This is difficult in the best of cases. Have we authentically preserved a computer game if we preserve only the graphics, or must we preserve the look and feel of the game in use?

Every solution changes the context of information in ways that affect its authenticity. One strategy tries to preserve the original equipment; another uses contemporary technology to emulate the original "look and feel" of the information in use; still another migrates the digital signal to new storage media.

Migration is not just a technical problem. Storage media for digital documents are not yet stable for long-term preservation. Magnetic storage media such as tape and discs eventually deteriorate. Moreover, hardware and software eventually become obsolete, hence very expensive to preserve and operate.

A Web archive must migrate from one technical environment to another as generations of technology succeed one another. Nevertheless, under today's law such migration could be a violation of copyright law because it involves copying the signal from one medium to another.

These problems are typical of those that occur in the early stages of every innovation, when getting to market quickly is more important than is perfecting the product. Digital information products are not designed for longevity, and even if they were, it is likely they would become obsolete quickly.

As a consequence, the technologies of digital preservation are complex and expensive. The problems are understood far better than are the solutions at this point, but it is already clear that a Web archive will require substantial investment in technological infrastructure and technical research and development, and that commercial entities are unlikely to lead this effort unless there is short term economic value in doing so.

Both archives and libraries collect, organize, preserve, and provide access to the documentary record. The distinguishing function of archives is to preserve the integrity of documents for the long run. Preservation for centuries invariably requires new technologies; hence, the Council on Library and Information Resources and other organizations are investigating long-term storage and migration of data.

While the technical problem of preservation is difficult, it is well understood. The problem of access, by contrast, involves legal and economic issues that have not yet been adequately explored. While print archives provide a useful model, the economic and legal environments surrounding print are quite different from those surrounding digital documents.

Economic and legal issues cannot be separated. In 1998, the Digital Millennium Copyright Act (DMCA) gave copyright owners rights to protect their works in digital formats. The DMCA implements the 1996 WIPO

Copyright Treaty and WIPO Performances and Phonograms Treaty. Among the purposes of these treaties was harmonizing copyright policy around the world to encourage global commerce in digital information.

As a public policy, the DMCA was focused upon making the Internet safe for intellectual property. If digital information is easily moved from place to place on a network, such movement is considered to be copying and is protected by copyright. If Internet information is easily accessed, making it difficult for a rights holder to control distribution, the DMCA encourages the development of technical protection services (such as encryption) by making it illegal to develop technologies to break them.

For printed information, copyright policy has balanced information markets with public goods, such as education, the First Amendment, and libraries to provide access to information.

— The first-sale doctrine allows libraries to circulate copyrighted works to library patrons. In the digital realm, however, information may be licensed by contract rather than sold under copyright. With licenses, the provisions of the contract determine the uses that are allowed, which are unlikely to include library circulation or fair use. While printed works may also be sold with "shrink-wrap" licenses, the print market has not accepted them as readily as have markets for digital information.

— The fair-use doctrine allows for copying for personal educational purposes, within limits that are designed to protect information markets from damage. Here again, if licenses govern commerce in digital information, these copyright provisions do not govern the contractual agreement reached between buyer and seller.

The Digital Dilemma makes a constructive case for extending the fair-use doctrine to digital information in the future. The rationale for the market approach, embodied in the DMCA, was twofold.

— First, new information markets are expensive to develop, and from the industry perspective, public interest doctrines such as first sale and fair use are taxes on this investment.

— Second, the global scale of the Internet means that millions of copies can be made and distributed in seconds, causing economic damage that cannot be repaired. Thus, while copyright laws governing print place emphasis upon ex post facto remedies such as litigation, the DMCA emphasizes prevention.

Every digital copy, perhaps even copies made temporarily for system management purposes, thus requires the permission of the copyright holder. The DMCA explicitly allows archives to make digital copies of print works for the purpose of preservation. To prevent illegal copying, the DMCA encourages the use of technical protection services such as encryption by making it illegal to use software to break them, and also making it illegal to develop and distribute such software.

Software developers feel that this provision raises free-speech issues and perhaps property issues if it makes it illegal for the owner of a legal copy to make a backup. Congress recognized the complexity of some of these issues, empowering the LC to advise Congress whether this provision in Section 104 prevents noninfringing uses of certain classes of copyrighted works.

Print archives are permitted to collect copyrighted materials and copy them for preservation purposes. For example, it is legal to copy print materials from one medium to another as part of a migration strategy over time, but it may not be legal to do so with digital collections, or to reformat them (e.g., from CD-ROM to a hard disk).

Differences between the production and distribution of printed and digital works raise additional legal issues for Web archives. When something is published in the print world, it is registered for copyright; thereafter, the laws governing it are largely unambiguous. On the Internet, it is not always clear when something has been "published." At this point, it is not clear to most users whether placing information on the Web places it in the public domain or under copyright protection.

The Digital Dilemma concludes that the Web is copyrighted in principle, but notes public confusion on the issue and explores ambiguities that make it unclear whether archives have the right to make preservation copies and preserve them using migration strategies. In the print world, it has been possible to develop a copyright regime that balances the needs of markets and those of archives.

The Internet makes it difficult simply to transfer copyright doctrine from the print to the digital environment. Yet many of the problems for the Web archive outlined earlier seem to be unanticipated consequences of laws intended to support the digital marketplace and might, in principle, be resolved by negotiation. This process might begin by discussing the possible damage to the marketplace caused by long-term archives and seeking solutions.

Inevitably, a Web archive will be a new kind of organization, one that responds to the problems and interests surrounding the Web. It may not be a place at all-it may be a function distributed among institutions over many locations on a global network. The starting point for building a Web archive is to envision organizational strategies to manage this process.

Two organizational strategies are emerging-one from the archival and library professions and the other from computer scientists. These strategies are not opposites and are not mutually exclusive, but contrasting them helps frame the strategic choices. In US, one library and archival strategy for organizing digital archives is presented in Preserving Digital Information, a report of the Task Force on Archiving of Digital Information, published by the Commission on Preservation and Access and the Research Libraries Group.

One technical strategy is offered by the library community, which has developed sophisticated cataloging strategies. The MARC record is used to build print library catalogs that may be searched by users to identify the best information resources. MARC records include fields to describe every aspect of printed documents; the Dublin Core metadata project is defining a standard for cataloging digital documents.

Computer scientists funded by the National Science Foundation (NSF) Digital Library program are developing a second model. While the Dublin Core is designed to enable searches of library catalogs of digital collections, the NSF digital library projects are developing search engines that directly parse the digital documents themselves.

Records identify the best information source described in a catalog, while search engines and data-mining technologies go to the source itself. Each has its advantages. The point is that these technologies are optimized for two different kinds of archive. The computer science paradigm allows for archiving the entire Web as it changes over time, then uses search engines to retrieve the necessary information.

An archival catalog supports high-quality collections built around select themes, saving only the Web sites judged to have potential historical significance or special value, and describing these special qualities in collection records and catalogs that could be searched. This is a fundamental debate about the nature of the Web as a technical object as well. The librarian tends to look at the content of the Web page as the object to be described and preserved.

The computer scientist tends to look at the Web as a technology for linking information-a system of relationships (hence the name "Web"). This implies not only a difference in scale: it is a difference in philosophy. Should Web archives include everything or only carefully selected samples? Should the end user make decisions about the quality of the Web page, or should they be made by a selector who chooses which Web pages to save?

Costs of Digital Library Projects

The potential benefits of digital access are considerable. Patrons, who previously traveled to a repository of rare books or a microfiche room at a research library, instead can access historical information from their desktop. This dramatically decreases the time and effort patrons spend traveling to the source of the information. This also dramatically increases the potential benefits to new patrons, who can now access historical texts that previously were only available at sites too distant for them to consider. The economic question is whether the cost of digitization is low enough to justify this future stream of benefits.

Digital texts in a networked environment hold the promise of lower cost access to information by a greater number of users than can be provided by printed texts. Projects such as The Making of America, Project MUSE, JSTOR, and the Early Canadiana Online project etc offer access to digital texts over the Internet to millions of potential users. These digital projects also offer the promise of lower costs by avoiding the cost of printing and shipping multiple copies of a text for patrons.

Let us examine the economics of digital, microfiche, and print access for the Early Canadiana Online (ECO) project as an example. ECO is a digital library of selected books and pamphlets from pre-1900. The ECO project includes over 3,000 titles and 500,000 images.

Cost Estimates of Early Canadiana Online (ECO)

Estimating the costs of digital projects is necessary to determine efficient investments in digitization of print or microfiched information products. The primary goals of the project are to estimate and compare the costs of three methods of information delivery; print, microfiche, and digital. Cost data was collected from the ECO project partners: The University of Toronto, Laval University, and the Canadian Institute for Historical Microreproductions (CIHM). The cost of construction of a new electronic library at the University at Albany was also used.

Cost of Print

Table 1 shows the cost estimates for book storage and access. These costs are based on the cost of the Thomas Fisher Rare Book Library at the University of Toronto. Construction costs are based on the 1999 library construction project at the University at Albany. Special environmental controls used in a rare book library imply that the construction costs in Table 1 may underestimate the actual construction costs. All costs are shown in Canadian dollars. The exchange rate used is $1.5257 Canadian dollars (CD) per US dollar.

Table 1. Annual Cost of Book Storage and Access

	Cost	Cost per volume (cost/volume)	Cost per use (cost/use)
Construction, utilities & maintenance	$1,586,056	$3.17	$ 72.51
Salaries	$1,105,031	$2.21	$ 50.52
Equipment & supplies	$ 255,799	$0.51	$ 11.69
TOTAL	$2,946,885	$5.89	$134.72

In Table 1 the cost per use is derived by dividing the cost by the number of requests for the year. This inflates the cost per retrieval by adding the costs of storage into the equation. However, it is important to note that the "service" of a library is the use of its materials. All costs when divided by the use of those materials gives an average cost for service which will be higher than separating out only part of these costs for retrieval.

For a comparison with the estimates cited by Bowen, Lesk, and Getz, an estimated 80% of salaries at the Thomas Fisher Rare Book Library is for access. Taking 80% of salary costs yields an estimate of $40 per transaction for labor, still significantly higher than other estimates. However, a rare book library has concerns of preservation that require additional staff care and monitoring for patron access. In addition, this estimate includes the total cost of administration, vacations, and benefits for employees rather than the marginal cost of retrieval based on a staff member's time spent multiplied by his salary.

Table 1 does not include the cost of purchasing a book. This is important although it will be a small percentage of total costs once the purchase price is amortized over the expected life of storage and use of the book. For example a rare book that costs $500 but is expected to last 100 years in storage has an annual cost, when amortized, of $4.80. Table 1 also does not include the value of the land. This can be significant but is different depending on the location of the library.

Cost of Microfiche

The annual costs of microfiche storage and access at the University of Toronto are shown in table 2. Cost per volume is based on a 216 page text, the average size of a text digitized in the Yale Open Book Project. As with Table 1 these costs represent the average cost per unit for storage or access. Just as the cost of purchasing a book is not included in Table 1, the cost of purchasing the microfiche is not included in Table 2. Both the cost of storage per volume and the cost per use are significantly lower for microfiche than for rare books. This is not surprising since microfiche is intended to provide access to and storage of information at a lower cost than print.

Table 2 Annual Cost of Microfiche Storage and Access

	Cost	Cost per volume (cost/volume)	Cost per use (cost/use)
Construction, utilities & maintenance	$ 170,527	$0.06	$2.71
Salaries	$ 251,602	$0.09	$4.00
Equipment & supplies	$ 34,423	$0.01	$0.55
TOTAL	$ 456,552	$0.16	$7.26

The cost per use is derived by dividing the total costs of microfiche storage and access by total use. This assumes that the value of microfiche storage is for access to patrons. If salaries and equipment are the only costs for access, and 80% of salaries are for access, then the cost per transaction can be estimated as $3.75, which is comparable to estimates of the costs of book retrieval. Both retrieval functions are similar in that staff must locate, check out, and reshelve the requested materials.

Table 2 does not include the subscription price of the microfiche to the library. These costs are part of the economic cost of producing microfiche and are shown in Table 3. To avoid double-counting, these costs are not shown in Table 2. The costs of microfiche production are shared costs. Library subscription fees, grants and donations are used to jointly finance the production of the microfiche as a public good.

Table 3 includes all economic costs of microfiche production including the value of space CIHM uses at the National Library of Canada. While this space is donated to CIHM, it still represents an economic cost of producing microfiche. As with previous tables, the average cost of production is derived by dividing total costs by number of units.

Table 3. Cost of Microfiche Production(all costs are average cost estimates)

	Cost	Cost per fiche	Cost per image	Cost per volume
Master Copies	$ 150,000	$ 16.07	$0.22	$ 46.88
Salaries	$ 602,932	$ 64.58	$0.87	$188.43
Equipment & supplies	$ 125,880	$ 13.48	$0.18	$ 39.34
Construction, utilities & maintenance	$ 187,066	$ 20.04	$0.27	$ 58.46
TOTAL (shared costs)	$1,065,878	$114.17	$1.54	$333.11
Cost of micro fiche reproduc tion & sales	$ 236,092			
TOTAL COST	$1,301,970			
Total cost per library (30-42 copies)	$43,399 -$30,999	$4.65 -$3.32	$0.06 -$0.04	$13.56 -$9.69
Annual cost per library (30-42 copies)	$2,254 -$1,487	$0.22 -$0.16	$0.01 -$0.00	$0.65 -$0.46

The first four rows of Table 3 show the cost of producing master copies of microfiche. The cost of producing master copies of microfiche is $114 per fiche, $1.54 per image, or $333.11 per 216 page volume. This is the cost of producing a set of master copies that are then used to produce additional microfiche copies for distribution to subscribing libraries. The cost of the master copies is a shared cost for all subscribing libraries.

If we compare the cost per volume of creating and storing a master microfiche copy relative to creating and storing a print copy, microfiche is expensive to create but has significant savings in storage ($0.16 per volume per year) relative to print ($5.89). However, at annual savings of $5.73 per year, it would take over 50 years to cover the cost of creation ($333.11) if the master copies were created solely for the use of one library.

Microfiche is produced by CIHM, not to have a single copy, but to provide multiple copies to libraries that would not otherwise have access to early Canadian literature. With a limited number of print copies, microfiche becomes a cost-effective alternative for providing access. CIHM produces several copies of each microfiche to sell as subscriptions for libraries throughout Canada, the United States, and the rest of the world. By purchasing a subscription, these libraries share the costs of the original microfiche production.

CIHM produces about 30 copies each year for library subscriptions and additional copies of individual microfiche at an additional cost of $236,092. The last two rows in Table 3 show how these costs can be shared among the subscribing libraries. If the full cost of microfiche production is averaged over the 30 copies, the cost of annual production is $43,399 per library. This includes the shared costs of production plus the costs of making copies. If an additional 12 copies of each fiche, on average, are sold the average cost is $30,999 per library.

The average costs per fiche, per image, and per volume for 30-42 copies are shown in the final three columns of Table 3. The sharing of the full costs of production among subscribing libraries reduces the cost to $0.04-$0.06 per image or $9.69-$13.56 per volume. This compares favorably to the cost of each library acquiring a printed manuscript. At an annual savings of $5.73 per volume for each library, it takes 1.7-2.4 years for the microfiche to cover the costs of creation ($9.69-$13.56).

Once produced, it is anticipated that a microfiche copy of a text will last for 100 years. The purchase of microfiche is an investment in an archival copy of materials that is expected to provide access for patrons to the information for many years. If the cost of the microfiche is spread out or amortized over a 100-year period, then the annual cost of microfiche production is only \$0.65-\$0.46 per 216 page volume per year. When this is added to the cost of storage from Table 2, the annual cost comes to \$0.81-\$0.62 per volume per year for producing, storing, and providing access to a text in microfiche format.

These costs indicate that when microfiche is produced in large numbers to accommodate several libraries, it costs significantly less to produce, store, and provide access to microfiche than to books. This shared cost per library declines further if the number of libraries acquiring subscriptions increases. In addition, the CIHM microfiche subscription provides access to a larger collection of texts than is likely to exist in any single library of rare books. These cost estimates show that microfiche is the more cost-effective alternative to library storage of print to provide patron access to out-of-print texts.

Cost of Digital Production

Digitization of texts may be able to provide even greater savings relative to microfiche and print. Unlike print and microfiche, which must be produced and delivered to a library, digital texts have the advantage of being stored remotely but accessed globally via the Internet. The cost of reproduction and distribution of digital information in a networked environment is zero. The only costs are the one-time fixed costs of producing and the annual fixed costs of storing the data. These fixed costs can be shared by the subscribing libraries. In theory this could drive the cost per library to a significantly lower level than with microfiche.

In the Early Canadiana Online Project, microfiche was converted to digital format. Microfiche was sent to Preservation Resources for scanning and the University of Michigan for optical character recognition. Cost estimates shown in Table 4 are based on contractual costs for scanning and OCR.

The total costs for production are \$236.08 per title or \$1.20 per image. Costs in the second and future years for digital storage and access are \$35.76 per title or \$0.18 per image. This includes the cost of salaries for maintaining the ECO Project database and annual costs of hardware storage. Although the cost of producing digital copy from fiche is less than the cost of microfiche, the cost of storage and access for digital, in the project, was more expensive. This is the result of costs averaging over a smaller number of available digital images which will be higher than the average cost per fiche in a university microtext room which contains hundreds of thousands of microfiche.

Table 4. Cost of Microfiche to Digital Production & Storage (all costs are average cost estimates derived by dividing costs by output)

	Cost	Cost per title	Cost per image	Cost per volume
Digitization	$ 439,548	$132.87	$0.67	$145.67
OCR	$ 159,098	$ 48.09	$0.24	$ 52.73
Salaries	$ 153,264	$ 46.33	$0.24	$ 50.79
Equipment & supplies	$ 7,975	$ 2.41	$0.01	$ 2.64
Construction, utilities & maintenance	$ 21,053	$ 6.36	$0.03	$ 6.98
TOTAL	$ 780,938	$236.08	$1.20	$258.82
Annual costs of storage & access	$ 118,290	$ 35.76	$0.18	$ 39.20

There are two factors that significantly lower the average cost per image of digital production and storage: the number of libraries subscribing to the database and the number of images stored. The production costs of the digital images are fixed costs that are constant regardless of the number of libraries that subscribe to the database. If there are 30 library subscriptions to the database the cost per library would be $8.63 per volume. An increase in the number of libraries or other organizations that subscribe to the database will decrease the "cost-share" for each organization. In addition, the annual cost of storage and access to the database is also a "shared" cost. If this cost is shared among 30 libraries it decreases to $1.31 per volume per library per year.

As the number of images available in the ECO Project increases, the cost per volume will also decline. Space costs (utilities, construction, etc.) and salaries for maintaining and updating the database and server constitute 97 percent of the costs of storage and access. These costs are incurred regardless of the number of images. Storage costs per volume are $0.90 of annual costs. As the number of images in the database increase, total storage costs will increase, but the average cost will continue to decline.

The cost estimates from Table 4 can be compared to similar recent studies estimating the cost of digital production. Estimates from studies at Cornell University and Yale University are shown in Table 5.

Table 5. Cost of Digital Image Production

	Cost per Image	Cost per Volume	
Early Canadiana Online	$ 1.20	$258.82	Average cost estimate
Yale	$ 0.40	$ 83.96	Marginal cost estimate
Cornell	$ 0.43	$ 91.37	Marginal cost estimate

These earlier studies show a significantly lower cost of digitization. The Cornell study created digital copies from paper while the study at Yale created digital copy from microfiche. The major difference between the Early Canadiana Online Project and these earlier studies is the method used for estimating costs. Both the Yale and Cornell studies estimated costs by timing staff scanning pages of print or microfiche. These studies are based on the marginal cost of scanning images and producing digital copy.

The cost estimates for the ECO project are average costs based on dividing total project costs by the number of images, titles, or volumes. The ECO Project cost analysis includes the full cost of producing digital copies and mounting the database on a server for access over the Internet. The ECO project is larger in scope, number of titles, and number of images. ECO costs include all salaries, space costs, and outsourcing of digitization and OCR. Therefore, this cost analysis should be viewed as a liberal cost estimate of a large digitization project with Internet access to the database.

Cost of Access to Digital Information

The cost of access to digital information is difficult to quantify. Access to digital information includes the personal computer, network connection, and space used by the patron. Since these are all fixed costs of access that a patron or library must incur regardless of what information is accessed, the marginal cost of accessing any image or database is zero.

We can attempt to quantify the average cost per use to the library of providing access to digital information. This is shown in Table 6.

Table 6. Cost of Access to Digital Images

	Cost	Cost per internal use	Cost per use
Construction, utilities&maintenance	$186,274.25	$0.01	$0.00
Salaries	$114,000.00	$0.01	$0.00
Equipment & supplies	$398,000.00	$0.03	$0.01
TOTAL	$698,274.25	$0.04	$0.01

Table 6 includes the cost of computers within the library, staff to maintain the server and network, and the cost of space for each computer. Cost per use is shown in terms of internal use and all uses of library databases regardless of the source. Internal use is defined as the number of unique and significant hits to the library server which originate from within the library (0.3 million per week). Use is the number of hits regardless of source (1.2 million per week). Regardless of which definition of use is applied, access to digital documents comes at a very low average cost per use. This is significantly lower than the average cost per use for microfiche or rare books.

Table 6 also illustrates the importance of understanding the difference between total, average and marginal costs. It shows the total and average costs per use. The total cost of providing electronic access within a university library is significant, but the high level of use of terminals within the library results in a very low average cost per use. The marginal or additional cost for each patron's use is zero. All costs in Table 6 are fixed costs, incurred regardless of whether a patron uses a terminal or not. Investments in information technology within university libraries can be expensive although digital documents in a networked environment come at a zero marginal cost of distribution.

User Costs of Access

The final economic cost of access is the cost to the user. With print and microfiche the user must travel to the library to use the information. Any library will have only a limited collection of print titles. To read other titles in print from the collection, a patron may have to travel to another research library. With the CIHM microfiche collection, a research library can offer patrons access to a greater number of titles than are typically available in print, although the patron must still travel to the library to access the microfiche.

Digital copies are accessible to all patrons of subscribing libraries with a network connection. This increased accessibility of the collection to patrons may result in a greater number of subscribing libraries and greater access to the CIHM collection of materials.

The cost to patrons of using information is the opportunity cost of their time spent in acquiring and consuming it. The value of access to information by patrons is reflected in the demand for using the database.

In theory if the user has a cost of time of $10 per use of a manuscript in a rare books library, he may only use the manuscript 5 times a month. If the patron's opportunity cost of time spent consuming the information decreases, then use will increase.

Microfiche is easier and takes less effort to use than books in a rare book library. Microfiche delivery by library staff takes less time than retrieval of a rare book. Once a patron understands how to use a microfiche reader, he can view several books with relative ease. In addition, patrons do not have to travel to another library to view early Canadiana texts if their library holds the entire CIHM collection on microfiche. If we assume that the cost to a patron of accessing an Early Canadiana text on microfiche is $5, then patron use of the microfiche will increase to 30 times a month.

Finally, digital access lowers the opportunity cost of access to the information even further. Digital access enables patrons to view the information from their personal computer in their home or office, or from a computer terminal in the library. Instant access to a large collection of images from the CIHM collection means faster, searchable access to the images.

To patrons, the time savings from digital access has two parts. First, there is the value to patrons of lower cost access to images they would have traveled to the library to view on microfiche. If a patron would have used microfiche 30 times a month at a cost of $5 per use, and this cost declines to $2 per use in digital form, then this patron has a $3 lower cost of access for 30 uses, or has decreased his cost by $90 a month. Second, there are additional uses of digital access that provide additional benefits to patrons. These additional uses can be assigned an average value of $1.50 each, or one-half of the value of lower cost access to the first 30 uses a month. If use increases to 50, the additional 20 uses per month would provide a benefit to this patron of roughly $30. The total value to this patron would be $120; the $90 in lower costs plus the additional $30 in benefit from an increase in access.

During this Early Canadiana Online (ECO) project, patron use of the print, fiche, and digital collection was observed. Patrons were also asked questions about their use and travel time to the library. Annual use of the collection at the University of Toronto and Laval University increased from 2984 for print and microfiche to an estimated 7030 uses of the digital texts. Travel time to the library for print and microfiche patrons varied from less than 30 minutes to more than one day, with 90 percent of patrons needing one hour or less. If we assume that digital access saves print and microfiche patrons 30 minutes of travel time and that the value of this time is $10 per hour, then the annual economic savings of increasing uses from 2984 to 7030 equals $25,035. This represents a lower-end estimate of the savings from accessing the CIHM collection online versus traveling to the library to use the microfiche or print. Some patrons are likely to save more than 30 minutes of travel time. Other patrons are likely to have an opportunity cost of time greater than $10 per hour. Most significantly, use of the Early Canadiana Online collection is likely to increase as more scholars and students are made aware of it.

Digital information provides greater access to information at a lower cost. However, funding the production, archiving, and access to the information requires creative financing, including value based pricing of information as well as the solicitation of grants and donations. Information production and access comes at a cost. An accurate measurement of the full economic costs of different methods of information delivery is essential in determining the most cost-effective method. The lower cost of digital production will continue to result in more information products appearing in digital format on the Internet.

References

Bertot, John C., "Libraries and Networked Information Services: Issues and Considerations in Measurement." *Performance Measurement and Metrics*, 2004.

Bishop, Ann Peterson. "Document Structure and Digital Libraries: How Researchers Mobilize Information in Journal Articles." *Information Processing and Management* 35 May 1999.

Schwartz, Candy. "Digital Libraries: An Overview." *The Journal of Academic Librarianship* 26, November 2000.

Shiri, Ali. "Digital Library Research: Current Developments and Trends." *Library Review* 52, no. 5, 2003.

Smith, Abby. *Strategies for Building Digitized Collections*. Washington, DC: Digital Library Federation, Council on Library and Information Resources, 2001.

7

Challenges of Online Cataloguing

The Library of Congress have identified many challenges that must be met if large and effective digital libraries are to be created during the 21st century. In some cases, there may be no technology solution to the challenge, but through sharing of ideas, new thinking may emerge to help institutions such as the Library of Congress formulate policy on these important issues. The challenges may be grouped under the following broad categories building the resource, interoperability, intellectual property, providing effective access, and sustaining the resource. The Library hopes that creative and innovative minds can devise solutions to these challenges.

Building the Resource

In order to build a comprehensive resource, historical materials now in analog form (e.g., books, journals, laboratory records, sound recordings, manuscripts, photographs) must be converted. Today, the technology for digital conversion is, at best, emergent and often forces a library to choose between risking damage to precious originals or producing the highest quality reproductions. There are few established standards or best practices and a shortage of tools for the objective measurement of reproduction quality. There is a need for more automated support for capturing in explicit data structures the navigational and organizational clues implicit in printed works through page numbers, tables of contents, and indices.

Providing access to library collections is labor-intensive. In order to apply scarce resources to the digitization of significant quantities of content, it is often necessary to reduce the level of detail offered in accompanying catalogues or indexes. Can automated tools permit the incorporation of factual knowledge (e.g., France is in Europe; Leontyne Price is an opera singer.) into descriptive information, indexing, or search and retrieval systems? Could such bodies of factual knowledge be shared or assembled cooperatively and distributed?

Can the digital library take advantage of distributed expertise? Among millions of users, there will be those who can enhance the description or cataloguing of an item, thus improving the next researcher's chance of finding it. Collaborative tools could allow far-flung professional colleagues, e.g., faculty or graduate students in the nation's universities, to provide excellent enhancements to materials they employ for their own advanced research. Less expert users (schoolchildren familiar with buildings in photographs, or individuals who recognize a family member in a group picture) can also add value to the resource. What filters, methods for attributing enhancements without violating privacy, or other protections against misuse could support this enhancement of the resource?

Interoperability

How can a distributed resource like the National Digital Library be assembled to create a virtual unity? What types of protocols and what degree of standardization on types of digital objects will achieve a balance between feasibility of widespread implementation and coherence of access? Should unified searching use an approach like that found in the Z39.50 standard (distributed search) or the approach used by World Wide Web search engines (distributed indexing)? How can distributed digital libraries best safeguard the rights associated with content (including rights of privacy and conditions imposed by donors as well as copyright) while still providing the broadest possible access?

Intellectual Property

A key element for digital libraries is appropriate recognition and protection of legal rights such as copyright, publicity, privacy, matters of obscenity, defamation intellectual property protection as well as less legalistic but serious concerns associated with the ethics of sharing or providing access to folk or ethnographic materials. The vision for digital libraries includes fluid, easy access to a wide variety of materials. This is often in conflict with the duties of libraries and archives entrusted with care and management of materials that may be subject to privacy rights or other needs for security.

Efforts to formulate digital libraries will be delayed or frustrated in the absence of a common, responsible framework of rights, permissions, and restrictions that acknowledges the mutual needs of rights-holders and users of materials in digital libraries. The challenge here is, in part, to develop mechanisms, perhaps social expectations independently or in combination with technical means, regarding acceptable levels of access (for example where privacy rights are at issue) and use (such as the extent or permissible copying and dissemination). Could responsible practices include acceptable use policies, codes of practice, and standard contracts that begin to establish norms of behavior by people creating and using digital library resources? How can authors, creators, researchers, publishers (who may require some control over how the information is made available or used) and digital libraries develop reasonably administrable means to maintain appropriate stewardship without focusing only on work in the public domain (or items not otherwise subject to legal protection)?

Materials currently available on the Internet from the American Memory collections range from items for which the Library is unaware of any copyright or other legal concerns to items where permission was sought from copyright or other rights' holders for inclusion in the Library's website. American Memory materials also encompass a wide range of media such as printed text, photographs, prints, sound recordings, and film. Applicants are encouraged to explore the more technical challenges in the context of the legal concerns and should carefully consider the "access statements" as well as the Copyright and Restriction Statements on the American Memory homepage and on most collection homepages. Note that the Library cannot provide legal advice to applicants regarding the contents of the collections beyond these statements.

Effective Access

A user looking for an item in a library catalogue should be able to identify it without regard to whether it is available in its original physical form or as a digital or microfilm reproduction. Intellectual descriptions of originals and reproductions should be presented in a fully integrated way. During the current experimental period, however, many digitization efforts are disconnected from traditional library services. Even when appropriate catalogue records exist, digital content may fail to connect to potential users because individual items in digital collections can not be retrieved directly or are not identified appropriately to support links from traditional catalogues or bibliographic indexes.

A digital library that provides diverse content will be characterized by heterogeneity in original format, in digital format and resolution, and in the level of detail and format of descriptive information that is available to support access. This heterogeneity may be seen in the historical collections on-line at the Library of Congress, which typify the larger class of materials that are likely to form part of any digital library, however defined. The National Digital Library Program offering includes books, articles, pamphlets, personal papers, legislative documents, prints, architectural drawings, photographs, maps, sheet music, sound recordings, and movies. Some text materials have been re-keyed and marked up in Standard Generalized Markup Language (SGML), some have been captured as bit-mapped images, and some are available in both forms. Pictorial images have been captured at various spatial and tonal resolutions. Some collections have detailed catalogues or indexes, while others are described in brief and superficial ways. The Library of Congress is building a generic repository that can store objects in any format, and represent relationships between objects, such as a sequence of page-images forming a book, which might also have been transcribed and marked up in SGML.

In the face of great diversity of content and description, special problems attend to the development of a coherent approach to indexing and presenting retrieval results. It is important that any approach allow all the information available to be used to aid retrieval rather than force the user who wants to search across the entire resource to rely on some lowest common denominator of descriptive information.

How many different ways can users explore and discover content? What capabilities will permit users to customize the interface and specify preferences that affect retrieval results? Will teachers benefit from tools that support group projects or collaboration with colleagues? By whom might these tools be developed? How can differences in vocabulary be resolved? For example, how might an interface translate the search terms selected by today's users into the language of older historical documents? How might the vocabulary of, say, teachers looking for material to illustrate broad topics in a prescribed curriculum be mapped to the vocabulary of the cataloguers who describe individual items?

Today, each content item in most digital libraries is represented in multiple forms or versions. The multiple forms exist to serve varieties of users, function as archival masters, and reduce download time and transmission loads on networks. A content provider may produce large and small versions of images; compressed and uncompressed versions of images, texts, audio, and video; texts formatted for browser software and also formatted for preservation or publication; and materials both in proprietary formats and in public or "open" formats. This burden of plural production and maintenance results from the fact that today many digital objects are hard to transform on the fly. What technologies can be developed to make digital objects malleable, migrate-able, and transformable? Similar capabilities are also needed to ensure the preserving of digital content for posterity.

Sustaining the Resource

The creation and maintenance of digital libraries is very expensive. Costs are incurred for production, for ongoing provision of access, and for preservation of the digital information. The cost to develop and operate a distributed architecture for long-term archiving, migration, and backup of digital materials will be high. Since the resource is distributed among providers, the net cost tends to be disguised. Libraries would benefit from better estimates of costs and trends in cost for production and maintenance of a corpus of digital information.

Issues in Serials Cataloguing

Serials are an essential and integral component of every major research library collection because the information they contain reflects the most current developments in all fields of activity. The basic nature of the serials publishing process insures that their "sequential products" are distributed in a timely fashion; timeless is fundamental to their relevance. It logically follows that efficient processing of these materials is key to providing the necessary timely access to them.

Cataloguing rules set only three basic criteria of a serial publication:

— it is issued in parts;

— each part carries a number or date that uniquely identifies it;

— the publication is intended to continue indefinitely.

Within these basic requirements one finds material that differs as widely as one can imagine. Many government documents are issued serially and contain unique information that only such an agency could develop (e.g., CIA reports). On the other extreme one finds more ephemeral material that is generated by individuals with desktop publishing capabilities (e.g., family-specific genealogical information). From annual reports to car repair manuals, the serials catalogue typically handles a great variety of material that presents numerous challenges and also leads to an exposure to a wide body of knowledge.

Recent history only reinforces the significance of serial publications. The price explosion of scholarly journals in the 1980s forced libraries to reevaluate their collections and to economize. The public outcry that followed reductions in serials' subscriptions only underscored the basic value of the literature. Some libraries were compelled to cooperate more with other libraries in their region, to identify their singular and collective strengths, and to focus their acquisitions policies accordingly.

Most recently we have seen several new technologies dramatically affect the serials publishing industry. Various types of electronic publications and computer formats have presented new challenges to serials cataloguing. The same technologies offer new capabilities to researchers that were barely imagined ten years ago. Some serial titles are not available exclusively through telefax distribution or an online system. CD-ROM products and other "computer-form" serials defy our understanding of the basic characteristics of serials. As publishers continue to use emerging technologies we find our field of librarianship confronted with providing the best and most timely access to these materials.

Serials are different. They don't always look or behave like other types of publications. Here are some of the characteristics of serials that distinguish them from monographic publications.

— They have a remarkable propensity for change.

— Serials are issued on a continuing basis, often with a regular frequency.

— Many serials do not have a title page. Instead, the title is found on the cover or at the beginning of the text. This is particularly the case with periodicals (magazines, journals, etc.) and newsletters.

— Serials have designations—numbers or dates or combinations of both that distinguish the individual issues.

— Serials do not usually have personal authors. Most persons associated with serials are editors or compilers. Serials are more often the work of one or more corporate bodies that have "issued" the serial.

— Serials titles are often given in more than one place in the issue and sometimes in different forms.

— Serials are often related to other serials—as earlier or later titles, companions, sections, language editions, translations, etc. Serials may also be related to monographs.

— Serials may have supplements, indexes, reprints, or special issues or may, themselves, be a supplement, index, reprint, or special issue.

— Because serials are issued continuously, the information presented on them may change. Such changes may be in the title, issuing body, form of numbering, frequency, size and physical appearance, or just about anywhere else.

— How cataloguing a serial differs from cataloguing a monograph

Successive Entry Cataloguing

A new record is created each time the title changes or the corporate body used as main entry changes. This is called "successive entry cataloguing." Each successive entry record contains information relevant only to the span of issues covered by that record. The relationship of successive entry records is shown through linking entry fields. The record for the "dead" serial is "closed off"—i.e., data elements are added or changed in the record to show that the title is no longer current.

Description Based on the First or Earliest Piece

Serials consist of a succession of issues, but the basic description of the serial is created from one issue. The primary difference between *AACR2* and earlier rules is that under *AACR2* the description is based on the first or the earliest available issue. Every *AACR2* serial record must indicate the issue upon which the description is based, either in area 3 or in a note. Once a serial is described from the first issue, the "body of the entry " is not changed (except when closing off the record for a "dead" title). An indication of changes appearing on later issues, that do not require a new record, is given in the notes, as appropriate. Serials described from issues other than the first, however, may be "backed up" when the first piece is available.

Designations

In citing the issue upon which the description is based, the cataloguers also describes the designation system as it is given on the serial. The designation may be numerical (volumes, numbers, etc.), chronological (dates), or a combination of the two. Occasionally letters are used. Designations are essential to serials because they provide the only means for distinguishing the individual issue of the serial.

Uniform Titles

Because so many serials are entered under title according to *AACR2*, a mechanism for distinguishing serials with the same title was devised shortly after the adoption of the code. When two different serials have the same title, a "uniform title " is assigned consisting of the title proper and a qualifier.

Linking Entry Fields

Serials are often part of "family" relationships. They may have parents (earlier titles), children (later titles), siblings (other editions, splits, etc.), and cousins (other related works). *AACR2* specifies that these relationships be mentioned in notes. The USMARC-defined linking entry fields may provide such notes, when desired, as well as linking the related records in a database.

In general, information contained in serial records must be broad enough to pertain to the span of issues covered by each successive entry record or a subset of those issues. This is perhaps the most difficult concept for an experienced monograph cataloguers to grasp. Information that is specific to a single issue is usually omitted because it does not relate to the serial as a whole. For example, dates and numbers that represent the issue are dropped from the title statement, titles specific to one issue are omitted, and so forth. When information is given that relates to certain issues but not all, dates are given to indicate the span of issues to which the information pertains. Such dates are most often given with notes.

Serial vs. Monograph Cataloguing

When a title is catalogued as a serial, all issues are represented by one record—at least until the title changes. If successive issues are received, they can be checked-in and added to the shelf without further cataloguing. Other types of records (e.g., check-in records) are also created. If nothing else is received (i.e., the publication is really a monograph), nothing need be changed. Just think of it as a "dead" serial!

When a publication is catalogued as a monograph, however, and turns out to be a serial, the monograph records have to be canceled and the publication recatalogued as a serial. On the other hand, treatment as a monograph is preferable when it appears that each issue will have a different title. If separate records are going to have to be made for each issue due to constant title changes, it is more economical to catalogue as a monograph because the records do not have to be linked nor do check-in records or union list records need to be created.

Treatment as a serial assures that all issues will have the same call number and will be kept together on the shelf. Usually the title will also be accessible in sources other than the catalogue, such as union lists, check-in files, and so forth. The cataloguing record, however, will be less complete than individual monograph records would be, since one entry must serve for all uses. If there is important information that is specific to each issue, treatment as a monograph may be preferable. This is often case for monographic series whose individual titles may require separate subject headings and classification numbers to provide the appropriate level of access.

Organisation of Documents

The question whether a document collection not subject to security measures can be most effectively used where it is kept together and administered as a unit, or, on the other hand, where its contents are classed with unofficial works dealing with the same subject, has never been fully answered. In the area of United States government publications, this matter was discussed with inconclusive results in a group of four papers presented at a meeting of the Public Documents Committee of the American Library Association in the summer of 1950.

Since the records of a document collection maintained as a unit are relatively uncomplicated, the difficulties of its organisation inhere chiefly in devising a classification scheme sufficiently flexible to accommodate the publications of issuing bodies on various levels, and representing more than one government or international organisation. In 1952 such a system, purely alphabetic in plan, based entirely on standard corporate author headings, using a notation consisting of several Cutter numbers for each item, and compounded to express the alphabetic arrangement, was put into successful operation in the library of the University of New Mexico.

The organisation, administration, and use of document collections kept together as units and consisting of the publications of more than one government have been outlined and discussed in monographs by Anne E. Markley and Ellen Jackson. Both have emphasised the current tendencies toward the limited cataloguing of such collections and the use of existing bibliographies to implement the necessary control records. Earlier discussions of these trends are to be found in papers sponsored by the Public Documents Committee of the American Library Association in 1950.

In the postwar era two groups of documents have been brought forcibly to the attention of the library world. They are those commonly known as technical research reports and those pertaining to the work of international governmental organisations. The contents of these documents, the conditions of their use, and in some instances their actual physical form, have often made it expedient, if not actually obligatory, to maintain them in collections entirely distinct from the other holdings of the libraries possessing them.

Of technical research reports it is said "A new and important body of technical literature is arising parallel to an existing body in the fields of science and engineering. This new literature is largely separate because of mode of origin and security restrictions, and much of it has not yet been absorbed into university libraries." The maintenance of adequate records and control procedures on security classified reports is an operational problem of the greatest importance. The bibliographical services for the collection and dissemination of information on technical and scientific research in the United States have been substantially strengthened and increased in recent years through the efforts of agencies within the federal government.

The trends in the acquisition, processing, and reference use of report literature were sufficiently evident in 1952 to make welcome the sessions of an Institute on the Administration and Use of Technical Research Reports of the Science-Technology Division of the Special Libraries Association in New York in May of that year.

The limiting of the use of most report literature to a necessarily restricted clientele has made its organisation in collections the preoccupation of a relatively small group of librarians. The reverse is true of the unrestricted documents and publications of the United Nations and its specialised agencies, the distribution of which is on a worldwide basis.

The need for bibliographical controls over the documentation of the United Nations was recognised by the Organisation at a very early stage. The interest was intensified because the League of Nations had never established such controls except through the catalogues of sales publications. Although perfected by Marie J. Carroll, these still are incomplete as a bibliographical aid, since the voluminous League documentation not intended for sales purposes is omitted.

The need for means whereby United Nations documents could be acquired and organised effectively was also expressed by outside institutions and groups. During 1947 three conferences devoted to the distribution of documentary material were held in New York at the Woodrow Wilson Foundation, under the sponsorship of the Carnegie Endowment for International Peace and the World Peace Foundation. Matters relating to documents of the United Nations and specialised agencies were discussed at each of the meetings. In 1948, during the sessions of the United Nations Third General Assembly in Paris, a conference attended by delegates from ten European countries, together with officials of the United Nations, was held at the Paris office of the Carnegie Endowment for International Peace. At that session a series of recommendations on the distribution of United Nations documents and about their servicing and bibliographical implications was formulated."

In the years named and those following, persons having access to the complete documentation of the United Nations were making every effort to provide bibliographical and other aids to implement it both retrospectively and currently. The first major tangible result is the check list of United Nations documents undertaken by the United Nations Library in 1948. The first four fascicles were published in 1949. The project involves a retrospective bibliography by organs and sessions, covering the years 1946 to 1949, inclusive. At the time of writing seventeen sections of this series have been published. When completed the entire project will contain nineteen parts in thirty-three fascicles. The *United Nations Documents Index,* published monthly since 1950, lists, describes, and indexes by subjects all of the unrestricted documents and publications of the specialised agencies received in the United Nations Library.

In 1951, on the basis of experience, the United Nations Library found itself in a position to give constructive advice as to the most effective and economical means whereby the documents of the Organisation could be of the maximum use where they were assembled in a separate collection. This was done in the form of papers written by Fernando Caballero-Marsal, Harry N. M. Winton, and Jorgen K. Nielsen, three members of the library staff. One year later, in 1952, Carol C. Moor and Waldo Chamberlin of New York University issued their manual on the use of United Nations documents by research scholars and librarians having charge of full collections. Its most valuable feature is a bibliography containing references to complete works and periodical articles, intended to orient and guide those concerned with the organisation and reference use of documents in the international field.

While it is true that a considerable number of libraries throughout the world find need for full sets of unrestricted United Nations documents and publications, as well as those of the specialised agencies, there also is a group of institutions desiring to acquire such material on a highly selective basis. In many instances it is their practice to add the publications to already established collections of official and non-official works.

In the spring of 1953 the United Nations Library and the Library of Congress initiated together an enterprise whereby the former will select United Nations printed and processed documents and publications in all language versions that are believed to be of substantial and lasting interest, and the latter will catalogue the materials promptly and will sell the printed cards at the usual card prices. Such a service should assist those interested in acquiring materials from the United Nations on a basis of selectivity, and at the same time "will provide many libraries with an economical solution to the problem of cataloguing essential UN documents."

Issues in Cataloguing Non-book Resources

Non-book resources include material such as microfilms, microfiches, dissertations, posters, reports, slides, stamps, photos, maps, postcards, brochures, computer software, audio books, and other audio visual works. In the world of collection development, the acquisition of non-book materials is bringing more complexities to the process. When considering such materials for circulation, librarians must become familiar with a variety of issues as well as be prepared to explain them to an increasing number of curious patrons.

The pressure for organising nonbook materials has come with the development of large collections of such materials. When a catalogue is needed, rules for it inevitably are developed. The formulation of rules by individual libraries is the first step, and gradually uniform or commonly acceptable operations are incorporated into codes. This evolution is observable in tracing the history, growth, and trends in the cataloguing and classification of nonbook items, and specifically of archives, manuscripts, and audiovisual materials. The last-named are considered as including maps, pictures, phonorecords, and motion pictures. Excluded from this discussion are micro reproductions of printed matter, since, with relatively minor additions to provide for physical form, the rules for cataloguing books can be applied to them.

The terms "archives" and "manuscripts" mean different things to different people. Some maintain that "archives" should refer only to records of government agencies, and others that it should comprise those of societies, churches, universities, business firms, and even individuals, thus limiting the term "manuscripts" to one or more unrelated documents, historical or modern. A broader concept of "manuscript" is included in the Historical Records Survey's definition of it as "a handwritten or typed document (including letterpress and carbon copies) or a photographic reproduction of such a document."

In the nineteenth century and the early part of the twentieth, responsibility for preservation of archives and manuscripts in this country was largely assumed by historical societies and a few state and large research libraries. During this period greater emphasis was placed upon collecting and protecting them than upon organising them for use. The Public Archives Commission of the American Historical Association, established in 1899, was instrumental in bringing about significant legislation leading to the preservation and custody of state archival collections. The work of the Historical Records Survey stimulated interest in the guarding of public and private records.

Whether collections of private records are categorised as archives or manuscripts, the technique of cataloguing them is similar to that for public records. In both cases, it treats the files of an agency as a group and employs such finding media as check lists, inventories, indexes, calendars, and to a lesser extent card catalogues, and maintains the integrity of the original arrangement whenever possible. The chief difference is that certain additions are necessary for public records, because they are interrelated and complex, whereas private ones arc made up of unrelated series. The cataloguing of single documents, such as letters, or the analysing of isolated documents, likewise is similar. Where possible the cataloguing of a single manuscript follows the rules and principles for printed books.

Although the fourth edition of C. A. Cutter's *Rules for a Dictionary Catalogue* contains a section on the cataloguing of both private and public manuscripts, prepared by Worthington Ford, the first systematic handbook was J. C. Fitzpatrick's *Notes on the Care, Cataloguing, Calendaring and Arranging of Manuscripts,* issued by the Library of Congress in 1913 and appearing in a third edition in 1928. In this work the author warns that the first handling of a mass of manuscripts is often crucial, since it reveals hints of value in the final archival plan and the dating and identifying of the miscellany of the collection. Chronological arrangement within groups is recommended.

In 1936 a useful handbook on the care of manuscripts was issued by the Minnesota Historical Society, setting forth the treatment of materials in its collection. In that library manuscripts are divided into nine main groups, as follows;

1. Personal papers;
2. Records of organisations;
3. Miscellaneous records;
4. Transcripts and photo-static copies;
5. Calendars and field reports;
6. Secondary material;
7. Broadsides;
8. Autographs; and
9. Manuscript maps.

The arrangement of each group varies. Catalogue cards are made for each collection, and calendar cards for personal papers. Later accounts of this collection have appeared in professional literature.

About the same time, the Historical Records Survey, originally established in 1935 to survey local public records, produced manuals of instruction on the preparation of guides, inventories, and calendars which also serve as helpful aids to the cataloguing and classifying of manuscripts.

When the H.R.S. was abolished, in 1942, more than 1,200 inventories, calendars, transcripts, and other publications had been issued."

The opinions concerning the treatment of manuscripts differ considerably. Calendars, for example, are thought by some to be desirable only in exceptional cases. Certain librarians have preferred printed guides, rather than detailed card catalogues or calendars. Chronological arrangement within a collection appears essential for easy use.

Although references to individual library procedures have been largely omitted from this review, since they are available in *Library Literature,* mention should be made of Harvard's recent approach. When the Manuscripts Department was created there in 1948 it was found that manuscripts catalogued before 1940 were treated according to a variety of methods, while those acquired after 1940 were listed but not catalogued. Since the old catalogues could not be consolidated, it was decided to start a new one. In it descriptions of the collections are expressed in simplest terms, in the belief that the reader will prefer to be guided to, not told all about, the materials. The original arrangement by linguistic and geographic areas has been retained, but some new categories, such as music and graphic arts, have been added. Within each class, arrangement is by serial number.

The Library of Congress has been currently engaged in drafting tentative rules for the cataloguing of single manuscripts and manuscript collections. These have been sent out for criticism, and when in final form will be submitted to the A.LA. Division of Cataloguing and Classification for its approval. In England, J. L. Hobbs has recommended that manuscript cataloguing conform as closely as possible to the Anglo-American code.

European interest in archival control is older than American. In the discussion of classification and arrangement of archives at the first meeting of the Conference of Archivists called by the Public Archives Commission in 1909, it was advocated that the principle of *respect des fonds,* or *principe de la provenance,* be observed. Prior to the nineteenth century the materials in European archives were arranged in accordance with some predetermined scheme of subject matter. When the principle of *respect des fonds* was adopted in France in 1841, the records of each political unit or *fond* were thereafter to be segregated, but those of the agencies within each political unit were to be arranged by subject. In 1874 the Prussians went further providing that not only records of each political division but also those of each subordinate one were to be kept separate. The extension of *respect des fonds* has come to be known as *Provenienzprinzip* or principle of provenance. Within each agency the "original organisation" given to its records in the registry office is to be maintained, under the principle known as *Registraturprinzip.* Such methods were immediately accepted in the Netherlands and given theoretical justification in a manual issued by three Dutch archivists—Muller, Feith, and Fruin—which became the modern archivists' bible. A translation into English of the second edition was published in 1940. The principle developed by the Prussian and Dutch archivists appears to have mainly an academic interest for American archivists, since public records in the United States are not organised by registry offices before being transferred to the National Archives.

In 1936 tentative catalogue rules of the Archives Division of the Illinois State Library, representing the result of several years' experimentation in adapting Library of Congress rules to the cataloguing of archives, were issued. The types of records made were an inventory shelf list on sheets, a dictionary catalogue on cards, and a name index. Calendars were made for each volume or unit but not for each piece. In actual practice, however, it was found that subject reference to classification groups was more useful.

Perhaps the most important single event in American archival history was the establishment of the National Archives in 1934. This created problems in archival organisation on a large scale. In a paper on cataloguing at the National Archives, J. R. Russell described the card catalogue, which was planned as a guide to groups of records and not to single pieces, and made with main entry under the name of the agency whose archives were listed. According to him the catalogue card resembled in form that for printed books, and a card list of subject headings was started. Accession cataloguing was the first step; division cataloguing or series cataloguing, the second. Division cataloguing grouped all records of a government subdivision together. The items were given series cataloguing rather than division cataloguing if the division contained documents on a variety of subjects.

R. R. Hill, writing about classification at the National Archives, observed that it was still in the experimental stage, there being no precedents of sufficiently universal application to offer guidance. He indicated that the practice for European archives was kept in mind and its limitations recognised. The classification reflects the government organisation, though the picture cannot be complete because of governmental changes. The steps in classifying archives are an examination of the materials, a study of the history of the agency and of its records, and a determination and analysis of each unit. The basic unit of classification is a group or series of records.

It was decided at the National Archives in 1940 that the card catalogue was not a useful finding medium and it was therefore discontinued. The Catalogue Division then devoted its time to the preparation of indexes to records. In 1941 a new program of finding media was begun. The work of preparing them was transferred to the custodial divisions, and the divisions of cataloguing and classification were abolished.

The Committee on Archives and Libraries established by the A.L.A, in 1937 arranged programs on archives at annual conferences from 1937 to 1940. Papers on cataloguing and classification were presented, and are available in the published proceedings of the sessions. It was brought out that a manual of cataloguing and classification for archives was needed, but that more experience in the handling of such records was necessary before a standard handbook could be compiled.

A recent development in archival work is concern for records management, with a view to eliminating unnecessary record-making and filing of papers. Articles on this subject by E. T. Leahy and Helen Chatfield appeared in 1949 and 1950. A comprehensive program for the management of federal records was authorised by the Federal Property and Administration Services Act of 1949. It established the National Archives and Records Service under the newly created General Services Administration to administer the National Archives and a Records Management Division.

Another recent development is the inauguration of training courses for archives administration. The first of these was given at Columbia University in 1938/39. Courses have been offered since at other institutions.

Management of Catalogued Collections

The prime duty of all libraries is to incorporate of books and other materials into a library's catalogued collections in such a fashion that the reader may readily ascertain what the library's holdings are and get hold efficiently of the particular item he wants to use. Classifying, shelf-listing, descriptive cataloguing, and subject cataloguing are the principal processes involved in accomplishing this function. In libraries these duties are assigned to a catalogue department, although it is frequently made responsible also for certain others more or less closely related to these major functions.

Because of the number and diversity of the elements on which organisation of cataloguing work may be based, the pattern of individual departments is usually complex. Among these elements the following are considered to be especially important: function, subject, language, form or type of material, degree of difficulty of material, and level of treatment to be accorded various categories of material. Theoretically, the organisation of work in catalogue departments along strictly functional lines seems both natural and logical. Yet few departments have set up separate divisions for classifying, descriptive cataloguing, and subject cataloguing. A stronger preference has been shown for a scheme whereby one group does the descriptive cataloguing and a second the classifying and subject cataloguing, the logic for combining the latter two processes being that both require subject analysis. But in most libraries each cataloguer performs all three of the basic operations, and the organisation patterns in their catalogue departments therefore follow other lines.

Particularly in libraries where organisation of readers' services by subject fields is emphasised, for example, in public and university libraries set up on the subject-divisional plan, and in university libraries with college and departmental libraries serving special subject areas, the division of work in catalogue departments is likely to be primarily according to subject. The important advantage this kind of organisation holds over one developed along functional lines is that, since it involves most, if not all, of the cataloguing staff, a higher degree of subject specialisation can be achieved than in a special subject cataloguing unit made up of a relatively small number of workers. Although there appears to be no common agreement as to the level in the departmental structure where subject specialisation should occur, the importance of making definite provision for it is increasingly recognised. Not only have library survey reports generally urged the management of cataloguing with reference to subject, but reorganisation plans of catalogue departments indicate that more libraries are accepting the idea.

The outstanding example illustrating this trend is the reorganised Preparation Division in the Reference Department of the New York Public Library, which, prior to a survey by a firm of management engineers, had been set up primarily around form of material. The Preparation Division now is divided into a Cataloguing Branch and a Preparation Branch. On the recommendation of the surveyors, the Cataloguing Branch was organised around subjects rather than forms of material. According to R. E. Kingery, Chief of the Preparation Division, the recommendation was based on the view "that the cataloguing job is a whole job of planning approaches between a piece of material and its potential users, that the job should not be broken up as it had been on the basis of subject analysis vs. description, and that the significant differences among materials, in terms of use, lie in differences in subject and not differences of form." In line with this theory, Kingery reports, cataloguers now handle materials within a subject area "regardless of form of material, and... do the whole job of catalogue planning for that material, including subject analysis and description."

Libraries acquiring much material in foreign languages must have on their staffs cataloguers with a knowledge of these languages. Some catalogue departments set up special units to handle all foreign publications. Both the Chicago Public Library and the Los Angeles Public Library have such units in their catalogue departments, and the Descriptive Cataloguing Division of the Library of Congress contains a Foreign Language Section and a Slavic Language Section.

Although in the cataloguing of foreign materials language facility is more useful than subject specialisation, in the catalogue departments of university libraries the formal unit for cataloguing all foreign language publications is the exception rather than the rule. The explanation may be that in these libraries, where increasing emphasis is given to subject specialisation, cataloguers generally have a working knowledge of two or more of the principal foreign languages and so can handle the bulk of such material without particular difficulty. Moreover, they may go to a language specialist of the department for assistance whenever necessary. The cataloguing of most materials in the minor or dead languages, however, is usually assigned to cataloguers with the special language facilities required.

With respect to form or type of library materials, the organisational structure of catalogue departments most commonly includes a special unit for the cataloguing of serials. The fact that in the larger departments the serial cataloguing section is commonly one of the principal units is due both to the phenomenal growth in importance and mass of serial publications, and to realisation that the physical and bibliographical peculiarities of serials make specialisation with them sound administrative practice.

The use of the degree of difficulty of material as an element in determining basic organisation of cataloguing work is excellently demonstrated by the reorganisation some years ago of the catalogue department of the Harvard College Library. In this department, Susan M. Haskins reports, the staff was organised into two major groups. One handles material which can move along rapidly, such as titles for which Library of Congress cards are available, nonfiction which presents no special difficulties, other editions, second copies, and books which are to be sent directly to the New England Depository Library. The other group catalogues the more difficult material involving research problems, unusual languages, and so forth. The second group only is organised along the traditional lines of subject and language.

Manifestly the many and varied publications which flow into libraries are not all equal in value or importance, and therefore need not all receive equal treatment. Hence the level of treatment to be accorded certain categories of library materials is an additional element influencing the organisational patterns of catalogue departments. For example, a special unit may be made responsible for the processing of pamphlets and similar ephemera, and another for the cataloguing of rare books and manuscripts. The developing trend for applying brief or limited cataloguing techniques to older and less important publications has resulted in the creation in some catalogue departments of special units to handle such materials.

Traditionally, much importance has been attached in libraries to the value of accuracy and consistency in cataloguing records. To attain these twin objectives, it has been the policy in many catalogue departments to revise in detail the work of even experienced cataloguers. Approaching their work conscientiously, the catalogue revisers spent much time covering the same ground as the cataloguer and correcting minor errors which might have been rectified more cheaply by proofreaders. Forced by the economic exigencies of the times to scrutinize the effects of these practices on cataloguing costs and the flow of material through the department, library administrators came to the conclusion that, all things considered, the premium they were paying for accuracy and consistency was too high and that, in the interests of economy and efficiency, a major shift in emphasis was necessary. This has been accomplished in many catalogue departments:

1. By depending on proofreaders to discover and correct minor errors,
2. By revising closely only the work of the less experienced personnel,

3. By letting cataloguers take the initiative in consulting revisers when their help was needed and in this way placing more responsibility for good work on those doing the original cataloguing, and
4. By limiting such overall revision as remains necessary to a quick examination of entries, classification, and subject headings.

This policy has been followed for some years in the Catalogue Department of the University of Illinois Library, and is very similar to the scheme advanced by the surveyors of the Los Angeles Public Library in conjunction with their proposal for the reorganisation of the cataloguers into subject units under the supervision of senior cataloguers.

Administrators of catalogue departments have long recognised the importance of differentiating clearly between professional and clerical duties for the purposes of efficient management. However, despite the increasing attention given in libraries to job analysis and position classification, the evidence shows that in many catalogue departments the lines between professional and clerical processes have not yet been sharply drawn. Obviously, where this has not been done, all attempts to arrive at defensible ratios of professional to clerical personnel must rest on guesswork.

Some notion of the size and nature of this problem may be gained from the data presented in the 1951 survey of personnel in catalogue departments in public libraries which was conducted by a committee of the American Library Association Division of Cataloguing and Classifications. According to the answers supplied by 108 libraries, only two of the duties defined as professional were not also performed by nonprofessional workers, and 5 per cent of all duties listed as professional were also performed by nonprofessional personnel. An analysis of the staff involved in the performance of nonprofessional duties in the catalogue departments of 110 public libraries revealed that all nonprofessional operations were carried on by both groups; further, 26 per cent of the answers from these libraries indicated that nonprofessional duties were performed by professional cataloguers. The conclusion that professional personnel is often wastefully employed in catalogue departments is rather obvious. Evidence produced by the survey showing that large libraries experience least difficulty in separating clerical from professional duties is scarcely surprising. Despite the somewhat discouraging picture drawn by these facts, there is considerable evidence in library survey reports, as well as in the published accounts describing reorganisation of work in individual catalogue departments, to indicate that much real progress has been achieved in the past decade in differentiating professional and clerical duties and in making use of clerical personnel for cataloguing operations not requiring professional training.

Accessioning of Books

The accessioning of books is not regarded by all librarians as a logical function of the catalogue department. Actually, in many libraries it is performed in the order department or in a special unit. The formal register of accessions, for so many years looked upon as a basic and essential record for any properly managed library, appears to be on the way out. In fact, quite a few libraries have abandoned both the accession book and the use of accession numbers in the individual books. Others have decided on one of several possible compromises, such as:

1. Adapting other library records, e.g., bills, lists, order cards, or shelflist cards, to serve the purposes of a standard accession record, or
2. Continuing the stamping of accession numbers in the books themselves, thereby preserving their value as a means for positive identification of particular volumes or copies, but without listing books in an accession register nor noting their accession numbers on shelflist cards.

That simplification of accession records and procedures, if not their complete elimination, is a growing trend in libraries, is suggested by the fact that nearly all library surveys have recommended it wherever the surveyors encountered the traditional accession records.

The taking of inventory of the library's book stock by the circulation department and other readers service units can readily be defended on the ground that they have a custodial responsibility for the books shelved in their departments. However, in many libraries this duty is delegated to the catalogue department, presumably because it makes and maintains the shelf list and catalogue and often keeps the accession record, and therefore should withdraw the notations of items established as lost in the inventory process. Moreover, it may be reasoned, the catalogue department is the logical department to correct any errors or discrepancies that may be discovered in the course of inventory.

Particularly in very large libraries, the trend is away from complete periodic inventories, for the simple reason that they no longer can be afforded. In some such libraries formal checking is attempted only in reference and reading rooms and for departmental collections. Larger libraries which have not abandoned the taking of inventories of their central collections, tend to carry them out at longer intervals, rather than annually, or to assign relatively small staffs to carry them on continuously.

One of the most significant recent developments in American librarianship has been the grouping in numerous individual libraries of all services in two divisions, viz., technical services and readers' services. The underlying administrative philosophy aims primarily at reducing the span of control of the top administrator and promoting effective oversight, coordination, and integration of the various services carried on in the organisational units brought together by the change. The services commonly regarded as technical include acquisitions, cataloguing, binding, and photographic reproduction, and the act whereby they are placed in a single large division recognizes the close relationship of their individual functions and the operations involved in performing them.

Costs of Cataloguing

The growing concern of library administrators over mounting cataloguing costs is matched by a similar concern over the problem of cataloguing arrears. The most inclusive definition of cataloguing arrears includes all acquired materials which are to be incorporated in a library's organised collections but are not being processed currently.

It is a truism that a library's acquisitions are limited only by the size of its book fund and its ability to secure materials by gift and exchange. But the flow of accessions often is increased substantially by administrative action and policies. For example, the librarian may succeed in getting a sizeable increase in the regular allowance for books, or he may manage to have the book fund supplemented by special appropriations or monetary donations, or he may promote an active gift and exchange program leading to large gift collections. If, when any of these things happen, he does not provide the additional personnel needed to take care of the increased accumulations, he either creates an arrears problem for the library or makes an existing one worse.

The general tendency to put the blame for uncatalogued arrears on the catalogue department is quite understandable, since getting the libraries acquisitions catalogued is its chief responsibility. Moreover, it cannot hope to escape criticism for being behind in its work unless it has taken all steps necessary to maintain high efficiency. But if, despite good organisation, sound procedures, efficient techniques, and satisfactory morale, a catalogue department is unable to bring its accumulated arrears under control, the solution to the problem must be found in providing more cataloguing personnel or in adopting a more realistic acquisitions program.

The catalogue departments of a number of libraries have experimented with various methods for reducing cataloguing arrears or preventing them. The Division of Cataloguing and Classification devoted a session to consideration of the problem at the 1951 A.L.A. conference. Papers presented at that meeting reported on efforts to deal with arrears at the University of California at Los Angeles, Yale University, the University of Pennsylvania, the Brooklyn Public Library, and the Library of Congress. These papers, as well as a statement on arrears at Colombia University were published in the Fall 1951 issue of the *Journal of Cataloguing and Classification.* In the same year A. D. Osborn reported on the way Harvard had attacked the matter, and a few months later Alice T. Paloney came out with an article telling how the Los Angeles Public Library avoids arrears entirely.

Although tackling a common difficulty, the methods developed by these libraries have varied considerably. A comparison shows differences in the organisation of the material in arrears, in the use of personnel, in the kind of cataloguing treatment given, and in the application of special techniques. The significant thing about these experiments is that they all have proved worth while, some beyond all expectation. In view of the results there can be little doubt that more and more libraries, seeing they cannot hope for sufficient personnel to process arrears by normal cataloguing methods and routines, will use the lessons reported above to deal with their own arrears.

Maintenance of Catalogues

Before the development of card catalogues the problem of catalogue maintenance was comparatively insignificant. With few exceptions libraries were so small that the remedy for an inadequate catalogue was to make a new one. In the Harvard College Library, for example, there were no fewer than thirteen catalogues in succession before the present public and official catalogues were created about 1913. Naturally then, there was no established program of catalogue maintenance to carry over from the nineteenth century, nor was the need of it apparent in the early days of this century. In fact, to some extent it might be said that the very idea of taking steps against obsolescence and of allowing for depreciation was alien to the thoughts of twentieth-century cataloguers who, in the face of all cataloguing history, thought they could make their records with workmanship of so high a quality that these would endure indefinitely.

Not until the present has the necessity for a regular program of catalogue maintenance become apparent. The age, complexity, and size of existing catalogues are the principal factors in bringing about this development, As might be expected, the largest libraries have had to face the problem first and most seriously. Simultaneously, yet independently, the Library of Congress, the New York Public Library, and the libraries of Harvard and Yale Universities all set to work to formulate a plan for the future of their catalogues.

The most ambitious proposal to date is the one at the Library of Congress, which would take over eleven years to carry through and would cost almost $750,000. There the main or public catalogue (incidentally the official catalogue too) would be edited because of:

> ...Unreconciled changes in cataloguing policies, rules, and procedures and imperfections in the adequacy of the maintenance of this catalogue over the years. In addition, heavy use over a long period has taken a toll of some of the cards. There has been no provision of systematically organised guide cards. Filing errors are too frequent. In short, the use of the catalogue by readers and staff alike is continually impeded by conflicts between the cards in the catalogue, by cards with wrong call numbers, by cards with no call numbers, and by cards which are misfiled or missing from the catalogue altogether. Editing the catalogues will not only correct the important respects in which the catalogue is in a rundown condition but will also offer an opportunity to institute methods of counteracting in some degree the increasing difficulty of its use (due to its continual growth) such as simplifications in filing arrangement and the provision of helpful guides to the user where they are most needed. As the trays are edited, it is planned that filing in them in the future will be completely revised in order to prevent the recurrence of the filing error rate which is in excess of 5%.

Business practice generally allows for depreciation of equipment, But libraries have failed in their budgets to provide for the depreciation of their principal tool, the card catalogue. The cumulated effect of this neglect is now making itself felt, as can be seen from studies in several of the largest libraries. Sooner or later institutions of various sizes will have to face the problem squarely too. In an older library with but a single cataloguer the problem may even be disproportionately greater than in the large and middle-sized library, where the budget may be sufficient to allow for extra help when necessary.

Filing

The obvious point at which to attack the problem of catalogue maintenance is filing, for any general review of a catalogue should be undertaken in conjunction with revised filing rules and a complete refilling of all cards, as the Library of Congress has indicated. Simplification in filing are called for because technicalities not readily grasped by readers or staff make consultation of a catalogue difficult and lead to errors in filing. Some of these technicalities derive from the days of the classified catalogue. Under the influence of Charles Ammi Cutter, classified arrangements were introduced into the emerging dictionary catalogue, and the resulting departures from a straight alphabetical arrangement have died hard. The *A.L.A. Rules for Filing Catalogue Cards,* published in 1942, straddled the issue by providing numerous alternative rules and by recommending straight alphabetical arrangement primarily for the smallest libraries only. In truth, it is the largest libraries that require straight alphabetical filing most.

Failure to come to grips with this fundamental issue was undoubtedly a significant factor in the subsequent trend towards division of library catalogues. Automatically, by dividing their catalogues, libraries were able to dispense with many of the classified arrangements. So the filing was simplified. And whenever the filing is simplified, consultation of the catalogue should become easier for readers and staff alike. But even this trend left untouched another basic matter, namely, the contribution that letter-by-letter filing might make towards solving problems of arrangement. American librarians have given scant attention to letter-by-letter filing, which has found some acceptance in Great Britain. Thereby they have lost some theoretical insights which might have resulted from a careful comparison of the word-by-word and the letter-by-letter systems. More particularly, for divided catalogues the letter-by-letter system might have much to offer.

It would be of considerable value if studies existed to show whether the revision of filing is less of a burden under letter-by-letter filing. In theory, it should be; for theoretically letter-by-letter filing should require practically no revision except to catch gross errors due to mistakes by workers. Word-by-word filing adds a plethora of technicalities, so that faults in filing may be due either to the human equation or to a failure to grasp or consistently follow a technicality.

The descriptive cataloguer has quite generally overlooked the need for a clear, unambiguous, and close-knit filing medium. Fortunately most catalogue entries have one naturally, but in any large catalogue tens of thousands of imprecise entries are a constant source of trouble and error. For instance, a wooden entry like the following suggests an autobiography:

> Descartes, Rene, 1596-1650 Descartes.
>
> But what is really meant is either
>
> Descartes, Ren£, 1596-1650
>
> [Works] or
>
> Descartes, Rene, 1596-1650
>
> [Selections]

This type of entry is also fairly common in the field of art, and difficulties naturally ensue. In the Fogg Art Museum at Harvard they have been sidestepped by not considering the artist as the author of a volume of reproductions. In general we have paid attention to the problem of books without authors, but no systematic study has been made of the problems that arise in connection with books without titles. The following represent some of the more obvious types of entry that cannot be filed without interpretation.

Heading	*Actually Filed as*
Bronte	Bronte
De La Mare	Delarnare
Eckhart, Meister	Eckhart
Huntington, A. M., ed.	Huntington, A. M.
Jones, Mrs. Colonel	Jones
New York. Metropolitan Museum of Art	New York City. Metropolitan Museum of Art
Terry, Dame Ellen	Teny, Ellen
Williams, William, called Pant-y-celyn, 1717-91	Williams, William, 1717-91

It should be clear from the foregoing that we consider cooperative cataloguing a part of centralised cataloguing as long as it is coordinated by a central agency and its product is distributed from a single point. There are, however, certain advantages in having the work originate as cooperative cataloguing that should not be overlooked. These may be listed as follows:

1. The cataloguing can be done without the expense, hazards, and delay of sending the books to the central agency.
2. Specialised subject and linguistic competence of scholars available as consultants to cataloguers throughout the country, more extensive than could ever be available at a central point, can be used.
3. The major financial burden for the participating institutions is included in their salary budgets and thus to some extent more subject to local control.
4. More prompt and satisfactory cataloguing can result from cooperative work on certain types of publications by getting them catalogued at their source of publication; e.g., state documents in the various state capitals, municipal documents in the issuing cities, doctoral dissertations in the libraries of institutions granting the degrees.
5. A wholesome, critical attitude toward the end product results only from the effort of many cataloguing establishments in applying the same rules and following the same policies.
6. National understanding of the difficulties and complexities of cataloguing would receive little nourishment if a central cataloguing agency were to solve all the problems alone.

References

Cutter, C. A.: Dr. Hagen's Letter on Cataloguing. *Library Journal,* 1:216-220, Feb. 1877.

Grove, Pearce, S., and Clement, Evelyn G., eds. *Bibliographic Control of Nonprint Media.* Chicago, ALA, 1972.

Hensel, Evclyn. "Treatment of Nonbook Materials," *Library Trends* 2:187, Oct. 1953.

Haskins, Susan M.: Sometime New in Cataloguing. *College and Research Libraries,* 6:291-321 I, Sept. 1945.

Whitney, J. L.: On the Cost of Catalogues. *Library Journal,* 10:214-216, Oct. 1885.

Works, G. A.: *College and University Library Problems.* Chicago, American Library Association, 1927, p. 114.

Bibliography

American Library Association. Catalogue Code Revision Committee: *A.L.A. Catalogue Rules; Author and Title Entries.* Prelim. American 2d ed. Chicago, The Association, 1941.

Anglo-American Cataloguing Rules. North American Text. Chicago, ALA, 1967.

Bertot, John C., "Libraries and Networked Information Services: Issues and Considerations in Measurement." *Performance Measurement and Metrics*, 2004.

Bishop, Ann Peterson. "Document Structure and Digital Libraries: How Researchers Mobilize Information in Journal Articles." *Information Processing and Management* 35 May 1999.

Blandford, Ann, and George Buchanan. "Usability of Digital Libraries: A Source of Creative Tensions with Technical Developments." *TCDL Bulletin*, Summer 2003.

Bliss, H. E.: *The Organisation of Knowledge in Libraries,* 2d ed., rev. New York, H, W. Wilson, 1939.

Chan, Lois Mai. *Cataloguing and Classification: An Introduction.* New York: McGraw-Hill, 1994.

Cutter, C. A.: Dr. Hagen's Letter on Cataloguing. *Library Journal,* 1:216-220, Feb. 1877.

Fayen, Emily Gallup. *The online catalogue : improving public access to library materials.* White Plains, NY : Knowledge Industry Publications, 1983.

Fellows, Dorcas. *Cataloguing Rules with Explanations and Illustrations.* 2d ed. New York, H. W. Wilson, 1922.

Godden, Irene P. ed. *Library technical services : operation and management.* 2nd ed. Sydney : Academic Press, 1991.

Grove, Pearce, S., and Clement, Evelyn G., eds. *Bibliographic Control of Nonprint Media.* Chicago, ALA, 1972.

Hanson, James C. M. *Catalogue rules; author and title entries.* Chicago: American Library Association. 1908.

Haskins, Susan M.: Sometime New in Cataloguing. *College and Research Libraries,* 6:291-321+, Sept. 1945.

Hensel, Evelyn. "Treatment of Nonbook Materials," *Library Trends* 2:187, Oct. 1953.

Hunter, Eric Joseph and KGB Bakewell. *Cataloguing*. London : Clive Bingley, 1979.

Intner, Sheila S. and Jean Weihs. *Standard cataloguing for school and public libraries*. Englewood, Colorado : Libraries Unlimited, 1990.

Kessler, Jack, *Internet digital libraries: the international dimension*, Boston and London: Artech House.

Liu, Ying, and Anita S. Coleman. "Communicating Digital Library Services to Scientific Communities." *LIBRES* 14, no. 1, 2004.

Michelle Q. Wang Baldonado and Steve B. Cousins. Addressing heterogeneity in the networked information environment. *New Review of Information Networking*, 2:83-102, 1996

Norris, Dorothy M.: *A History of Cataloguing and Cataloguing Methods, 1100-1850.* London, Grafton and Co., 1939.

Pearson, Dora M.: Library Reclassifies Books. *Library Journal,* 74:919-923, June 15, 1949.

Racine, Drew. ed. *Managing technical services in the 90's*. Sydney : The Howarth Press, 1991.

Sayeis, W. C. B.: An *Introduction to Library Classification.* 8th ed, London, Grafton and Co., 1950.

Schatz, Bruce R. "Information Retrieval in Digital Libraries: Bringing Search to the Net." *Science*, 17 January 1997.

Schwartz, Candy. "Digital Libraries: An Overview." *The Journal of Academic Librarianship* 26, November 2000.

Shiri, Ali. "Digital Library Research: Current Developments and Trends." *Library Review* 52, no. 5, 2003.

Smith, Abby. *Strategies for Building Digitized Collection*s. Washington, DC: Digital Library Federation, Council on Library and Information Resources, 2001.

Suleman, Hussein,et.al., "Networked Digital Library of Theses and Dissertations: Bridging the Gaps for Global Access—Part 1: Mission and Progress." *D-Lib Magazine* 7, September 2001.

Taylor, Arlene G., David P. Miller, and Arlene G. Taylor. *Introduction to Cataloguing and Classification.* 10th ed. Westport, Conn: Libraries Unlimited, 2006.

Tillett, Barbara B. "FRBR and Cataloguing for the Future," *Cataloguing & Classification Quarterly*, v. 39, no. 3/4, p. 205-216.

U.S. Library of Congress. Descriptive Cataloguing Division: *Rules for Descriptive Cataloguing in the Library of Congress.* Washington, D.C., 1949.

Universal Decimal Classification. Complete English ed. 4th international ed, BS 1000. 669 Metallurgy. London, British Standards Institute, 1949.

Whitney, J. L.: On the Cost of Catalogues. *Library Journal,* 10:214-216, Oct. 1885.

Works, G. A.: *College and University Library Problems.* Chicago, American Library Association, 1927, p. 114.

Wynar, Bohdan S. *Introduction to cataloguing and classification.* 6th ed. Littleton, Colorado : Libraries Unlimited. 1980.

Index